Company Secretarial Handbook

Westby Nunn's COMPANY SECRETARIAL HANDBOOK

Eighth edition

C N GORMAN BA LL B (CANTAB)
Solicitor

A V BARKER MA (CANTAB)
Solicitor

 Oyez Longman

© Oyez Longman Publishing Ltd 1983
21/27 Lamb's Conduit Street
London WC1N 3NJ

ISBN 85120 698 0

First Published   1926
Eighth edition   1983

Set in Times by
Kerrypress Ltd, Enterprise House,
7 Gordon Street, Luton, Beds. LU1 2QP
and printed in Great Britain by
Butler & Tanner Ltd, Frome and London

CONTENTS

v

CONTENTS

CONTENTS

PREFACE TO THE EIGHTH EDITION

The previous edition of this work was necessitated *inter alia* by the passing of the Companies Act 1976: this new edition follows upon two further Companies Acts, those of 1980 and 1981, each considerably longer and more complex than the 1976 Act. The 1980 Act was concerned principally to implement in the United Kingdom the provisions of the EEC Second Directive on Company Law relating to the establishment of public companies: in addition the opportunity was taken to introduce into companies legislation further provisions regarding the duties of directors and conflicts of interest and to make 'insider dealing' an offence. The 1981 Act again resulted principally from a requirement to implement an EEC Directive – the Fourth Directive on the harmonisation of company accounts – but likewise covered much further ground, particularly in relation to the purchase by a company of its own shares and more stringent rules for the disclosure of interests in voting shares of public companies. Neither of the new Acts can readily be regarded as straightforward in its provisions or easy to assimilate or apply: it is significant that the 1981 Act effected amendments even to a number of the provisions of the 1980 Act.

The net result, so far as this work is concerned, has been that substantial re-editing and, in a number of areas, rewriting has been required. The object of the work remains, as before, to provide a reasonably practical guide to the requirements of the Companies Acts and related matters for company secretaries and others engaged in company administration: it does not in its present edition, any more than in previous editions, purport to be a comprehensive treatment of companies legislation currently in force, still less of all the arcane provisions of the most recent Acts – for this company secretaries should continue to have recourse to the standard works on company law or to their professional advisers. It is nevertheless hoped that it will continue to provide assistance on a day-to-day basis and a signpost in cases of difficulty, and will be of direct practical relevance in a number of commonly encountered situations.

Assistance in the preparation of the new edition has been given by our colleagues S.H. Rajani (Chapter 12) and G.N.Russell. Errors or omissions which remain – we think it unlikely that we have yet achieved perfection – are ours alone, and if drawn to our attention or that of the publishers will be noted for future editions, as will any suggestions for improvement.

It is to be hoped that there will be a moratorium on new companies legislation whilst the latest Acts continue to be digested: but a sonsolidation of the current nine or so relevant Acts has been promised, and if this comes to fruition the present text will again require material re-editing.

April 1983.

C.N. Gorman
A.V. Barker

TABLE OF CASES

TABLE OF STATUTES

TABLE OF STATUTES

TABLE OF STATUTORY INSTRUMENTS

CHAPTER 1

INTRODUCTION

Companies Acts 1948 to 1981

The statutory provisions which govern the formation, conduct and winding-up of registered companies are contained mainly in the Companies Acts of 1948, 1967, 1976, 1980 and 1981. In the pages which follow these are referred to individually as 'the 1948 Act', 'the 1967 Act' and so on and together as 'the Acts'. References to sections or Schedules of the Acts are given with the year of the relevant Companies Act first, eg 1948 s 2 and 1981 Sched 2. References to regulations (eg 'reg 110') are, unless the contrary is stated, to those contained in Table A to the 1948 Act (see p 7). Where company forms are referred to (eg Form 47), these indicate the official number (normally derived from the Companies (Forms) Regulations 1979 and later Companies (Forms) Regulations).

Unless otherwise stated, references to 'the Secretary of State' are to the Secretary of State for Trade, and references to 'the Registrar' are to the Registrar of Companies.

Copies of the Acts are an essential part of the working equipment of every company secretary. Secretaries of companies any part of whose securities are listed on The Stock Exchange should also have a copy of The Stock Exchange's publication, *Admission of Securities to Listing* (see p 44) commonly known as 'the Yellow Book'. In the Yellow Book will be found the Listing Agreement, a resolution required by The Stock Exchange to be passed by the board of a company whose securities are listed on the Exchange.

Delivery of documents to Registrar of Companies

Regulations may be made prescribing requirements as to size, durability and legibility of documents delivered to the Registrar (1976 s 35) and the Registrar may accept for registration any material other than a document (such as information on microfilm) of a kind approved by him (1976 s 36).

A person persistently in default in relation to the requirements of

1

the Acts as to the delivery of documents to the Registrar may be disqualified for a period not exceeding five years from holding office as a director or liquidator, or receiver or manager of the property of, a company, or from being concerned or taking part in any way in the promotion, formation or management of a company (1948 s 188). Any person acting in contravention of such an order may be fined or imprisoned (1948 s 188(6)). The Secretary of State is required to maintain a register of such disqualification orders for the time being in force and such register is open to inspection (1976 s 29) on payment of the prescribed fee (now 5p).

The Companies Registry

The address of the Registrar of Companies (or, colloquially, the Companies Registry) for England and Wales is Companies House, Crown Way, Maindy, Cardiff CF4 3UZ (telephone Cardiff (0222) 388588) although company searches and delivery of documents may still be made at Companies House, 55–71 City Road, London EC1Y 1BB (telephone 01–253 9393).

NB Hereafter 'file' naturally means 'deliver to the Registrar of Companies for registration'.

Scottish companies

This book deals with English law: in most but not all respects Scottish company law which applies to companies registered in Scotland is the same or very similar. The office of the Registrar of Companies for Scotland is 102 George Street, Edinburgh EH2 3DJ (telephone 031–225 5774/5).

THE SECRETARY

Every company must have a secretary. There can be joint secretaries (see 1948 s 200(3)).

Appointment of secretary

The directors of a *public* company (see p 9) must take all reasonable steps to secure that the secretary or each joint secretary is a person who appears to them to have the requisite knowledge and experience to discharge the functions of secretary and who is qualified in one of the following ways:

(a) On 22 December 1980 he was secretary or assistant or deputy secretary of the company.

(*b*) For at least three of the five years before his appointment as secretary he was secretary of a public company.

(*c*) He is a member of:
    The Institute of Chartered Accountants in England and Wales,
    The Institute of Chartered Accountants of Scotland,
    The Association of Certified Accountants,
    The Institute of Chartered Accountants in Ireland,
    The Institute of Chartered Secretaries and Administrators,
    The Institute of Cost and Management Accountants, or
    The Chartered Institute of Public Finance and Accountancy.

(*d*) He is a barrister, advocate or solicitor called or admitted in any part of the United Kingdom.

(*e*) By virtue of his holding or having held any other position or being a member of any other body he appears to the directors capable of discharging those functions (1980 s 79).

Subject to the above rules, any person may be appointed secretary, including a corporation, save that the secretary may not be (*a*) a person who is also the company's sole director (1948 s 177(1)) or (*b*) a corporation the sole director of which is a sole director of the company (1948 s 178(*a*)). In addition, since an officer of a company or a partner or employee of an officer may not be its auditor (1948 s 161(2)), and for this purpose 'officer' includes a director, manager or secretary (1948 s 455(1)), it follows that, for example, the auditor may not also be the secretary. There is nothing to prevent the company's solicitor from being the secretary.

The statement of particulars to be delivered on application for registration of a company (Form 1) must contain the name and relevant particulars of the first secretary, or the first joint secretaries, and on the company's incorporation he or they are deemed to have been appointed as such (1976 s 21). Any appointment by the Articles is void unless the person appointed is also named in the statement of particulars (1976 s 21(5)). Each subsequent appointment of a person to the office of secretary is usually made by the directors of the company in exercise of the power conferred on them by the company's Articles (eg reg 110); though it seems that they may make the appointment even if the Articles do not specifically confer such a power on them.

Where there is more than one director, the secretary may also be a director of the company; but where a provision in the Acts requires a thing to be done by or to a director *and* the secretary, the thing cannot be done by or to the same person acting as both director and secretary (1948 s 179).

An assistant or deputy secretary is not one of the principal officers of the company (see the definition of 'officer' in 1948 s 455(1)). However if the office of secretary is vacant, or there is for any other reason no secretary capable of acting, anything required to be done by or to the secretary may be done by or to his deputy or assistant, or, if there is no such deputy or assistant capable of acting, by or to any officer of the company authorised generally or specially in that behalf by the directors (1948 s 177(2)). In other circumstances a deputy or assistant secretary can perform a function of the secretary if the Articles permit and provided that the function is not required by statute to be carried out by the secretary.

Every appointment of a secretary must be recorded in the register of directors and secretaries and notified to the Registrar of Companies (see pp 140 to 142).

Change of secretary

A secretary appointed by the directors may be dismissed by them, but if such dismissal breaks his contract of service he may have a claim against the company for breach of that contract. The termination of a secretary's appointment must be recorded in the register of directors and secretaries and notified to the Registrar of Companies (see p 142).

Status of secretary

The secretary is an officer of the company (1948 s 455(1)) with ministerial and administrative functions; but he does not have, by virtue of his office, managerial functions, although in practice he is frequently given, expressly or impliedly, considerable managerial authority and responsibility. As the chief administrative officer of the company he has ostensible authority to enter into contracts connected with the administrative side of the company's affairs, eg for the employment of staff or the hiring of cars to meet customers (*Panorama Developments (Guildford) Ltd* v *Fidelis Furnishing Fabrics Ltd* [1971] 2 QB 711); but depending on the circumstances and any course of dealing his authority may not extend to concluding managerial contracts, eg the borrowing of money, for which he would have to be given authority by the board of directors.

The secretary may or may not be a servant of the company: this is a point of some importance to him in the event of a receiver being appointed or the company being wound up, for only if he is a servant is he entitled to rank as a preferential creditor in respect of his remuneration. If he is a full-time employee of the company with more or less regular hours then he is an employee and a preferential creditor; but if, for example, he is a practising solicitor or accountant who acts as secretary and does the work in his own time, he is not an employee and not a preferential creditor (*Cairney* v *Back* [1906] 2 KB 746).

Liabilities of secretary

Many important duties are imposed on secretaries by the Acts, and in many cases serious penalties may be incurred if these duties are not carried out. Some of the penalising sections make the secretary liable only if he is knowingly or wilfully a party to the default, and it is not possible to make any general statement as to what degree of inaction constitutes this form of default; but in most cases where a secretary had called the attention of his directors to the fact that a certain duty had to be performed and had continued to remind them that it had not been performed, he would probably be deemed to have done what was within his power to carry out the duty.

Like all other employees of the company, a secretary may be liable to the company for damage resulting from his own negligence; and any provision in the Articles or any contract with the company which purports to exempt any director, manager or officer of the company from liability in respect of negligence, default, breach of duty or breach of trust is void (1948 s 205). However the court can relieve him from responsibility in certain cases (1948 s 448).

Failure to draw the attention of the directors to the company's insolvency or likely insolvency, and the consequences of continuing in business, can amount to negligence but mere silence and omission do not necessarily bring the secretary within the provisions of 1948 s 332 ('fraudulent trading') (*Re Maidstone Buildings Provisions Ltd* [1971] 1 WLR 1085).

It is also possible for a secretary to incur liability to third parties in respect of contracts entered into ostensibly on behalf of the company, if sufficient care is not taken; though, if such contracts are made in the name of the company and it is made quite clear that the secretary is acting only as the company's agent, he should avoid personal liability. Care should be taken in signing bills of exchange and cheques. The words 'for and on behalf of —— —— Ltd' should always be written under the secretary's signature. It is not sufficient to use the formula 'John Smith, secretary of —— —— Ltd'. The word 'Limited' must not be omitted (*Atkins & Co* v *Wardle* (1889) 58

LJQB 377) (see further p 17). The above of course applies mutatis mutandis in the case of a public company.

THE MEMORANDUM AND ARTICLES

The secretary should acquire a thorough knowledge and understanding of the company's Memorandum and Articles of Association, for upon these documents the conduct of the company's business and many of the rights, duties and liabilities of directors and members of the company depend. Rights of members may also be affected, however, by resolutions which nevertheless are not required to be annexed to the Articles. Thus an ordinary resolution under Table A, reg 2, would not have to be filed unless it was within the terms of 1948 ss 63(2) or 143(4) or 1980 s 27(2) (see pp 100 to 102).

Every company must have a Memorandum of Association, which must state the name of the company, whether the registered office is to be situated in England (which includes Wales, the alternative wording 'England and Wales' being permitted), Wales or Scotland, the objects of the company, that the liability of members is limited (if it is), and the amount of the share capital (if any) (1948 s 2 and 1976 s 30). A company whose Memorandum of Association states that its registered office is to be situated in Wales may have its Memorandum and Articles, and may deliver documents to the Registrar of Companies, in Welsh but accompanied by a certified English translation (1976 s 30).

That part of the Memorandum which lays down the objects of the company is of particular importance, for a company is able to pursue only those objects which are either expressly set out in its Memorandum or are reasonably incidental thereto. Anything done or attempted to be done which is not in pursuance of these permitted objects is said to be ultra vires the company; and contracts which are such ultra vires objects may be void. Moreover, the officers of the company by whom such ultra vires contracts are made may incur personal liability in respect thereof to outsiders and may find themselves liable to compensate the company for any loss which it has sustained. The European Communities Act 1972 s 9 limits the application of the ultra vires doctrine in cases where third parties deal with the company in good faith. (see *International Sales & Agencies* v *Marcus* [1982] 3All ER 551 and *Barclays Bank Ltd* v *TOSG Trust Fund*, 27 February 1981, unreported) but the doctrine continues to apply, for example, as regards the liability of the officers to the company. It remains important, therefore, for the secretary to be wholly familiar with the objects.

In construing the objects clause of the Memorandum certain general principles should be borne in mind. In *Cotman* v *Brougham* [1918] AC 514, a provision for each object to be treated as a main object was held by the House of Lords to be effective; and one empowering the company to carry on any ancillary business which 'in the opinion of the directors' could be advantageously carried on was upheld in *Bell Houses Ltd* v *City Wall Properties Ltd* [1966] 2 QB 656. In *Introductions Ltd* v *National Provincial Bank Ltd* [1970] Ch 199 a borrowing provision in the objects clause was, however, held to be a power rather than an object and accordingly, despite a *Cotman* v *Brougham* and a *Bell Houses* provision, exercisable only for the purposes of its true business objects; and even where a transaction is within the scope of an express object, it may be voidable if no reasonable person could have concluded that it was entered into for the benefit of the company (*Charterbridge Corporation* v *Lloyds Bank Ltd* [1970] Ch 62 and see *Re Halt Garage* (1964) Ltd [1982] 3 All ER 1016 and *Rolled Steel Products* v *British Steel Corporation* [1982] Ch 478).

The Articles of Association provide the machinery for the conduct of the company's affairs, laying down regulations, eg for the summoning and holding of meetings of members, the appointment, retirement and powers of directors, the keeping of accounts, and the issuing of shares. In 1948 Sched 1 there is a model set of Articles of Association known as Table A. This forms the Articles of a company registered after 30 June 1948 if no special Articles are registered; and, even where special Articles are registered, those regulations of Table A apply which are not expressly excluded or contradicted by the special Articles (1948 s 8).

Table A, as it appears in 1948 Sched 1 (as amended by later Companies Acts), differs considerably from the forms of Table A which appeared in earlier Companies Acts, and care must be taken to ascertain which form of Table A, if any, is applicable to a particular company. Companies formed before 1 July 1948 are not governed by Table A in the Act of 1948 unless they take steps after that date to adopt that version of Table A (1948 s 459(14)). Companies formed under the Acts of 1862, 1908 or 1929 may still be governed by the version of Table A adopted when the company was formed, unless steps have been taken to exclude them or adopt a later version of the Table. Many of the provisions in these earlier versions of Table A were, however, overridden by the 1948 Act. Considerable care must, therefore, be taken in applying these earlier versions of the Table.

Part II of the 1948 Table A applied only to private companies and has been repealed for new companies by the 1980 Act: it will however, unless excluded, continue to apply to private companies registered before 22 December 1980.

Certificate of incorporation

When the Memorandum and Articles have been registered with the Registrar of Companies and other preliminary requirements have been fulfilled (see Chapter 2) a certificate of incorporation is issued by the Registrar (1948 s 13). This certificate fixes the date on which the company comes into existence and is conclusive evidence that the requirements of the Acts have been fulfilled (1980 s 3(4)).

Copies of Memorandum and Articles

If any member of the company so requires, he must be sent a copy of the Memorandum and Articles and a copy of any Act of Parliament which alters the Memorandum (1948 s 24). A fee of not more than 5p may be charged for the Memorandum and Articles. The published price of the Act of Parliament may be charged. Every copy of the Memorandum issued must contain all alterations made prior to the date of issue and every copy of the Articles must embody or annex special resolutions for the time being in force which will include those altering the Articles (1948 ss 25 and 143(2)).

TECHNICAL TERMS

In studying the Memorandum and Articles and the Acts and applying their provisions to the practical problems he encounters, the secretary must ensure that he understands the meaning of many important technical terms which are freely used. Many of these will be explained in the text as they are encountered; but some are so important and frequent that they are explained here.

Members

The term 'member' is defined by 1948 s 26, which states that the subscribers to the Memorandum of a company shall be deemed to have agreed to become members of the company, and on its registration shall be entered as members in its register of members; and that every other person who agrees to become a member of the company, and whose name is entered in the register of members, shall be a member of the company.

'Member' is not synonymous with 'shareholder'. A company limited by guarantee, for instance, may have members who hold no shares. Moreover, a person who possesses a share warrant (see p 55), though he is a shareholder, is not a member, except to the extent he may be deemed to be under the Articles (1948 s 112(5)).

If the number of members of a company is reduced below two and the company carries on business for more than six months while the number is so reduced, every person who is a member of the company during the time that it carries on business after those six months and knows it has only one member is liable (jointly and severally with the company) for the payment of the debts of the company contracted during that time (1948 s 31).

Companies and bodies corporate

The Acts refer sometimes to 'companies' and sometimes to 'bodies corporate'. Where the term 'company' is used in the Acts, it usually means a company formed and registered under the 1948 Act or a previous Companies Act (1948 s 455(1)). There are, however, many other types of corporate bodies, which, though they are not directly governed by these Acts, are referred to in them. Such are companies formed by Royal Charter or by special Act of Parliament or incorporated outside Great Britain. All these are included in the phrase 'bodies corporate'. In some places in the Acts 'company' includes any such body corporate, eg in the definition of 'subsidiary' and 'holding company' in 1948 s 154 and in 1980 Pt V relating to insider dealing.

Public and private companies

A public company is a limited company with a share capital (whether limited by shares or guarantee) whose Memorandum states that it is to be a public company and which has been registered or re-registered at the Companies Registry as a public company after 22 December 1980, the date on which the provisions of the 1980 Act relating to classification of companies came into effect (1980 s 1(1)). A public company must satisfy minimum capital requirements explained below. The name of a public company must end with 'public limited company' or its Welsh equivalent (or certain abbreviations thereof) (see p 17).

Any company which is not a public one is a private one (1980 s 1(1)). Most companies are private ones. Since the 1980 Act it is no longer necessary for the Articles of a private company to restrict the right to transfer shares, put a basic limit of fifty on the number of members and prohibit any offering of its shares or debentures to the public—although it may include any of such matters in its Articles if it wishes and the prohibition on a private company's offering its securities to the public is now set out in 1980 s 15.

A company can be initially formed as a public company only if its share capital as stated in its Memorandum is at least 'the authorised minimum', a figure which is currently £50,000 but can be varied by statutory instrument (1980 ss 3 and 85). Further, a company registered as a public one on its original incorporation must not do business or exercise any borrowing powers until the Registrar has issued it with a certificate under 1980 s 4 (or it has re-registered as a private company). This certificate is obtained only if the Registrar is satisfied that the company has *allotted* share capital in nominal amount of at least the authorised minimum and there is delivered to him an application and statutory declaration (Form 8) stating this and certain other matters. (Shares allotted under an employees' share scheme are taken into account for this purpose only if paid up as to at least a quarter of nominal amount and the whole of any premium.)

If an old public company (ie one which was a public company within the meaning which that expression had before 22 December 1980) proposes to re-register as a public company within the new meaning of that expression, the share capital requirements are more onerous. Not only must it have an allotted share capital in nominal amount of at least the authorised minimum but:

(1) its shares or such of them as are needed to satisfy the authorised minimum (called below 'the necessary shares') must be paid up to the extent of at least one quarter of nominal amount and the whole of any premium;

(2) if the necessary shares have been fully or partly paid up, as to nominal amount or premium, by an undertaking to do work or perform services, the undertaking must have been performed or otherwise discharged; and

(3) if the necessary shares have been allotted as fully or partly paid up, as to nominal amount or premium, otherwise than in cash and the consideration for the allotment is or includes any other undertaking, *either* the undertaking must have been performed or otherwise discharged *or* there must be a contract under which it must be performed with five years (1980 s 8).

If a private company other than an old public company proposes to re-register as a public company, the share capital requirements are more stringent still. Not only must the company have an allotted share capital in nominal amount of at least the authorised minimum but, with certain exceptions, the requirements numbered (1), (2) and (3) above must be satisfied not just in respect of the shares needed to make up the authorised minimum but in respect of all the company's allotted shares (1980 s 6).

Holding companies and subsidiaries

The Acts often refer to holding companies and subsidiaries. The meaning of these terms is contained in 1948 s 154.

Prima facie, a company is deemed to be a *subsidiary* of another company if, but only if, one of the following conditions is fulfilled:

(a) if the other company is a member of it *and* controls the composition of its board of directors; *or*

(b) if the other company holds more than half in nominal value of its equity share capital; *or*

(c) if the company is a subsidiary of a third company which is that other company's subsidiary.

For the purpose of this definition one company is deemed to control the composition of another's board of directors if, but only if, the controlling company, by the exercise of some power exercisable by it without the consent or concurrence of some other person, can appoint or remove the holders of all or a majority of the directorships; and a company is deemed to have power to appoint to a directorship if:

(a) a person cannot be appointed a director without the exercise in his favour by the company of such a power as is mentioned above; *or*

(b) a person's appointment to a directorship follows necessarily from his appointment as director of the controlling company; *or*

(c) the directorship is held by the controlling company itself or by its subsidiary.

For the purposes of the definition of a subsidiary, the expression 'company' includes any body corporate (eg a statutory or chartered company may be a subsidiary of a registered company); and the expression 'equity share capital' means the issued share capital of a company excluding any part thereof which, neither as respects dividend nor as respects capital, carries any right to participate beyond a specified amount in a distribution (1948 s 154(5)). It includes, for instance, ordinary share capital and participating preference share capital; and, if preference shares are given the right, expressly or by necessary implication, to participate on a winding-up in the distribution of surplus assets, it would include the preference shares. Only a close study of the Memorandum and Articles can determine what is and what is not part of the equity share capital.

In determining whether or not one company is a subsidiary of another, any shares held or power exercisable by that other (ie by the company suspected of being a holding company) in a fiduciary capacity are to be treated as not held or exercisable by it. In other words, such shares or powers will not help to tip the scale in favour of the company being a subsidiary.

On the other hand, shares held or powers exercisable by any person as a nominee for the suspected holding company (except where the suspected holding company is concerned only in a fiduciary capacity) are generally to be treated as held or exercisable by the suspected holding company; and shares held or powers exercisable by, or by a nominee for, a subsidiary of the suspected holding company (not being a subsidiary concerned only in a fiduciary capacity) are to be treated as held or exercisable by the suspected holding company. But shares held or powers exercisable by any person by virtue of the provisions of any debentures of the suspected subsidiary, or of a trust deed securing any such debentures, are to be disregarded; and any shares held or power exercisable by, or by a nominee for, the suspected holding company or its subsidiary (not being within the above-mentioned rule concerning debentures) are to be treated as not held or exercisable by the suspected holding company if the ordinary business of the company or its subsidiary, as the case may be, includes the lending of money *and* the shares are held or the power is exercisable by way of security only for the purposes of a transaction entered into in the ordinary course of the business (1948 s 154(3)).

The following examples may assist:

Example A.
Company A has a share capital consisting of 1,000 shares of £1 each all of the same class. Company B holds and owns 501 of these shares. A is a subsidiary of B.

Example B.
Company A has the same share capital as in the previous example; but of the 1,000 shares only 60 have been issued. Company B holds and owns 35 of these shares. A is a subsidiary of B.

Example C.
Company A has a share capital consisting of 1,000 shares, divided into 600 ordinary shares of £1 each and 400 preference shares of £1 each. All shares of both classes have been issued. The preference shares carry a fixed cumulative dividend, but are not entitled to any further share in profits. On a winding-up they will give the holders a right to repayment of paid-up capital but no further right to participate in profits or assets. Company B holds and owns 320 of the ordinary shares. Since only the ordinary shares are 'equity share capital', A is a subsidiary of B.

Example D.

The facts are as in the last example, but the preference shares give the holders the right on a winding-up to share in surplus assets, if any, pari passu with the ordinary shares. In this case the preference shares are part of the 'equity share capital', so that, if B holds only 320 ordinary shares and no preference shares A is *not* a subsidiary of B.

Example E.

Company A has a share capital consisting of 1,000 ordinary shares of £1 each (all issued). Company B holds and owns 501 of these shares. B also has a share capital consisting of 1,000 ordinary shares of £1 each (all issued). Company C holds and owns 501 of these shares. A is a subsidiary of B. In addition A and B are subsidiaries of C.

Example F.

Company A has a share capital consisting of 1,000 shares of £1 each of a single class, only 600 being issued. Company B holds 100 shares in its own right and 306 shares under the terms of a trust deed in trust for, but not as nominee for, company C. A is *not* a subsidiary of B, since all except 100 of the shares held by B are held in a fiduciary capacity. Nor is A a subsidiary of C, since C does not hold shares in A.

Example G.

If in the last example the terms of the trust deed, under which B holds the 306 shares in A, provide that C may direct B as to the manner in which its voting powers shall be exercised, this does not apparently make any difference, since, though this gives C virtual power to control the composition of A's board of directors, C is not a member of A.

Example H.

If, however, in the last two examples B holds shares of A 'as nominee for' C, then A will be a subsidiary of C, though *not* of B.

Example I.

Company X has an issued share capital consisting of one non-voting £1 ordinary share, 500 'A' ordinary shares of £1 each and 500 'B' ordinary shares of £1 each. All the shares rank pari passu in all respects except that the 'B' shares confer on the holders the right to appoint a majority of the directors. If company Y holds the non-voting ordinary share and all the 'A' shares, and company Z holds all the 'B' shares, company X is a subsidiary of both Y (which holds more than half X's equity share capital) and Z (which is a member of X and controls the composition of its board of directors).

Example J.

Company X has an issued share capital of 500 'A' ordinary shares of £1 each and 500 'B' ordinary shares of £1 each ranking pari passu save that holders of 'A' shares are entitled to appoint three directors to represent 'A' shareholders and holders of 'B' shares are entitled to appoint three directors to represent 'B' shareholders. If company Y holds all the 'A' shares and company Z holds all the 'B' shares, X is a subsidiary of neither Y nor Z.

A company is deemed to be the *holding company* of another company if, but only if, that other company is its subsidiary (1948 s 154(4)).

CHAPTER 2

FORMATION OF A COMPANY

Formation

A company comes into legal existence upon the issue of a certificate of incorporation, which is obtained by filing with the Registrar of Companies the following documents:

(1) A Memorandum of Association.

(2) Articles of Association (if desired), signed by each subscriber to the Memorandum and attested by at least one witness.

(3) Statement on formation of a limited company with a share capital-stamped £1 for every £100 or part of £100 of issued capital (Finance Act 1973, s 47 and Sched 19) (Form PUC 1). The Registrar will in practice accept a 'nil' return and no duty is payable if only subscribers' shares are taken up.

(4) A statement of the first registered office and the names and particulars of the first directors and secretary, signed by or on behalf of the subscribers to the Memorandum of Association, containing a consent to act signed by each person named as a director or secretary (1976 ss 21 and 23) (Form 1).

(5) A statutory declaration, by a solicitor engaged in the formation of the company or by a person named in the statement of particulars (see (4) above) as a director or secretary of the company, as to due compliance with the requirements of the Acts (Form 41a) (1980 s 3(5)).

Registration fees in accordance with the regulations for the time being in force must be paid when the documents are lodged.

Before any documents are filed, or even prepared, a search should be made at the Companies Registry to ascertain whether there is already a company registered with the same name or one very similar. The registration of a company with the same name as one already registered is prohibited (1980 s 22(1)(*c*)) and if a company is registered with a name which in the opinion of the Secretary of State is too like the name of an existing company the Secretary of State may within a year of its formation require the new company to change its

15

name (1980 s 24(2)). Certain minor matters (eg 'The' at the beginning of a name and 'Company' or 'Limited' (or abbreviations thereof) at the end of a name) are disregarded in determining whether two names are the same (1980 s 22(3)).

Registered office

Every company must at all times have a registered office to which all communications and notices may be addressed (1976 s 23).

The Memorandum of Association states in which part of Great Britain the registered office is to be situated (ie England (which expression includes Wales), Wales or Scotland). The intended situation of a company's registered office on incorporation must be specified in the statement of particulars to be delivered on application for registration (Form 1) and notice of any change in the situation of the registered office must also be given to the Registrar within fourteen days of the change (1976 s 23) (Form 4a). The country of registration of the company, its registered number, and the address of its registered office must be shown in legible characters in all business letters and order forms (European Communities Act 1972, s 9(7)). Following the removal of the Companies Registry to Cardiff, the appropriate designation for the place of registration of a company registered with the Registrar for England and Wales is 'Registered in England and Wales' or 'Registered in Cardiff' or 'Registered in Wales'. However, the Registrar would not take objection to use of the expressions 'Registered in England' or 'Registered in London' (*Law Society's Gazette*, 23 March 1977, p 243).

Name

The name of every company must be painted or affixed and kept painted or affixed outside every office or place of business in a conspicuous position and in easily legible letters (1948 s 108). In addition, the name must be mentioned in all business letters, notices and other official publications of the company, and in all bills of exchange, promissory notes, endorsements, cheques and orders for money or goods which purport to be signed by or on behalf of the company, and in all invoices, receipts and letters of credit of the company (1948 s 108). A company with 'Cyfyngedig' as its name's last word must also publicise in English the fact that the company is limited (1976 s 30(5)). Similarly a public company which ends its name 'Cwmni Cyfyngedig Cyhoeddus' must publicise in English the fact that it is a public limited company (1980 s 77).

Directors and officers of the company may incur severe criminal penalties if these provisions are not complied with. Further, where the default consists of signing a bill of exchange, promissory note, cheque or order for money or goods, the officer signing will be personally liable for the amount thereof if payment is not made by the company (1948 s 108(4)). In *Durham Fancy Goods Ltd* v *Michael Jackson (Fancy Goods) Ltd* [1968] 2 QB 839, it was held, however, that the plaintiff, who had himself incorrectly prepared a form of acceptance in the name of 'M Jackson (Fancy Goods) Ltd' for signature by a director was estopped from enforcing personal liability under s 108 (contrast *Maxform SpA* v *Mariani* [1979] 2 Ll Rep 385). Note that a default will be committed under these provisions if the *full* name of the company is not included, so that the omission of the word 'Limited' may render the directors and officers liable (*Atkins & Co* v *Wardle* (1889) 58 LJQB 377, *British Airways Board* v *Parish* [1979] 2 Lloyd's Rep 361); though liability will not be incurred merely by abbreviating 'Limited' to 'Ltd' (*Stacey & Co* v *Wallis* (1912) 106 LT 544) or 'Company' to 'Co' (*Banque de l'Indochine et de Suez SA* v *Euroseas Group Finance Co Ltd* [1981] 3 All ER 198). Signature of a cheque with the omission of an ampersand in the company's name can result in personal liability under s 108 (*Hendon* v *Adelman* (1973) 117 SJ 631).

If an existing company knows in time of the formation of a new company with the same or a very similar name it may ask the Secretary of State to exercise his power under 1981 s 24(2) to require the new company to change its name. Otherwise action may be taken for an injunction to restrain the new company from allowing its name to remain on the register in the offending form and to restrain it from passing off (*Exxon Corporation* v *Exxon Insurance Consultants International Ltd* [1981] 1 WLR 624): a similar remedy is available where an unincorporated partnership or an individual attempts to deceive the public by adopting a name similar to that of an existing company. Arrangements can be made with the Registrar, however, for the name of an existing company to be adopted by another company (whether existing or newly formed) subject to the existing company first, or simultaneously, changing its name.

A public company (which is necessarily a limited company) must have at the end of its name 'Public Limited Company' or the abbreviation 'plc' (which abbreviation, it appears, can be rendered in upper or lower case letters, or with the p in upper case and the l and c in lower case, and with or without intervening spaces or full stops) or, if its Memorandum states that its registered office is to be situated in Wales, their Welsh equivalents 'Cwmni Cyfyngedig Cyhoeddus' or

'CCC' (1980 ss 2(2) and 78). A private limited company must normally have as the end of its name 'Limited' or 'Ltd' or, if its Memorandum states that its registered office is to be situated in Wales, 'Cyfyngedig' or 'cyf' (1948 s 2(1)(*a*) and 1980 s 78).

However, a private company limited by guarantee (or a private company limited by shares which before 26 February 1982 had a licence under 1948 s 19, now repealed, to omit 'Limited' from its name) need not comply with the above, provided its Memorandum or Articles:

   (i) require it to apply its profits in promoting its objects;
  (ii) prohibit payment of dividends to members; and
 (iii) require it on a winding-up to transfer surplus assets to a body with similar objects or charity (1981 s 25).

In practice a statutory declaration must be filed at the Companies Registry as provided in 1981 s 25(4) before a company may be formed or may change its name as permitted by 1980 s 25.

By s 9(7)(*c*) of the European Communities Act 1972, a limited company exempt from the obligation to use the word 'Limited' (or an equivalent) as part of its name must state that it is a limited company on all business letters and order forms.

A company may not be registered with a name:

   (i) which includes otherwise than at its end 'Limited', 'Unlimited' or 'Public Limited Company' or their Welsh equivalents or their abbreviations;
  (ii) the use of which would in the opinion of the Department of Trade be a criminal offence;
 (iii) which in the Department's opinion is offensive; or
 (iv) except with the Department's approval which (*a*) would in its opinion be likely to give the impression that the company is connected with Her Majesty's Government or any local authority or (*b*) includes any word or expression specified in the Company and Business Names Regulations 1981 (SI 1981 No 1685 as amended by SI 1982 No 1653) (such as Royal, United Kingdom, England, Insurance, Chamber of Commerce and University) (1980 s 22).

The Department may also direct a company to change its name within a specified period of not less than six weeks if the Department is of the opinion that the name by which a company is registered gives so misleading an indication of the nature of its activities as to be likely to cause harm to the public (1967 s 46). Application may be made to the court within three weeks to set the direction aside (ibid). An oversea company may be restrained from carrying on business in

Great Britain under its corporate name if registration under that name would not have been permitted had it been a British company (1976 s 31).

Particulars on business letters, order forms etc

A company must also state in legible characters on its business letters and order forms (in addition to its name, and the fact that it is limited if it has 'Cynfyngedig' at the end of its name, or is exempt from ending its name with 'Limited' or 'Cynfyngedig'—see above):
  (a) the country in which it is registered, eg England, England and Wales, Wales or Scotland;
  (b) its registered number;
  (c) the address of its registered office; and
  (d) if it is an investment company within the meaning of 1980 Pt III the fact that it is such (European Communities Act 1972 s 9(7)).

Further, a public company which ends its name with the Welsh equivalent of 'public limited company' (or its abbreviation) must state that it is a public limited company in English in legible characters on all its prospectuses, bill heads, letter paper, notices and other official publications and similarly in a conspicuous notice at every place where it carries on business (1980 s 77).

Business names

Following the repeal of the Registration of Business Names Act 1916, trading by a company under a name, called below a business name, other than its corporate name is controlled by 1981 ss 28 to 30 (except where a company merely adds to its corporate name an indication that its business is carried on in succession to a former owner of the business, eg 'X Limited, successor to J Smith'). A company may not trade in Great Britain under a business name which would be likely to give the impression that the business is connected with Her Majesty's Government or a local authority or includes a word or expression specified in the Company and Business Names Regulations 1981 (SI 1981 No 1685 as amended by SI 1982 No 1653) save that:
  (i) a company which acquires a business may carry it on under its former lawful business name for a year; and
  (ii) a company may continue to carry on a business indefinitely under the name under which it lawfully carried it on immediately before 26 February 1982 (1981 s 28).

Seal

Every company must have a corporate seal, on which its full name must be engraved in legible characters (1948 s 108(1)(*b*)). Care should be taken to prevent unlawful use of the seal, eg by its being kept under lock and key or so constructed that it can be used only if one or two locks are released.

The regulations in the Articles or Table A for affixing the seal to a document should be observed carefully, for any illicit affixation may be ineffective and may render those responsible liable for breach of warranty of authority.

It is commonly provided in the Articles that the seal is to be used only by authority of the board of directors and that every document to which the seal is affixed must be signed by one director and the secretary or by two directors (see also reg 113) although modern Articles often provide for the sealing of share and debenture certificates without signature or with facsimile signatures. In no circumstances should the seal be used unless authority has previously been obtained from a properly constituted meeting of the board of directors or a committee duly authorised in that behalf. The authority may however be a general one authorising affixation of the seal to a category of documents: a separate authority is not needed for each specific transaction.

A minute of the resolution of the board or committee, authorising the affixing of the seal, must be entered in the minute book.

A document or proceeding requiring authentication by the company may be signed by a director, secretary, or other authorised officer, and need not be under its common seal (1948 s 36).

If Articles permit it, a company may have a seal for use out of the United Kingdom (1948 s 35). In addition the Stock Exchange (Completion of Bargains) Act 1976 provides that a company may have, for use for sealing securities issued by it and documents creating or evidencing securities so issued, an official seal which is a facsimile of the common seal of the company with the addition on its face of the word 'Securities'. See further p 53.

It is advisable to maintain a sealing register in, for example, the following form, in which are entered particulars of all documents to which the seal is affixed:

Sealing register

No of entry	Document sealed	Date of resolution to seal	Date of sealing	Sealed in presence of and document signed by

Contracts

Of necessity a company must make all contracts through the medium of an agent. If contract is of such a nature that, if made between individuals, the law would require it to be in writing under seal, it should be made under the common seal of the company. If, however, the law would require the contract if between individuals to be in writing signed by the parties to be bound, it may be made on behalf of the company in writing signed by any person acting under its authority, express or implied. And the contract, if made between individuals, could be made orally, then it may be made orally on behalf of the company by any person acting under its authority, express or implied (1948 s 32).

It is not always essential for the validity of a contract made on behalf of the company that the company should be described with complete accuracy (*F Goldsmith (Sicklesmere) Ltd* v *Baxter* [1970] Ch 85).

Commencement of business

A private company may commence business as soon as a certificate of incorporation has been issued; but a company originally formed as a public company may not do business or exercise any borrowing powers until the Registrar has issued it with a certificate under 1980 s 4 (or it is re-registered as a private company). The Registrar issues this certificate on receipt of an application (which incorporates a statutory declaration) (Form 8), if satisfied that the company fulfils the share capital requirements for a public company.

Pre-incorporation contracts are not binding on, and cannot be ratified by, a company although they can be taken over by novation. However, by s 9(2) European Communities Act 1972, a pre-incorporation contract can impose personal liability on the person purporting to act for the company in entering into it: for an illustration see *Phonogram Ltd* v *Lane* [1982] QB 938.

A company which does not commence business within one year after its incorporation or which being a public company originally formed as such is not issued with a certificate under 1980 s 4 within that time may be wound up by the court (1948 s 222).

Transfers of non-cash assets by subscribers

1980 ss 26 and 27 impose certain requirements relating to expert valuation where a public company formed as such contracts with a subscriber to its Memorandum for the transfer by him during the first two years in which it is entitled to do business of non-cash assets for a consideration to be given by the company equal to or greater than one-tenth of its issued share capital.

CHAPTER 3

ISSUE OF SHARES

AUTHORITY TO ALLOT AND PRE-EMPTION RULES

1980 ss 14 and 17 to 19 deal with authority to allot shares and rights of pre-emption of existing shareholders. The following explanation of these provisions is necessarily a summary. The application of the sections and the preparation of resolutions and other drafting affected thereby will often require professional advice. Particularly complex problems can arise in connection with, eg, convertible loan stocks. Listed companies will have to bear in mind also The Stock Exchange's pre-emption requirements set out in the Yellow Book (see p 1) and the views expressed by institutional investors' representative bodies on resolutions under ss 14 and 18.

Authority to allot shares

A company's Articles usually give the power to allot shares to the directors. However by 1980 s 14 the directors may not allot relevant securities unless they are authorised to do so by a resolution of the company in general meeting (which may be an ordinary resolution) or the Articles. 'Relevant securities' means: ·

(a) shares in the company other than those which under its Memorandum are taken by the subscribers or shares allotted pursuant to an employees' share scheme (defined by 1980 s 87(1)); and

(b) any right to subscribe for, or convert any security (such as loan stock) into, shares within (a) above.

Moreover, for the purposes of 1980 s 14 'allotment' is deemed to occur where any such right is granted, following which actual allotment of the shares pursuant to that right is not regarded as an allotment for the purposes of s 14.

A s 14 authority may be given for a particular transaction or be general; it may be subject to conditions or unconditional. Whether contained in the Articles or not the authority must state the maximum amount of relevant securities which may be allotted under it and a date on which it will expire. An authority may not last beyond five years from its grant, but an allotment can be made after its expiry if it results from an offer or agreement made by the company before such expiry and the authority allows the company to make an offer or agreement which would or might require such an allotment. An authority can be revoked or varied by the company in general meeting and also renewed under similar rules for up to a further five years any number of times.

A resolution to give, vary, revoke or renew a s 14 authority may, even if it alters a company's Articles, be an ordinary resolution. But whether the resolution is ordinary or special it must be filed at the Companies Registry.

An allotment of relevant securities which contravenes s 14 is not void or voidable but may involve the directors in criminal liability.

Pre-emption rules

By 1980 s 17, except with the sanction of a special resolution, any equity securities which a company proposes to allot wholly for cash must be offered first to its existing equity shareholders pro rata. There are detailed provisions relating to the manner in which the offer is made and the period for which it must remain open.

To decide what are 'equity securities' it is necessary first to consider the meaning for the purposes of the section of 'relevant shares': a share will be a relevant share unless (i) its right to participate in both dividends and capital is limited to specified amounts or (ii) it is held by a person who acquired it pursuant to an employees' share scheme or if it has not been allotted it is to be allotted pursuant to such a scheme. 'Equity securities' are then defined as relevant shares (except subscribers' shares or bonus shares) or a right to subscribe for, or convert any securities into, relevant shares. A similar rule to that explained above in connection with s 14 applies in construing the meaning of allotment in ss 17 to 19. An offer required by s 17 must be made to holders of relevant shares and to holders of 'relevant employee shares', shares which would be relevant shares if they were not held by a person who acquired them pursuant to an employees' share scheme.

There are provisions which apply where a company's Memorandum or Articles contain similar pre-emption rights and which enable a private company to exclude s 17 by its Memorandum or Articles.

Under 1980 s 18 where directors have a general s 14 authority they may be given power by the Articles or by special resolution to allot equity securities pursuant to that authority as if:

(*a*) the pre-emption rule in s 17 did not apply; or

(*b*) it applied with such modifications as the directors determine. There are broadly similar powers of disapplying the pre-emption rule in relation to particular allotments but in this case there is a requirement that disapplication be recommended by the directors and certain information circulated to shareholders. There are transitional provisions to cover the case where a company is at the time when the rules become applicable to it subject to an obligation inconsistent with them.

CONSIDERATION FOR AN ALLOTMENT OF SHARES

Subject as mentioned below, shares, including any premium on them, may be paid up in money or money's worth (including goodwill and know-how) (1980 s 20(1)).

Any shares taken by a subscriber to the Memorandum of a public company in pursuance of his undertaking in the Memorandum, and any premium thereon, must be paid up in cash (1980 s 29).

A public company may not accept as payment for its shares, whether as to nominal amount or premium, an undertaking that work will be done or services performed (1980 s 20(2) and (3)). Except in pursuance of an employees' share scheme, a public company may not allot a share unless at least a quarter of the share's nominal value and the whole of any premium is paid up (1980 s 22). A public company may not allot shares as fully or partly paid, as to nominal amount or premium, otherwise than in cash if the consideration is or includes an undertaking which will or may be performed more than five years after the allotment (1980 s 23). If any of these rules are broken, the shareholder is liable to pay to the company in cash immediately the amount involved or the deficiency, as the case may be, with interest.

Except where the consideration for the allotment is wholly or partly the acquisition of shares in another company pursuant to an offer made to all its shareholders (or all its shareholders of a class) or the acquisition of all the assets and liabilities of another company, a public company must not allot shares as fully or partly paid, as to nominal amount or premium, otherwise than in cash unless the consideration for the allotment has been valued, a report on such value has been obtained in accordance with the detailed requirements of 1980 ss 24 and 25 from a person qualified to be the company's auditor and a copy of the report has been sent to the proposed allottee. Infringement involves the allottee in liability to pay to the company the amount involved in cash with interest. A copy of any such report must also be filed at the Companies Registry with the relevant return of allotments.

Under 1980 s 28 the court has limited powers to grant relief from liabilities imposed by the above rules.

THE PROSPECTUS

What is a prospectus?

1948 s 455 defines a prospectus as any prospectus, notice, circular, advertisement, or other invitation, offering any shares or debentures of a company to the public for subscription or purchase. The key phrase is 'to the public'; for if the offer is not made to the public, the document will not be a prospectus as defined by the Act; though, on the other hand, if it is made to the public, it will be a prospectus as so defined, whatever form it may take, and even if it bears the words 'private and confidential'.

The offer can be made by the company itself by means of a direct invitation to the public: but it is frequently made, eg, by an issuing house by means of an 'offer for sale' (see below) or 'placing' of the shares or debentures. A prospectus can only be issued in relation to a public company: private companies cannot invite public subscriptions (1980 s 15).

1948 s 55 provides that any reference in the 1948 Act to offering shares or debentures to the public shall, subject to any provision to the contrary, be construed as including a reference to offering them to any section of the public, whether selected as members or debenture holders of the company concerned or as clients of the person issuing the prospectus or in any other manner. (The definition also applies for 1980 s 15). This means that the statutory requirements as to prospectuses cannot be avoided by limiting the offer to a specified section of the public.

On the other hand, the section goes on to state that, if an offer can properly be regarded, in all the circumstances, as not being calculated to result, directly or indirectly, in the shares or debentures becoming available for subscription or purchase by persons other than those receiving the offer or invitation, or otherwise as being a domestic concern of the persons making and receiving it, the offer will not be regarded as a prospectus and in particular a provision in a company's Articles prohibiting invitations to the public to subscribe for shares or debentures shall not be taken as prohibiting the making to members or debenture holders of an invitation which can properly be regarded as aforesaid.

Furthermore, an offer of or invitation to subscribe for shares or debentures of a private company will, unless the contrary is proved, be treated as being a domestic concern of the persons making and receiving it if:

(a) made to any member of the relevant class (ie existing members or employees of the company, their families and existing debenture holders); or

(b) the shares or debentures are to be held under an employees' share scheme.

This provision applies even if the offer or invitation can be renounced in favour of any other member of the relevant class or a person entitled to hold shares or debentures under the scheme.

It is necessary to judge each case on its merits and determine, having regard to all the circumstances, whether or not an offer is made to the public.

Where a company allots shares or debentures to an issuing house, which then offers the shares or debentures for sale to the public, the offer would not, without 1948 s 45, be a prospectus issued by the company; but s 45 provides that if the shares or debentures are allotted, or the company has agreed to allot them, with a view to their subsequent offer for sale to the public, the consequential offer for sale is to be deemed to be a prospectus issued by the company. Moreover, unless the contrary is proved, the fact that an offer for sale is made within six months after an allotment, or that at the time of the offer for sale the consideration for the shares or debentures is still unpaid, is evidence that the allotment was made with a view to the subsequent offer for sale.

An offer for sale of this nature must on registration (see below) be signed by two directors of any company or by not less than half the partners of any firm by which it is made (ie, in the above example, of the issuing house); but a director or partner may sign by an agent authorised in writing (1948 s 45).

Registration of prospectus

Every prospectus issued by or on behalf of a company or intended company must be dated, and the date, unless the contrary is proved, is taken to be the date of the publication of the prospectus (1948 s 37). On or before the date of publication a copy must be delivered to the Registrar of Companies for registration (1948 s 41). This copy must be signed by every person named in the prospectus as a director or proposed director or by his agent authorised in writing, and must have endorsed on or attached to it (a) any requisite consent of a person as an expert and (b) in the case of a prospectus 'issued generally' (ie to persons who are not existing members or debenture holders of the company (1948 s 455(1)) a copy of, or memorandum in respect of, any contract required to be mentioned in the prospectus (see 1948 Sched 4, para 14), and any statement concerning adjustments made in compliance with 1948 Shed 4, para 29.

In addition, every prospectus must on the face of it state that a copy has been delivered for registration to the Registrar, and specify any documents required to be endorsed thereon or attached thereto (1948 s 41(2)).

Form and contents of prospectus

Generally, every prospectus issued by or on behalf of a company or by or on behalf of any person who is or has been engaged or interested in the formation of the company must contain the particulars listed in 1948 Sched 4 (1948 s 38), and any condition requiring an applicant for shares or debentures to waive compliance with this requirement is void (ibid). The Sched 4 requirements are designed to ensure that the prospective investor receives the material information necessary to enable him to decide whether or not to invest; but these requirements do not apply (a) to an issue to existing members or debenture holders of a prospectus relating to shares in or debentures of the company, whether an applicant will or will not have the right to renounce in favour of other persons, or (b) to the issue of a prospectus relating to shares or debentures which are or are to be in all respects uniform with shares or debentures previously issued and for the time being listed on a prescribed stock exchange (1948 s 38(5)). In 1973 the constituent members of the Federation of Stock Exchanges of Great Britain and Ireland were amalgamated into a single organisation entitled The Stock Exchange which is the only prescribed stock exchange for the purposes of s 38 (The Companies (Stock Exchange) Order 1973 (SI 1973 No 482)).

Moreover, where (a) it is proposed to offer any shares in or debentures of a company to the public by a prospectus issued generally, and (b) application is made to The Stock Exchange for the shares or debentures to be listed on it, and (c) a certificate of exemption from the general requirements as to prospectuses is given by The Stock Exchange, then, provided that the terms prescribed by The Stock Exchange are complied with, the prospectus need not be in the form prescribed by s 38, which will accordingly not apply to any issue of these shares or debentures (1948 s 39). In such a case the prospectus must be filed with the Registrar, but it may be in the form prescribed by The Stock Exchange.

Where the statutory requirements must be complied with, the following particulars listed in 1948 Sched 4 must be included in the prospectus:

(1) *Particulars concerning shares*

(*a*) The number of founders, management or deferred shares, if any, and the nature and extent of the interest of the holders in the property and profits of the company (Sched 4, Pt I, para 1).

(*b*) The amount payable on application and allotment on each share including the amount, if any, payable by way of premium; and, in the case of a second or subsequent offer of shares, the amount offered for subscription on each previous allotment made within the two preceding years, the amount actually allotted, and the amount, if any, paid on the shares so allotted including the amount, if any, paid by way of premium (Sched 4, Pt I, para 6).

(*c*) Particulars as to the minimum subscription (Sched 4, Pt I, para 4).

(*d*) The number and amount of shares or debentures which within the two preceding years have been issued, or agreed to be issued, as fully or partly paid up otherwise than in cash; and in the latter case the extent to which they are so paid up; and in either case the consideration for which those shares or debentures have been issued or are proposed or intended to be issued (Sched 4, Pt I, para 8).

(*e*) If the share capital of the company is divided into different classes of shares, the right of voting at meetings of the company conferred by, and the rights in respect of capital and dividends attached to, the several classes of shares (Sched 4, Pt I, para 17).

(*f*) The number, description and amount of any shares in or debentures of the company, which any person has or is entitled to be given an option to subscribe for, together with the following particulars of the option:

(i) The period during which it is exercisable.

(ii) The price to be paid.

(iii) The consideration, if any, given or to be given, for it or the right to it.

(iv) The names and addresses of the persons to whom it or the right to it was given, or, if given to existing shareholders or debenture holders as such, the relevant shares or debentures (Sched 4, Pt I, para 7).

(2) *Particulars as to directors*

These particulars are not required where a prospectus is issued more than two years after the date when the company is entitled to commence business (Sched 4, Pt III, para 22).

(*a*) The names, descriptions and addresses of directors or proposed directors (Sched 4, Pt I, para 3).

(*b*) The number of shares, if any, fixed by the Articles as the qualification of a director (Sched 4, Pt I, para 2).

(*c*) Any provision in the Articles as to the remuneration of directors (ibid).

(*d*) Full particulars of the nature and extent of the interest, if any, of every director in the promotion of, or in the property proposed to be acquired by, the company (Sched 4, Pt I, para 16).

(3) *Particulars as to property*

(*a*) As respects property purchased or acquired by the company, or proposed to be purchased or acquired, which is to be paid for wholly or partly out of the proceeds of the issue offered for subscription, or the purchase or acquisition of which has not been completed at the date of the issue of the prospectus:

   (i) The names and addresses of the vendors.
   (ii) The amount payable in cash, shares or debentures to each vendor.
   (iii) Short particulars of any transaction relating to the property completed within the two preceding years in which any vendor or any person who is, or was at the time of the transaction, a promoter or director or proposed director of the company had any interest (Sched 4, Pt I, para 9);

but not in the case of property the contract for the purchase or acquisition of which was entered into in the ordinary course of the company's business, the contract not being made in contemplation of the issue nor the issue in consequence of the contract; or as respects which the amount of the purchase money is not material (ibid).

(*b*) As respects any property to which the last paragraph applies, the amount paid or payable as purchase money in cash, shares or debentures specifying the amount, if any, payable for goodwill (Sched 4, Pt I, para 10).

(4) *Particulars as to formation expenses etc*

(*a*) The amount of underwriting commission paid within the two preceding years (except to sub-underwriters) (Sched 4, Pt I, para 11).

(*b*) The amounts or estimated amounts of preliminary expenses and expenses of the issue and the persons by whom such expenses have been paid or are payable (Sched 4, Pt I, para 12; but also see Sched 4, Pt III, para 22).

(5) *Particulars as to promoters*

Any amount paid or benefit given within the two preceding years or intended to be paid or given to any promoter, and the consideration for it (Sched 4, Pt I, para 13).

(6) *Particulars as to contracts*

The dates of, parties to and general nature of every material contract within the last two years not being a contract entered into in the ordinary course of the company's business (Sched 4, Pt I, para 14).

A material contract may be defined as one which could reasonably be regarded as likely to influence a person in deciding whether or not to apply for shares.

A copy of each such contract, or, in the case of a contract not in writing, a memorandum giving full particulars thereof, must be delivered to the Registrar before the prospectus is issued, either by endorsement on or attachment to the prospectus; and, if the contract is wholly or partly in a foreign language, a written translation certified in the prescribed manner must be so delivered (1948 s 41(1)). These may be inspected only during the fourteen days beginning with the date of the publication of the prospectus or with the permission of the Department of Trade (1948 s 426(1)).

(7) *Other particulars*

(*a*) The names and addresses of the auditors, if any (Sched 4, Pt I, para 15).

(*b*) The time of the opening of the subscription lists (Sched 4, Pt I, para 5).

(*c*) In the case of a company which has been carrying on business, or of a business which has been carried on for less than three years, the length of time during which it has been carried on (Sched 4, Pt I, para 18).

Reports to be included in prospectuses

Prospectuses which must observe the above requirements must also contain the following reports:

(1) A report by the auditors of the company with respect to (*a*) the

profits or losses of the company in respect of each of the five financial years immediately preceding the issue of the prospectus; (*b*) the assets and liabilities of the company at the last date to which accounts have been made up; and (*c*) the rates of dividend, if any, paid by the company in respect of each class of shares in respect of each of those five years. For details see Sched 4, Pt II, para 19.

Where the company has subsidiaries, the report must also deal with the combined profits and losses of the subsidiaries so far as they concern members of the company, or with the profits or losses of each subsidiary individually, or with the combined profits or losses of the company and the subsidiaries. Assets and liabilities of subsidiaries must be dealt with similarly (ibid).

(2) If the proceeds of the issue of the shares or debentures are to be applied in the purchase of any business, a report by named accountants on the profits or losses of the business in respect of each of the five financial years immediately preceding the issue of the prospectus and on the assets and liabilities at the last date to which the accounts of the business were made up (Sched 4, Pt II, para 20).

If the proceeds of the issue are to be applied in any manner resulting in the acquisition by the company of shares in any other body corporate, and that other body corporate will become a subsidiary of the company, a similar accountants' report must be made indicating a number of particulars concerning the other body corporate and its subsidiaries (Sched 4, Pt II, para 21).

These accountants' reports must be made by persons qualified for appointment as auditors of companies (see p 158), and must not be made by an officer or servant, or partner or employee of an officer or servant, of the company, its subsidiary or holding company or another subsidiary of its holding company; for this purpose 'officer' includes a proposed director but not an auditor (Sched 4, Pt III, para 30).

Reports of experts in prospectuses

A prospectus must not be issued purporting to contain a statement by an expert unless (*a*) he has given and has not, before delivery of a copy of the prospectus for registration, withdrawn written consent to its issue with the statement included in the form and context in which it is included; and (*b*) a statement that he has given and not withdrawn his consent appears in the prospectus. For this purpose 'expert' includes an engineer, valuer, accountant and any other person whose profession gives authority to a statement made by him (1948 s 40).

Issue of forms of application

Generally it is unlawful to issue any form of application for shares in or debentures of a company unless the form is issued with a prospectus which complies with 1948 s 38 (ie it contains the particulars listed in Sched 4) (1948 s 38(3)). But this prohibition does not apply if the form of application is issued either (*a*) in connection with a bona fide invitation to a person to enter into an underwriting agreement; or (*b*) in relation to shares or debentures which are not offered to the public (ibid). Nor does it apply where the company has, on the certificate of The Stock Exchange, obtained exemption from the obligation to comply with s 38 or where the company issues a prospectus in the circumstances referred to in s 38(5) (see p 28).

Liability for false statements and omissions in prospectuses

Where a prospectus includes any untrue statement, any person who authorised its issue is liable to criminal penalties, unless he proves that the statement was immaterial or that he had reasonable grounds for believing and did believe up to the time of the issue of the prospectus that the statement was true (1948 s 44). But a person is not deemed to have authorised the issue of a prospectus merely because he consented to the inclusion of a statement made by him as an expert (ibid).

In addition to the above criminal liability, a civil liability to pay compensation may be incurred by directors of the company, persons who authorised themselves to be named as directors or proposed directors, promoters, experts and other persons who have authorised the issue of the prospectus. All such persons are prima facie liable for any damage suffered by persons who subscribed for shares or debentures on the faith of the prospectus, provided that the damage has been caused by an untrue statement in the prospectus or in any report or memorandum appearing on the face of the prospectus or by reference incorporated therein or issued therewith (1948 ss 43 and 46).

In order to escape from this prima facie liability the person sued must establish one of the defences set out in s 43(2).

Whether or not a statement in a prospectus is a mis-statement for the purpose of imposing a liability under the above provisions is a question of fact; but it is made clear that a statement is deemed to be untrue if it is misleading in the form and context in which it is included (1948 s 46).

The non-disclosure of a material fact, which renders the terms of the prospectus misleading, may give rise to an action for deceit if the non-disclosure is deliberate or reckless.

Any person who takes shares or debentures on the faith of a prospectus from which omissions have been made is entitled to recover damages from the persons responsible for its issue: but only if he is able to prove that the facts omitted were of a material nature and that actual damage has been suffered through the omission. But no person responsible for the issue of the prospectus shall be liable for an omission who is able to prove that:

(1) he was not cognisant of the matter omitted; or

(2) the omission arose from an honest mistake of fact on his part; or

(3) the omission was immaterial or ought to be excused (1948 s 38(4)).

APPLICATIONS FOR SHARES

Where a company issues a prospectus inviting the public to subscribe for shares, the document is usually accompanied by a form of application similar to that shown on p 229. A form of application for debentures is somewhat similar.

It is usual for payment of application moneys to be made to receiving bankers appointed for the purpose, who should be instructed to open accounts for moneys so payable, though payment is sometimes made to the company, when the wording of the form of application must, of course, be adjusted.

These forms of application constitute written offers to take shares or debentures in the company, and no binding contract exists until a letter of allotment has been posted to the applicant.

Where a prospectus is 'issued generally' (see pp 27 and 28) and is subject to the requirements of 1948 s 38 (see pp 27 and 28) an application for shares or debentures cannot be revoked until after the expiration of the third day after the date of the opening of the subscription lists, unless, before that date, some person has given public notice with a view to avoiding liability for mis-statements in the prospectus (1948 s 50(5)). The date of the opening of the subscription lists, for this purpose, is deemed to be the third day after the date on which the prospectus is first issued (see p 35).

In other cases an application may be withdrawn at any time before the posting of the letter of allotment (*Re Imperial Land Co of Marseilles, Harris' Case* (1872) 7 Ch App 587) unless by a collateral contract the applicant agrees for consideration that his application shall not be withdrawn.

An application for shares will lapse if allotment is not made within a reasonable time (*Ramsgate Victoria Hotel Company* v *Montefiore* (1866) 4 H & C 164).

ALLOTMENT AND ISSUE OF SHARES

Allotment

The allotment of the shares or debentures must be made by properly recorded resolutions at a properly convened and properly constituted meeting of directors or of a duly authorised committee. Where the securities are offered otherwise than by an offer for sale by an issuing house, the secretary should prepare lists of applicants showing the number of shares or debentures each has applied for in order to enable the directors at the meeting to determine which, if any, of the applications it is advisable to reject.

The date of the allotment (which includes sale of the shares where the prospectus is in the form of an offer for sale) requires careful calculation where the prospectus is 'issued generally', ie issued to persons who are not existing members or debenture holders of the company; for in such a case no allotment may be made until the third working day after the day on which the prospectus is first issued, or such later day as may be specified in the prospectus (1948 s 50) ('the date of the opening of the subscription lists'). 'The day on which the prospectus is first issued' means the date of its first issue as a newspaper advertisement unless it is not so issued at all or is not so issued before the third working day after first issue in some other way, in either of which cases the day of first issue in some other way applies. A working day means any day except a Saturday, Sunday or bank holiday in any part of Great Britain.

Failure to comply with these requirements, which apply only where there has been a prospectus 'issued generally', does not invalidate the allotment; but it renders the company and its officers liable to a fine.

Minimum subscription

Where shares are first offered to the public for subscription, no allotment may be made unless the minimum subscription has been applied for and the sum payable on application in respect of such minimum has been received by the company (1948 s 47). A sum is treated as received if a cheque for it has been received and there is no reason to suspect that the cheque will not be paid.

1948 Sched 4, Part I, para 4 requires the sum fixed to represent the minimum amount which in the opinion of the directors is required to be raised by the contemplated issue to provide for:

- (a) the purchase of property to be purchased in whole or in part out of the proceeds of the issue;
- (b) the preliminary expenses and underwriting commission payable by the company;
- (c) the repayment of moneys borrowed for the above purposes; and
- (d) working capital.

It is not necessary to include in this minimum amount sums borrowed to provide the company with working capital, or the purchase price of property to be provided otherwise than out of the proceeds of the shares offered to the public; but if any of the four items described are to be provided otherwise than by means of the issue, the amount and sources thereof must be shown in the prospectus.

If, for instance, a company has contracted to purchase an existing business for an agreed sum of £700,000 on terms that (a) the agreed price shall be paid as to £400,000 in cash to be raised by an issue of shares and as to £300,000 by the allotment of fully paid shares of that nominal value, and (b) the preliminary expenses and underwriting expenses shall be payable by the vendors of the business, it is necessary to state in the prospectus the amount of the purchase price and the preliminary expenses and underwriting commission; but only the cash portion of the purchase price (£400,000) need be included in the minimum subscription.

A formula such as the following may be used to give this statutory information:

> The minimum amount which in the opinion of the directors must be raised by the present issue of shares in order to provide the sums required to be provided in respect of the matters specified in para 4 of Part I of the Fourth Schedule to the Companies Act 1948 is £500,000, made up as follows: (a) cash portion of the purchase price of property, £400,000; (b) preliminary expenses, *nil;* (c) underwriting commission, *nil;* (d) sums borrowed, *nil;* (e) working capital, £100,000. The balance of the purchase price of property will be satisfied by the allotment to the vendors of 300,000 fully paid ordinary shares of £1 each at par. Preliminary expenses and underwriting commissions amounting to £50,000 are payable by the vendors under Contract 7 above.

Shares to be allotted for a consideration other than cash cannot be included in the minimum subscription.

If the minimum subscription is not subscribed within forty days after the first issue of the prospectus, all moneys received from applicants must be returned to them; and, if any moneys are not returned within forty-eight days after the issue of the prospectus, the directors are jointly and severally liable to repay the moneys with interest at the rate of 5 per cent per annum from the forty-eighth day (1948 s 47(4)).

Partial subscription

In addition to the above requirements of 1948 s 47 share capital of a public company offered for subscription must not be allotted unless it is subscribed for in full or the offer states that it may be allotted even if it is not subscribed for in full (1980 s 16). 1948 s 47(4), summarised above in relation to minimum subscription requirements, applies also where these requirements are not satisfied, with additional provisions where applicable relating to the return of consideration other than cash or payment of its value.

Letter of allotment

To each applicant to whom the directors decide to allot shares a letter of allotment (pp 230 and 231) or share certificate should be forwarded at the earliest possible date. If the allottee is to have the power to renounce the allotment in favour of another person, the letter of allotment or share certificate should be renounceable.

According to the ordinary law of contract, a letter of allotment, being an acceptance of the applicant's offer to take shares, must be un-conditional and must not vary the terms of the application. Thus, no binding contract exists if a smaller number of shares is allotted than the number for which application is made, unless the applicant has agreed to accept a smaller number (*Re Barber* (1851) 20 LJ Ch 146). Usually the form of application is worded to cover this contingency; but care should be taken to see that the words are not struck out by the applicant.

If the number of shares applied for exceeds that to be allotted, care must be taken in carrying out the provisions of the prospectus with regard to the amount received. Normally, the amount paid will be applied towards the payment of the amount due on allotment and the balance returned to the applicant. The letter of allotment has to be altered or completed accordingly.

Before letters of allotment or certificates are posted, particulars should be entered in a list of applications and allotments.

If shares are to be listed on The Stock Exchange an undertaking has to be given that all letters of allotment will be posted simultaneously.

Letter of regret

Where an issue is over-subscribed, letters of regret should be sent to those applicants to whom shares are not allotted, accompanied by a cheque for the amount paid on application. A form such as the following may be adopted:

LETTER OF REGRET

—— PUBLIC LIMITED COMPANY
(Incorporated under the Companies Acts 1948 to 1981)
Offer of .... Ordinary
Shares of .... each at .... per Share

Dear Sir or Madam,

I refer to your application for Ordinary Shares in this Company and regret to inform you that in view of the over-subscription of the Offer, you have not been successful in obtaining an allotment of shares.

A cheque for £....., the sum paid by you on application, is enclosed.

Yours faithfully,

Secretary

Companies whose securities are listed on The Stock Exchange are required to issue letters of regret preferably at the same time as, but in any event not later than three business days after, allotment letters and if it is impossible to issue letters of regret at the same time as allotment letters, to insert in the press a notice to that effect so that the notice appears on the morning after the allotment letters are posted.

Return of allotments

Within one month of an allotment of shares, the secretary must file with the Registrar a return of allotments, stating the number and nominal value of the shares allotted, particulars of the allottees and the amount paid or due and payable on each share, on Form PUC 2 (issue wholly for cash) or PUC 3 (issue wholly or partly for consideration other than cash) (1948 s 52). Capital duty at the rate of 1 per cent is payable at the same time on the amount of the contribution to the assets of the company (FA 1973, s 47 and Sched 19). Where shares are allotted on renounceable documents, the Registrar of Companies will normally accept within one month of the last date for renunciation a further return including particulars of the renouncees and will not require particulars of the original allottees to be filed when the capital duty is paid. It is not necessary to give the occupations of the allottees but females should be described as 'Miss', 'Mrs' or 'Ms' as the case may require.

A return need not be filed in respect of the shares subscribed for in the Memorandum.

If shares are being allotted at intervals, a return of allotments should be made within one month of the first allotment and should include all shares allotted up to the date of filing. A further return will then be required within one month of the next allotment.

Where allotments are wholly or partly for a consideration other than cash, a contract in writing, constituting the title of the allottee, must be filed, together with a return stating the number and nominal value of the shares so allotted, the extent to which they are to be treated as paid up, and the consideration for which they have been allotted. If no such written contract exists, particulars of the verbal contract must be filed, stamped with the same stamp as would have been required had the contract been in writing (1948 s 52) (Form 52).

If default is made in complying with these provisions, every director, manager or secretary, who is knowingly a party to the default, will be liable to a fine; but the court may in certain circumstances grant relief from the penalty.

Allotment where Stock Exchange listing expected

Where a prospectus, whether issued generally or not, states that application has been or will be made for permission for the shares or debentures offered to be listed on The Stock Exchange, allotments made will be void if (a) the permission has not been applied for before the third day after the first issue of the prospectus, or (b) the permission has been refused before the expiration of three weeks from the date of the closing of the subscription lists or such longer period not exceeding six weeks as may, within the said three weeks, be notified to the applicant for permission by or on behalf of The Stock Exchange. But permission will not be deemed to be refused if it is intimated that the application for it, though not at present granted, will be given further consideration (1948 s 51).

Where permission has not been applied for as aforesaid or has been refused as aforesaid, the company must forthwith repay without interest all money received from applicants, and, if such money is not repaid within eight days after the company becomes liable to repay it, each director becomes liable to repay the money with interest at the rate of 5 per cent per annum from the expiration of the eighth day, unless he can prove that the default was not due to any misconduct or negligence on his part (ibid).

All money received from applicants in such cases must be kept in a separate account so long as the company may become liable to repay it; and any condition requiring or binding any applicant to waive compliance with the section is void.

Generally, the section applies only to allotments made in pursuance of applications received under the prospectus; but where an underwriter has agreed to take shares offered by the prospectus, he is, for the purposes of the section, deemed to have applied for the shares in pursuance of the prospectus.

Section 51 may also apply where shares are offered for sale.

Underwriting commission

Where shares are offered to the public, it is usual to underwrite the issue. In effect, the company insures itself against the risk of the public not applying for the shares by paying a premium to the underwriters, who, in consideration thereof, agree to take up such of the shares as may not be applied for by the public. The premium payable to the underwriters usually takes the form of a commission or percentage of the price at which the shares are issued, but no such commission can be paid unless it is expressly authorised by the company's Articles.

The rate of commission is a matter for arrangement between the company and the underwriters; but, notwithstanding any contrary provision in the Articles, in no case can it exceed 10 per cent of the price at which the shares are issued (1948 s 53). The Articles may fix a lower maximum rate than 10 per cent.

The amount or rate per cent of commission paid or to be paid must be disclosed (in the case of shares offered to the public) in the prospectus, if any, or (in the case of shares not offered to the public) in a statement in the prescribed form (Form 58) signed by all the directors or their agents authorised in writing and filed with the Registrar before the commission is paid.

Where any of the shares are 'firm underwritten', ie where it is stipulated in the underwriting agreement that a certain number of the shares are to be allotted to the underwriters irrespective of the number for which the public apply, the number of shares 'firm underwritten' must also be disclosed.

Moreover, if, although no public offer of shares is made, a circular or notice inviting subscriptions is sent out, the above particulars must be disclosed therein as well as in the statement in the prescribed form (1948 s 53).

Underwriting commission is a commission paid as consideration for an agreement to subscribe for shares; but sometimes (eg on a 'placing') a commission is paid to persons who procure subscriptions from others and here the same principles apply.

Brokerage

It is otherwise where brokerage (usually a small sum per share) is paid to recognised banks and stockbrokers through whom successful applications are made. Nothing in 1948 s 53 affects the power of a company to pay such brokerage as it was formerly lawful to pay and it was held in *Metropolitan Coal Consumers' Association* v *Scrimgeour* [1895] 2 QB 604 that the payment by a company of a reasonable amount of money by way of brokerage is perfectly lawful. In such cases the forms of application usually bear the stamp of the bank or broker.

Commission cannot, however, be paid to a private individual, not being a broker, for procuring a subscription for shares unless it is permitted by the Articles and disclosed under s 53 like underwriting commission (*Andreæ* v *Zinc Mines of Great Britain* [1918] 2 KB 454).

Financial assistance to subscribe or purchase shares

Only in certain circumstances may a company or its subsidiary give financial assistance, directly or indirectly, for the purpose of an acquisition or proposed acquisition of the company's shares or, such an acquisition having taken place and some liability having been incurred by anyone for the purpose of that acquisition, for the purpose of reducing or discharging that liability (1981 s 42). Financial assistance is widely defined and includes, for example, the making of a gift or loan, the giving of a guarantee, security, indemnity (of certain types), release or waiver or any other financial assistance which reduces a company's net assets. A transaction under which a company receives less than market terms, ie a partial gift, is probably a gift for this purpose.

The main exceptions may be roughly summarised as follows:

(*a*) If the offending purpose is not the principal purpose of the assistance or the giving of the assistance for that purpose is but an incidental part of some larger purpose and in either case the assistance is given in good faith in the interests of the company giving it.

(*b*) Distribution of a company's assets by way of an otherwise lawful dividend.

(*c*) A distribution in the course of winding-up the company.

(*d*) Allotment of bonus shares.

(*e*) A redemption or purchase of a company's own shares made under 1981 ss 45 to 61 (see p 76).

(*f*) Where a company's ordinary business includes lending money, doing so in the ordinary course of that business.

(*g*) Providing money in accordance with an employees' share scheme for the acquisition of shares in the company.

(*h*) Making loans to employees, other than directors, to enable the employees to acquire shares in the company for themselves.

(*i*) Subject to certain conditions, the giving of assistance by a private company for the acquisition of shares in itself or, if it is also a private company, its holding company (1981 ss 42 and 43).

The conditions mentioned in (*i*) above may in the case of a company assisting the purchase of its own shares be likewise roughly summarised as follows (further provisions applying where a company assists the purchase of shares in its holding company):

(i) The company must have net assets which are not thereby reduced or if they are reduced the assistance must be provided out of distributable profits.

(ii) The giving of the assistance must be approved by special resolution in general meeting unless the company is a wholly-owned subsidiary.

(iii) The directors must before the assistance is given make a statutory declaration giving certain particulars of the proposals and their opinion on certain points concerning the company's future ability to pay its debts (Form 59).

(iv) There must be annexed to this statutory declaration a report by the company's auditors stating that they have enquired into the company's state of affairs and are not aware of anything to indicate that the directors' opinion mentioned above is unreasonable.

(v) There are detailed requirements on the timing of the various steps involved, making documents available for inspection by members and filing documents with the Registrar (1981 ss 43 and 44).

There are certain rights for members of the company to apply to the court to cancel the resolution approving the assistance.

Issue of shares at a discount

Shares may not be allotted at a discount (1980 s 21). If they are, the allottee is, and a later holder may be, liable to the company for the discount and interest thereon. The company and any officer in default is liable to criminal penalties (1980 s 30).

Issue of shares at a premium

There is a basic rule that if shares are issued at a premium (ie for more than their nominal value), the premium must be transferred to a 'share premium account', which must be shown separately in the balance sheet (1948 s 56).

This share premium account is similar to the share capital inasmuch as it is not available for paying dividends and may not generally be reduced except in the manner in which share capital is reduced (see p 184). It may, however, be applied in paying up unissued shares to be issued to members of the company as fully paid bonus shares; in writing off preliminary expenses or the expenses of, or commission paid on, any issue of shares or debentures; or in providing any premium payable on redemption of debentures.

However, 1981 ss 36 to 41 give certain relief from the basic rule where, broadly:

(1) a company secures a 90 per cent equity holding in another company by an arrangement whereby it issues equity shares on or after 4 February 1981 in consideration of the issue or transfer to it of equity shares in that other company; or

(2) a wholly-owned subsidiary allots shares on or after 4 February 1981 to its holding company or another wholly-owned subsidiary in consideration of the transfer to it of shares in another subsidiary (whether wholly-owned or not); or

(3) a company issued shares before 4 February 1981, the consideration therefor was the issue or transfer to it of shares in another company, that other company was or thereby became its subsidiary and the premium or part of it was not transferred to share premium account but was so applied as to be unidentifiable at 4 February 1981.

(Where however advantage is taken of this relief in case (1) above, certain information must be given in a note to the company's accounts as required by the Companies (Accounts and Audit) Regulations 1982 (SI 1982 No 1092).)

Control of borrowing etc

Article 8A (as substituted by SI 1970 No 708, SI 1977 No 1602 and SI 1979 No 794) of the Control of Borrowing Order 1958 (SI 1958 No 1208) gives an exemption from the Order's basic provisions so that a company resident in the United Kingdom need not now apply for Treasury consent to the raising of money by the issue of shares or debentures. Where, however, the amount of the money to be raised by the issue of any sterling security is £3,000,000 or more, the timing of the issue must be approved by the Bank of England (on behalf of the Treasury) and the procedure is for the company's brokers to apply to the Bank of England through the Government broker for the necessary consent.

Stock Exchange listing and Unlisted Securities Market

Where a listing on The Stock Exchange is being applied for in connection with an issue of new shares, compliance with the relevant requirements set out in The Stock Exchange Yellow Book will be necessary. These requirements are extensive and detailed and a secretary will normally seek the assistance of the company's solicitors for an issue of this nature—as indeed he will normally do in connection with a prospectus issue even where no listing is to be sought.

The same applies where a company seeks to have its shares dealt in on The Stock Exchange's Unlisted Securities Market. In this case the company's board of directors must adopt a general undertaking which outlines the company's continuing obligations relating to the publication of information and similar matters for the protection of investors. The general undertaking is broadly similar to the Listing Agreement which appears in the Yellow Book and applies to listed companies.

CHAPTER 4

SHARES AND SHAREHOLDERS

CLASSES OF SHARES

Unless the Memorandum or Articles forbid it, the company's shares may be divided into different classes, eg into preference, ordinary and deferred shares (reg 2). The rights of the holders of shares of different classes are normally defined in the Articles.

Preference shares

Every company may issue preference shares, unless the Memorandum or Articles provide to the contrary (*Andrews* v *Gas Meter Co* [1897] 1 Ch 361).

Where shares are given preferential rights, these usually include a right to receive out of the profits of the company a certain fixed dividend, which must be paid before any dividend at all can be paid to the holders of ordinary or deferred shares. If the Memorandum or Articles do not provide otherwise, a preference dividend is assumed to be cumulative, ie any part of it not paid in any year is carried forward to the next year and must be paid to the holders of the preference shares before any dividend is paid to the other shareholders (or carried forward as arrears again). Usually the Articles will expressly provide whether preference shares are cumulative or non-cumulative.

In some cases, in addition to the fixed preferential dividend, the shares carry a right to participate with the ordinary shares in profits available for dividend after the preference dividend has been paid. Such shares are known as participating preference shares.

It is the practice for preference shares to be given, in addition to the right to a preference dividend, a preferential right to repayment of paid-up capital in the event of the company being wound up, ie the right to have capital repaid before any repayment can be made to holders of ordinary shares; but no such right is enjoyed unless it is given by the Memorandum or Articles. Where such a preferential right to repayment of capital is given, the right applies on a reduction of capital as on a liquidation. In *Scottish Insurance Corporation Ltd* v *Wilsons and Clyde Coal Co Ltd* [1949] AC 462 and in *Prudential Assurance Co Ltd* v *Chatterley-Whitfield Collieries Ltd* [1949] AC 512 the court approved as 'fair and equitable' reductions of capital whereby preference shares were paid off first even though this was opposed by some holders of preference shares.

Whether arrears of cumulative preference dividends which have never been declared are payable in a winding-up depends on the true construction of the Memorandum and Articles (see *Re Roberts and Cooper Ltd* [1929] 2 Ch 383; *Re Walter Symons Ltd* [1934] Ch 308; and *Re Wood, Skinner & Co Ltd* [1944] Ch 323).

Deferred shares

Deferred shares are usually given the right to an undetermined dividend out of profit available after a certain maximum dividend has been paid to the holders of the ordinary shares. The rights attaching to them are determined by the Memorandum or Articles.

Redeemable shares

Shares of any type may be redeemable. Since the 1981 Act shares need not be preference shares to be redeemable.

Classes of members of company without a share capital

Any company which does not have a share capital must file at the Companies Registry within one month particulars of the following, unless they appear in an amendment of its Memorandum or Articles or in a resolution or agreement which must be filed under 1948 s 143:

(1) the rights of any class of members which it creates (Form 67) (1981 s 102(1));
(2) the variation of the rights of any class of members (Form 68) (1981 s 102(2));
(3) the assignment of a name or other designation, or new name or other designation, to any class of members (1981 s 102(3)).

Such a company which had on 15 June 1982 any class of members with rights not stated in its Memorandum or Articles or any such resolution or agreement had to file particulars of such rights within three months of 15 June 1982 (Form 70) (1981 s 102(4)).

For amendment of the rights attaching to any class of shares, see p 187.

THE REGISTER OF MEMBERS

Maintenance of register

Every company must keep a register of members (1948 s 110) and enter in it:

(a) The names and addresses of the members, and, where applicable, the amount, distinguishing numbers and class of the shares held by each member and the amount paid or agreed to be considered as paid thereon.

(b) The date at which each person was entered in the register.

(c) The date at which any person ceased to be a member.

Additional columns are also usually provided for many other particulars it is found convenient to record.

Where the company has converted any shares into stock and given notice of the conversion to the Registrar, the register must show the amount of stock instead of the amount of the shares.

Where there are more than fifty members, if the register itself is not in such a form as to constitute an index, an index to the names of members in the register must be kept (1948 s 111), and within fourteen days of any alteration in the register the company must make any necessary alteration in the index. The index must be kept at the place at which the register is kept.

The register of members is prima facie evidence of any matter required or authorised to be inserted therein (1948 s 118).

If the name of any person is omitted from the register or has been entered therein when it ought not to have been, or if there has been unnecessary delay in recording that any person has ceased to be a member, the person aggrieved, any member or the company may apply to the court for rectification of the register (1948 s 116).

Form of register

The register and its index may be kept either by making entries in bound books or by recording the matters in question in any other manner (1948 s 436(1)). Loose-leaf or card index systems may, therefore, be employed; and by s 3 of the Stock Exchange (Completion of Bargains) Act 1976 any such register or record (including a register of debenture holders) may be kept otherwise than in legible form (eg on computer) provided that it is capable of being reproduced in legible form. Where entries are not made in bound books, adequate precautions must be taken to guard against falsification, and, if such precautions are not taken, directors and officers in default are liable to be fined (1948 s 436(2)).

The exact implications of this last subsection are difficult to ascertain; but it is suggested that loose-leaf registers and account books should not be employed unless they are provided with numbered pages and some locking device. In the case of a card index to the register of members, since falsification thereof cannot cause more than administrative inconvenience, it is suggested that such precautions are unnecessary.

Place at which register must be kept

The register of members must be kept at the registered office or at any office at which the work of making it up is done, provided that it is not outside the country, ie England (including Wales) or Scotland, in which the company is registered (1948 s 110(2)). Notice of the place at which the register is kept or of any change therein (Form 103) must be sent to the Registrar of Companies, unless it has been kept at the company's registered office (*a*) at all times since the company came into existence, or (*b*) in the case of a register in existence on 1 July 1948, at all times since then (1948 s 110(3)). An index to the register, and a duplicate of any dominion register (see p 49), must be kept at the same place as the register of members (1948 ss 111(3) and 120(3)).

Inspection of register

The register and any index must be open to inspection during business hours by any member of the company or the general public (1948 s 113). Members may inspect free of charge, but any other person may be charged a fee not exceeding 5p.

The company may by resolution in general meeting place reasonable restrictions on the times for inspection provided at least two hours are allowed in each business day.

In addition, any person may require a copy of any part of the register to be supplied on payment of 10p, or such less sum as the company prescribes, per hundred words or fraction of one hundred words. A person who inspects the register has no right to take extracts from, or make copies of, the register (*Re Balaghat Gold Mining Co* [1901] 2 KB 665).

Any copy that is required must be supplied within a period of ten days commencing on the day after the day on which the request is received by the company.

Where a company arranges for some other person to make up its register of members, and the register is kept at the office of such person at which the work is done, such person is liable, as if he were an officer of the company, if any person entitled thereto is refused inspection or copies of the register (1948 s 114).

Closing the register

On advertising its intention in some newspaper circulating in the district in which the registered office is situated, a company may close the register for a period or periods not exceeding thirty days in each year (1948 s 115). This power is sometimes exercised for a period preceding the annual general meeting to avoid the need to register transfers until after the declaration of a dividend.

Dominion register

A company which is empowered to and does carry on business in a dominion or colony may keep there a branch register of members resident there, called a dominion register. Notice of the situation of the office where such a register is opened, and of any change in its situation and of its discontinuance, must be given to the Registrar on the prescribed form within fourteen days (1948 s 119) (Form 29).

A duplicate of the dominion register must be kept at the same place as the principal register of members and a copy of every entry made in the dominion register must be transmitted to the company's registered office as soon as possible and entered in the duplicate register (1948 s 120(3)).

Notice of intention to close a dominion register must be advertised in a newspaper circulating in the district in which the register is kept (1948 s 120(2)).

DISCLOSURE OF INTERESTS IN SHARES

Notification of substantial interests

Part IV of the 1981 Act (ss 63–72) contains complicated provisions relating to the disclosure to a public company of notifiable interests in its relevant share capital. Relevant share capital means shares carrying rights to vote in all circumstances at general meetings. A notifiable interest is an interest in five per cent or more of any class of the company's relevant share capital. The figure of five per cent may be altered by statutory instrument.

Where a person:

(a) to his knowledge acquires any interest in shares comprised in relevant share capital or ceases to be interested in any such shares; or

(b) becomes aware that he has acquired any interest in such shares or has ceased to be interested in any such shares;

and:

(i)   he has a notifiable interest after but not before; or

(ii) vice versa; or

(iii) he has a notifiable interest before and after but the percentage
      levels (rounded down to a whole number) are at least one per
      cent different;

certain disclosure obligations arise. These also arise where otherwise
than in the above circumstances a person:

(a) is aware at the time it occurs of any change of circumstances
    affecting any fact relevant to the application of the above rules
    in relation to any existing interest of his in shares of any
    description; or

(b) otherwise becomes aware of any such fact.

(a) above would occur, for example, where shares which previously
had restricted voting rights were given voting rights in all
circumstances and thus became relevant share capital.

A person is deemed to be interested in shares if his spouse or infant
child or a body corporate which is under his effective control or in
which he can exercise one-third or more of the voting power is
interested in them. There are a number of further rules for
determining whether a person has an interest in shares. For example,
one is taken to have an interest in shares if one has entered into a
contract to buy them or is entitled to exercise or control the exercise
of any right conferred by the shares, but an interest as a bare trustee
(or nominee) or an interest in reversion or remainder is disregarded.

By 1981 s 67 if two or more persons make an agreement (which may
include arrangements not binding in law) which restricts their use,
retention or disposal of shares they may acquire in a company (the
target company) and any of them acquires an interest in the target
company's shares in pursuance of the agreement, each party to the
agreement, commonly known as a 'concert party', is deemed to be
interested in all shares in which any other party is interested. Each
member of the concert party must notify all other members of his
interests in the target company so that they can for the purposes of
their disclosure obligations take account of the shares in which they
are deemed to be interested by virtue of the concert party.

A person's duties where the disclosure obligations of Pt IV of the
1981 Act apply may be summarised as follows:

(1) Notify the class of relevant share capital concerned and either
    the number of shares in which he is interested or the fact that he
    no longer has a notifiable interest.

(2) Include in such notification (unless it states that he no longer

has a notifiable interest) particulars of the registered holders of
the shares concerned so far as he knows such particulars.

(3) Notify those particulars on learning them later.

(4) Notify any change in those particulars.

(5) If a party to a s 67 agreement, state certain further matters in his
notification, eg the names and addresses of the other parties.

(6) If his notification is because he or another has ceased to be a
party to a s 67 agreement, state this in the notification and, in
the latter case, identify that other.

All such notifications must be in writing and state the name and
address of the person giving them. If he is a director, the obligation
being fulfilled must be stated. Generally, these notification
obligations must be performed within the five days following the day
on which they arise.

A person who authorises another ('the agent') to acquire or dispose
of, on his behalf, interests in shares in the relevant share capital of a
public company (eg a person who delegates the management of investments to a stockbroker or bank) must secure that the agent notifies
him immediately of acquisitions or disposals which will or may give
rise to an obligation to make a notification.

Register of substantial interests

Every public company must keep a register for the purposes of the
above disclosure requirements and within three days inscribe in it all
information received in fulfilment of those requirements (1981 s 73).
The register must be kept at the same place as the register of directors'
interests (see p 143), must unless it constitutes such an index in itself
have an index of names therein and (save insofar as it contains information with respect to certain overseas interests) be open to
inspection by any member of the company or the general public in the
same way as the register of members (see p 48).

Investigation of interests

A public company may by written notice require anyone whom it
knows or has reasonable cause to believe to be or to have been within
the previous three years interested in shares in its relevant share
capital to confirm that fact or indicate whether it is or is not so and to
give certain further information as to his interest in such shares which
can include particulars of other persons so interested (1981 s 74).
Information acquired by a company by this procedure must be
entered in a separate part of the register of substantial interests (1981
s 75).

A company can be required to exercise its above power on the requisition of members holding at least ten per cent of such of its paid up share capital as carries the right of voting at general meetings (1981 s 76). The company must make a report of the information obtained in an investigation resulting from such a requisition: if the investigation takes more than three months an interim report must be made every three months. Such reports must be kept at the registered office and be open to inspection in the same way as the register of members.

NUMBERING OF SHARES

Prima facie every share must have a distinguishing number so that it is possible to ascertain precisely which shares each member holds; but if all the issued shares in the company or all the issued shares of a particular class are fully paid up and rank pari passu for all purposes, they need not (1948 s 74). If, after the distinctive numbering of shares of a class has been dispensed with, further shares of that class are created not ranking pari passu for all purposes then, strictly speaking, the original shares of the class should be renumbered unless the new shares are distinguished as a separate class until they are all issued and fully paid and rank pari passu with the original shares. Where, however, newly created shares are not pari passu only because they do not rank for a dividend which is declared shortly afterwards on the original shares of the class, the point is often ignored in practice.

SHARE CERTIFICATES

1948 s 80 requires every company within two months of an allotment or of receipt of a transfer to complete and have ready for delivery share certificates, unless the conditions of issue otherwise provide. Where a brokers transfer is used in conjunction with a stock transfer (see p 66), the two months begin to run from receipt of the later of the two transfers to be lodged (Stock Transfer Act 1963, s 2(3)(b)). A company need not, however, issue certificates for shares or debentures allotted or transferred to Sepon Limited, The Stock Exchange nominee used for the 'Talisman' computerised settlement system (Stock Exchange (Completion of Bargains) Act 1976, s 1).

Certificates are issued in accordance with the provisions of the Articles. Unless power is taken to affix mechanical signatures or to dispense with signatures or advantage is taken of the provision outlined below relating to use of a securities seal, they are usually signed by the secretary and one or more directors. It is the invariable practice for certificates to be sealed by the company, thus affording prima facie evidence of the title of the member to the shares (1948 s 81). Certificates for securities may also be sealed with a facsimile of the common seal with the addition on its face of the word 'Securities', called a securities seal (Stock Exchange (Completion of Bargains) Act 1976, s 2) and in the case of a company formed before 12 February 1979 (the date on which that Act came into force) no signatures are required if such a seal is used, notwithstanding anything in the Articles. The provisions of s 81 (evidence of title) extend to share certificates sealed with a securities seal.

Apart from the statutory obligation, The Stock Exchange requires companies whose securities are listed to issue certificates within one month of the expiration of any right of renunciation and within fourteen days of the lodgment of a transfer.

It is desirable to postpone the issue of certificates where fixed instalments are payable upon the shares within a short period, and in such cases it is usual to issue a renounceable letter of allotment (the form of which will vary substantially depending on the number of instalments involved).

The Yellow Book forbids a listed company to charge for the issue of a share certificate and other companies rarely make such a charge.

Share certificates for different classes of shares should be easily distinguishable, preferably by colour; and where further shares are issued of an existing class, but not ranking for the next dividend, it is advisable to defer the issue of certificates until after payment of the next dividend (if possible within the above time limits) or mark the certificates for the later shares appropriately. Listed companies must comply with certain rules laid down in the Yellow Book regarding the size of and details to be stated on share certificates.

Lost certificates

The Articles usually authorise directors to issue new certificates in place of those which have been lost, defaced or destroyed, but the power should be exercised with caution, as the company may incur liability to any person who suffers loss through such an issue. Before issuing a new certificate, adequate protection should be obtained, the applicant being required to enter into an agreement to indemnify the company for any consequential loss with one or more sureties to the indemnity (p 243). No fee may be charged in the case of listed securities.

Effect of certificate

The need for caution in issuing share certificates is emphasised by the effect which the certificate may have on the company.

Every sealed certificate issued by the company is, in the first place, prima facie evidence of the title of the person named therein to the shares concerned (1948 s 81 and Stock Exchange (Completion of Bargains) Act 1976, s 2) and the company may be estopped from denying that the person named in a properly issued certificate is entitled to the shares (*Re Bahia, etc Railway Co* (1868) LR 3 QB 584).

In addition the company may be estopped from denying that the amount specified as paid up in the certificate has been duly paid as against a holder who acts on the faith of the certificate (*Bloomenthal* v *Ford* [1897] AC 156).

But the company may not be bound by a certificate issued without the authority of the board of directors (*South London Greyhound Racecourses Ltd* v *Wake* [1931] 1 Ch 496).

SHARE WARRANTS

If the Articles permit, share warrants may be issued to the holders of fully paid shares under the company's seal (1948 s 83) and must be stamped with duty of an amount equal to three times the current rate of duty (see p 69) payable on a transfer of the shares or stock represented thereby at their market value (Finance Act 1963, s 59 (as amended)).

Warrants are made out to bearer and are negotiable instruments, transferable by delivery.

The conditions upon which such warrants are issued are laid down by the Articles which authorise the issue, and it is usual to supply a printed copy of these conditions to warrant holders on application or with the warrant. In the case of listed securities, The Stock Exchange requires the company to issue certificates in exchange for warrants (and vice versa if permitted) within fourteen days of the deposit of the warrants (or certificates) and to certify transfers against the deposit of warrants. The Stock Exchange also requires that no new share warrant is issued to replace one which has been lost unless it is proved to have been destroyed.

Subject to any provision in the Articles, the bearer of a share warrant is entitled to have his name entered on the register of members on surrendering the warrant for cancellation (1948 s 112(2)). The company is held responsible for any loss incurred by any person if the name of a bearer of a share warrant is entered in the register without the warrant being surrendered and cancelled (1948 s 112(3)).

Particulars of share warrants issued and surrendered must be included in the annual return.

Status of warrant holders

The holders of share warrants are not members of the company, but the Articles may provide that they may be deemed to be for all or only some purposes (1948 s 112(5)). The Articles cannot, however, provide that shares held by warrant shall count towards a director's qualification (1948 s 182(2)). If a holder is authorised by the Articles to attend and vote at meetings, it is usually necessary for the warrant holder to deposit his warrant with the company three days before the meeting.

Procedure on issue of warrants

The following is a summary of the usual procedure involved in the issue of share warrants to bearer:

(1) The applicant lodges with the company a form of application, his share certificate and a remittance for the stamp duty payable on the warrant and for the fee which is usually payable for its issue. The fee should be fixed by the board of directors if it is not specified in the Articles.

(2) A receipt is issued to the applicant in the following form, to be exchanged in due course for the share warrant:

Share warrant application receipt

.... *PLC*	...................................*PLC*
No..... .... 19.....	No..... .... 19.....
No of share certificate	Certificate No .... , in respect of
....	shares numbered .... to ...., has been
Name of member	deposited this day at the Company's office by ....
....	with an application for the issue of a share warrant to bearer.
	.... *Secretary*
[*Counterfoil retained by company*]	The share warrant will be ready on .... 19......

(3) Entry of the application is made in any register for this purpose. Check that there is no restraint on the registered shares, draw up the share warrant and cancel the share certificate.

(4) The company's seal is affixed (1948 s 83) in accordance with the Articles.

(5) The warrant is impressed with the stamp duty.

(6) The holder's account in the register of members is closed as if he had ceased to be a member, and the following particulars must be entered in the register:

(a) The fact of the issue of the warrant.

(b) A statement of the shares included in the warrant, distinguishing each share by number (if any).

(c) The date of the issue of the warrant (1948 s 112(1)).

(7) The necessary entries must be made in any register of share warrants.

(8) The warrant is forwarded to the applicant.

NOTICE OF TRUSTS

1948 s 117 forbids the entry on the register of members of any trust affecting the shares, whether express, implied or constructive. As a consequence the company is relieved from all responsibility to persons, other than the registered holders, who enjoy equitable claims over its shares. However, if notice is given to the company of any lien, charge or other claim over its shares, it may be helpful to inform the person giving the notice at once that the claim cannot be recognised.

Thus if A, the registered holder of shares, holds such shares as trustee in trust for B the trust is no concern of the company. A is the person capable of signing a form of transfer and liable for any sums due on the shares. But the claims of persons other than the registered holder must be recognised where a stop notice (formerly a notice in lieu of distringas) is issued under Order 50, rule 11, of the Rules of the Supreme Court.

Where such a notice is received and the registered holder subsequently attempts to transfer the shares concerned, notice of the intended transfer must be given to the person on whose application the notice has been issued, and no transfer must be registered within eight days of this latter notice. If, however, at the end of these eight days no order of the court restraining the transfer is issued, the transfer should be registered in the ordinary manner.

The rule that a company cannot take notice of a trust does not, however, enable the company to obtain priority over equitable interests of which it has received notice (*Bradford Banking Co* v *Briggs* (1886) 12 App Cas 29).

The receipt of information for the purpose of completing the register of directors' holdings or the register of substantial interests in voting shares of public companies does not constitute notice of a trust (1967 s 29(6) and 1981 s 73(4)). The same applies to information obtained by a public company in any investigation of interests in its voting shares under 1981 s 74 (1981 s 75(3)).

MEMBERS

Companies

A limited company cannot acquire its own shares for valuable consideration except:

(*a*) by a redemption or purchase in accordance with Pt III of the 1981 Act (see p 76);

(*b*) in a reduction of capital approved by the court (see p 184);

(*c*) in certain other cases involving an application to the court (see p 186); and

(*d*) by forfeiture of shares, or their surrender in lieu of forfeiture, for failure to pay sums due on them (1980 s 35).

Certain consequences are prescribed by 1980 ss 36 and 37 where shares in a company are acquired by the company itself or its nominee.

As a general rule, a body corporate cannot be a member of a company which is its holding company and any allotment or transfer of a company's shares to its subsidiary is void (1948 s 27). This general rule is subject, however, to the following exceptions:

(*a*) A subsidiary may acquire shares of its holding company in the capacity of a personal representative or trustee, provided that it is not beneficially interested. (The proviso does not apply where the beneficial interest is only by way of security for the purposes of a transaction entered into by the company in the ordinary course of a business which includes the lending of money.)

(*b*) A subsidiary which on 1 July 1948 was a member of its holding company may continue to be a member but may not vote at meetings of the holding company or at meetings of any class of members.

A nominee of a body corporate is subject to a similar restriction against being a member of the body corporate's holding company (1948 s 27(4)).

Apart from the above restrictions, any company may, subject to its Memorandum and Articles, hold shares in another company.

Transfers of shares by a company should be executed under its common seal.

A corporation which holds shares in a company may authorise any person it thinks fit to act as its representative at meetings (1948 s 139). The authorisation should be given by resolution of the directors or other governing body; and the person so authorised should prove his authority by producing a certified copy of the resolution. See p 238 for a form of authorisation. This person is not a proxy. He has the same powers of voting, etc, as the corporation would be able to exercise were it an individual (1948 s 139). The company cannot, therefore, insist that the representative's authorisation be lodged at the registered office before the meeting.

Partnerships

Since an English partnership has no corporate existence, the company may refuse to register a transfer into the name of such a partnership (*Re Vagliano Anthracite Collieries Ltd* (1910) 79 LJ Ch 769). The transfer should be executed in favour of all the partners (or up to four of them as trustees for all the partners) who should be registered as joint holders of the shares.

Minors

Subject to the provisions of the Articles a minor (a person under the age of eighteen—Family Law Reform Act 1969) may become a member of a company. The membership contract is voidable at the instance of the minor up to or within a reasonable period after attaining the age of eighteen and any sums paid to the company can then be recovered. Until repudiation, a minor has full powers of membership. If partly paid shares are transferred to a minor the transferor will remain liable for all future calls on such shares while they are held by the minor.

Joint holders

In the absence of other provisions in the Articles, where one of a number of joint holders of shares dies, the survivors acquire all the rights of the deceased holder, but a death certificate or grant should be required as evidence of the death.

Articles usually provide that where shares are held by persons jointly notices of meetings need to be sent only to the holder who is named first on the register, that dividends shall be sent to that person and that a receipt signed by any one of the joint holders shall bind the others. For this reason joint shareholders are entitled to require the company to register some of the shares with the name of one holder first and others with the name of another first (*Burns* v *Siemens Bros Dynamo Works (No 2)* [1919] 1 Ch 225).

A transfer of shares held jointly must be executed by all the registered holders but on the death of one, execution by the survivors is valid without the assent of the deceased holder's personal representative since the shares were held jointly and not, at any rate so far as the company is concerned, as 'tenants in common'.

Bankrupt members

If a member becomes bankrupt his shares vest in his trustee who is entitled to execute transfers. The trustee's title should be proved by production of the original court order appointing him, an office copy of the order or a copy of the *London Gazette* in which the appointment of the trustee is advertised.

If it is discovered that a shareholder is an undischarged bankrupt, dividends should not be paid to him. The existence of the dividend should be reported to the Official Receiver or the Department of Trade.

The trustee of a bankrupt shareholder enjoys a power of disclaimer where the shares are of an onerous nature as where calls are likely to be made. The exercise of this power, however, entitles the company to prove in the bankruptcy for any damages suffered through the disclaimer.

Proof may always be made for debts, calls actually due at the date of the commencement of the bankruptcy and the estimated present value of future calls; but the trustee in bankruptcy may set off against a call any debt due from the company.

Subject to compliance with the Articles, particulars of the bankruptcy and the name of the trustee should be entered in the register (reg 30, Table A). While the bankrupt's name remains on the register, unless the Articles provide otherwise, he is entitled to vote or tender a proxy at meetings (*Morgan* v *Gray* [1953] Ch 83), although his vote must be cast as his trustee directs. Until the trustee obtains registration of the shares in his own name, he cannot petition for compulsory winding-up (*Re HL Bolton Engineering Co Ltd* [1956] Ch 577, but see *Re Bayswater Trading Co* [1970] 1 All ER 608).

Marriage of members

If a woman on marriage changes her surname (as is usual but not obligatory) she should by producing her share certificate and marriage certificate have her name altered on the register and on her share certificate. If, however, she omits to do this she may on transferring the shares execute the transfer in her former name. But if her former name remains on the register dividend warrants will be made out in that name; after a few months she may have difficulty in paying them into her bank account if that is in her new name.

TRANSFER OF SHARES

The duties described below relating to the registration of transfers of shares, like other duties concerning the maintenance of the register of members and registration of transmission of shares, will often be performed by a separate registrar rather than the secretary, but for simplicity it is assumed here that the secretary does them. The duties will be the same if they are undertaken by a separate registrar, who may be another employee of the company or an independent company or firm providing the services of a registrar.

Notwithstanding anything to the contrary in the Articles, shares or debentures may only be transferred by an instrument in writing (1948 s 75), ie a verbal transfer is ineffective; but this rule does not extend to transmission by operation of law, eg on death or bankruptcy. An article providing for automatic transfer of shares on the death of a member is invalid (*Re Greene, decd, Greene* v *Greene* [1949] Ch 333).

The law and practice as to transfers has been radically altered by the Stock Transfer Act 1963 (called here 'the 1963 Act') and by The Stock Exchange's Talisman system, which are discussed below.

With regard to the form of a transfer Articles usually state merely that transfers must be in the usual form or such other form as the directors approve (see reg 23) and that the directors may refuse to recognise a transfer relating to more than one class of share (see reg 25).

Prior to the 1963 Act shares had to be transferred by a transfer executed by both transferor and transferee, each in the presence of a witness who also signed. (The transferee had to execute to signify that he agreed to become a member, as required by 1948 s 26(2).) Any additional requirements of the Articles (eg that the transfer be a deed) had to be observed: although this was rarely a requirement, transfers were usually by deed.

Fully paid registered securities of a company limited by shares are now almost always transferred by a stock transfer as permitted by the 1963 Act but the pre-1963 law continues to apply to transfers of other securities (eg partly paid shares or shares of an unlimited company, so that execution by the transferee is still necessary where transfer of the shares to him involves the possibility of liability for him). A transfer which could be effected by a stock transfer must however comply with the requirements of the 1963 Act as to execution and contents.

Where a stock transfer is not or cannot be used, material variation from the common form is necessary to justify refusal of registration (*Re Letheby & Christopher Ltd, Jones's Case* [1904] 1 Ch 815). Although both the transferor(s) and the transferee(s) must execute a transfer which is in a form other than a stock transfer, a person who is both a transferor and a transferee need execute only once.

The 1963 Act enables fully paid registered securities (including shares, stock, debentures, debenture stock, loan stock and bonds) of a company limited by shares to be transferred by a stock transfer as set out in Schedule 1 to that Act or any other form which complies with the Act as to execution and contents.

The 1963 Act also provides that where a stock transfer has been executed for the purpose of a stock exchange transaction (ie a transaction on The Stock Exchange), particulars of the consideration and of the transferee may either be inserted in that stock transfer or, where a block of securities is being transferred to several transferees not in joint account, inserted in separate brokers transfers (the 1963 Act s 1); however The Stock Exchange's Talisman system explained below has reduced the use of brokers transfers.

The above provisions of the 1963 Act have effect notwithstanding anything to the contrary in any enactment or instrument (eg Articles of Association) relating to the transfer of the securities concerned, but nothing in s 1 affects any enactment or rule of law regulating the execution of documents by companies or other bodies corporate, or any Articles of Association regulating the execution of documents by any particular company or body corporate (the 1963 Act s 2). Thus, transfers by companies and other bodies corporate should normally be executed under their common seal and provision in a company's Articles to the effect, eg, that a transfer by that company must be executed in a particular manner must be observed.

As to the stamping of transfers, see p 69. Articles sometimes empower the directors to authorise a fee (usually $12\frac{1}{2}$p) for the registration of a transfer but the practice of charging a fee is falling into disuse. Listed companies are required to register transfers and other documents relating to or affecting title without payment of any fee.

After a transfer has been registered the old share certificate and the transfer form should be carefully filed and preserved unless (as is often the case) power is taken in the Articles to destroy them after a specified period (eg six years). The new share certificates must be ready for delivery within two months after the date on which the transfer is lodged with the company (time beginning to run where a transfer is by stock transfer and brokers transfer only when both have been lodged) unless the terms on which the shares were issued otherwise provide (1948 s 80 and the 1963 Act s 2(3)(*b*)) or unless the transfer is to a stock exchange nominee (Stock Exchange (Completion of Bargains) Act 1976 s 1) (when no share certificate need be issued—see below under 'The Talisman system'). The Listing Agreement however reduces this two month period to fourteen days for listed companies and the general undertaking applicable to companies whose securities are traded on the Unlisted Securities Market does likewise for them.

Procedure on transfer in the simplest case

The simplest procedure for transfer occurs when in a non-market transaction (ie a transaction not made through The Stock Exchange) all the shares represented by one or more share certificates are transferred to one transferee. In such circumstances a stock transfer form is completed in full and the words in italics deleted. The form is then executed by the transferor and his agent (if any) places his stamp and the date in the box beside the transferor's signature. The form is then delivered, with the relative certificate(s), to the transferee who stamps it (see p 69). The person lodging the stock transfer for registration, if different from the transferee, places his stamp in the appropriate box at the foot of the form before lodging it, accompanied by the relative certificate(s), with the company secretary for registration. If the transfer appears to be in order it is, if necessary, presented to the board of directors for authorisation or refusal of registration. If the transfer is registered, the old certificate(s) are cancelled, a new certificate sealed and issued to the transferee and entries and adjustments made in the register of transfers and register of members.

Certification of transfers

The more complicated procedure of certification of transfers is needed in non-market transactions where:

    (i) although some of the shares represented by a certificate are transferred, others are retained, since the transferor will not be willing to part with possession of the certificate to the transferee, the transferee will if a sale is involved not be willing to part with the purchase price while the transferor retains possession of the certificate for all the shares and the company will not register the transfer unless the share certificate is delivered to it; or

(ii) some of the shares represented by a certificate are transferred to one transferee and others to a second transferee, since neither transferee will be willing for the other to have possession of the certificate for all the shares and if a sale is involved neither will part with the purchase price for the shares he has bought while the transferor keeps the certificate.

In either case the secretary will be called on to certify transfers, ie to sign certificates on transfers that the share certificates for the shares transferred have been deposited with him. The form of certificate is at the top right-hand corner of a stock transfer form. Transfers need not be stamped or dated, nor need the transferee's name be inserted, before certification.

A transfer is deemed to be certified if it bears the words 'certificate lodged' or words to the like effect, and a certification is deemed to be made by a company if the person issuing the instrument is a person authorised to issue certified instruments of transfer on the company's behalf, and the certification is signed by a person authorised to certify transfers on the company's behalf or by any officer or servant either of the company or of a body corporate so authorised. Moreover a certification is deemed to be signed by any person if it purports to be authenticated by his signature or initials (whether handwritten or not), *and* it is not shown that the signature or initials were placed there neither by himself nor by any person authorised to use the signature or initials for the purpose of certifying transfers on the company's behalf (1948 s 79).

The certification of a transfer by a company constitutes a representation by the company to any person acting on the faith of the certification that there have been produced to the company such documents as on the face of them show a prima facie title to the shares or debentures in the transferor named in the transfer; but they do not constitute any guarantee that the transferor has a title (ibid).

A person who acts on the faith of a false certification by a company made negligently has the same right of action as if the certification had been made fraudulently (ibid).

The fact that a transfer is certified by the secretary does not imply that the directors will approve the transfer, but if the directors are unlikely to approve it, it is advisable that the secretary should inform the person lodging it. Certification by the secretary of a transfer of what purports to be fully paid shares will, however, estop the company from denying that the shares are fully paid (*Re Concessions Trust, McKay's Case* [1896] 2 Ch 757); but certification will not estop the company from challenging the title of the transferor (*Bishop* v *Balkis Consolidated Co Ltd* (1890) 25 QBD 512).

(*a*) *Where the transferor is transferring to one person part only of the shares represented by a certificate*

A stock transfer form is completed in full and the words in italics deleted. The form is then executed by the transferor and his agent (if any) places his stamp and the date in the box beside the transferor's signature before lodging the form and the share certificate with the company for certification of the transfer.

The share certificate is retained by the company, a non-returnable balance ticket is issued to the transferor entitling him to apply for a new certificate for the shares which are not transferred, and the stock transfer form is certified and returned to the transferor. The form is then delivered to the transferee who stamps it (see p 69). The person lodging the stock transfer for registration, if different from the transferee, places his stamp in the appropriate box at the foot of the form before lodging the form for registration. The procedure thenceforward is the same as if all the shares represented by the share certificate had been transferred, except that on registration two new certificates will be issued, one to the transferee for the shares transferred, and the other to the transferor for those retained.

(*b*) *Where the transferor is transferring some or all of the shares represented by a certificate to more than one transferee*

The procedure is practically the same as in (*a*) above. Separate stock transfer forms will be executed for each transferee, and each form must be certified, a non-returnable balance ticket being issued to the transferor if he is retaining some shares.

The Talisman system

This computerised system operated by The Stock Exchange (and taking its name from Transfer Accounting Lodgment for Investors, Stock Management for jobbers) now deals with nearly all transactions effected on The Stock Exchange. The only securities not covered by Talisman are those of oversea companies and those represented by bearer certificates or renounceable letters of allotment or acceptance.

Under Talisman a special type of stock transfer form, called a 'Talisman Sold Transfer', transferring the securities to Sepon Limited, is completed. (Sepon Limited is a company owned by The Stock Exchange, the word Sepon denoting Stock Exchange Pool Nominees, and is below referred to simply as Sepon.) The Talisman Sold Transfer is then executed by the transferor and his broker places his stamp and the date in the appropriate boxes on the form before lodging the form and the relative certificate(s) with The Stock Exchange Centre. Provided the documents so lodged are found to be in order the Centre passes them to the company for registration of the transfer to Sepon and the securities comprised in such transfer are credited to the account of the selling broker until account day. On account day the securities comprised in the Talisman Sold Transfer are debited to the account of the selling broker and credited to the account of the buying jobber and the selling broker receives payment (on the jobber's behalf) from the Centre. The securities are then allocated between the persons to whom the jobber sold them and the Centre prepares 'Talisman Bought Transfers' from Sepon to those persons and lodges these with the company for registration in the normal way. Throughout the time while the securities are registered in Sepon's name Sepon holds them as nominee for the person entitled at the time. This central pooling system saves much certification work formerly undertaken by The Stock Exchange for companies.

A company need not issue a certificate for securities transferred to Sepon which is a 'stock exchange nominee' (1948 s 80 as amended by Stock Exchange (Completion of Bargains) Act 1976, s 1) but only in favour of the ultimate purchaser.

No stamp duty is payable on a Talisman Sold Transfer (Finance Act 1976, s 127(1) and Stock Exchange (Designation of Nominees) (Stamp Duty) Order 1979 (SI 1979 No 370)). Stamp duty on Talisman Bought Transfers is collected centrally for the Inland Revenue by the Centre but a company secretary is still responsible for seeing that such a transfer is properly completed as to the duty payable before he registers it.

A Talisman Sold Transfer need not specify the consideration or Sepon's address (Stock Transfer (Addition of Forms) Order 1979 (SI 1979 No 277), art 3(1)). A Talisman Bought Transfer need not be executed under hand but is sufficiently executed by Sepon if it bears a facsimile of Sepon's corporate seal, authenticated by the actual or facsimile signature of a director or the secretary of Sepon (ibid, art 3(2)).

If a Talisman Sold Transfer relates to only some of the shares represented by a share certificate a balance certificate is requested on the Talisman Sold Transfer. When the secretary registers the transfer he will issue a balance certificate in the name of the transferor. This is issued via the Centre to the transferor's broker: the shares represented thereby are never transferred into Sepon's name.

The system also includes arrangements for the settlement of claims to dividends and the like in respect of shares sold.

Certification of transfers by The Stock Exchange

Although the Talisman system has much reduced the amount of certification work undertaken by The Stock Exchange, The Stock Exchange Centre still certifies transfers of companies' securities arising from transactions on the Exchange in certain circumstances. (Before the introduction of Talisman certification work arising from such transactions was mostly performed by The Stock Exchange as an alternative to certification by the company.) The Centre can certify Talisman Sold Transfers against a balance certificate requested in respect of a previous transaction provided the Talisman Sold Transfer for that previous transaction has not been despatched by the Centre to the company for registration or against a Talisman Bought Transfer provided it has not been similarly despatched.

Where a holding is passing to two or more transferees, brokers transfer forms may still be used and certified in certain circumstances. Where brokers transfers are used a stock transfer form is completed as if for a non-market transaction, save that the words in italics are left in and the lower part of the form (where details of the transferee would be inserted) is cancelled. Brokers transfers completed as to Part 1 are then certified by The Stock Exchange Centre or by the secretary (usually the former) by being produced with the stock transfer and the certificate(s). If certification is by the secretary he retains the certificate(s) for the shares concerned and the stock transfer until he receives the brokers transfers for registration. If certification is by the Centre it forwards the certificate(s) and stock transfer to the secretary. Having been certified the brokers transfers are then delivered to the buying brokers who insert particulars of the transferees in Part 2, place their stamp upon them and lodge them with the company secretary for registration in the normal way.

Summary of variants of Stock Exchange transactions

In the case of Stock Exchange transactions, therefore, the secretary will most often receive for registration Talisman Sold Transfers accompanied by certificate(s) and Talisman Bought Transfers, but less frequently he may receive certified Talisman Sold Transfers, ordinary stock transfers or brokers transfers. Transfers will always be accompanied by certificate(s) or certified (either by the secretary or The Stock Exchange Centre). Where transfers are certified the certificate(s) will already have been lodged with the secretary.

Scrutinising of transfers

All transfers should be carefully scrutinised. The form of transfer must comply with the requirements summarised above and must be properly executed.

Generally, it will no longer be possible for the secretary to compare the signature of the transferor with the transfer giving rise to the holding since transfers do not require to be executed by the transferee. Sometimes transfers may be executed by a person who signs on behalf of the transferor; and in such a case the secretary must see that the power of attorney by which the authority is given is in order. Transfers of shares standing in the names of joint holders must be executed by all the holders. The secretary should check that the form is correctly dated and either sufficiently stamped (see p 69) or in the case of a Talisman Bought Transfer properly completed as to the duty payable.

Where the directors have power to refuse registration of a transfer the secretary should, in appropriate cases (eg where the shares are partly paid) and if possible, make inquiries as to the status of the transferee, for transfers of shares which are not fully paid should not be allowed to bankrupts, minors or 'men of straw'.

It is also important to consider the position of the transferor, for if calls are in arrear it may be desirable to refuse the transfer until payment has been made. The Articles may also give a lien on the shares for debts due to the company, although the Listing Agreement prohibits this for fully paid shares of listed companies. In particular, if there is a call or lien outstanding, the transfer should be refused if a receiving order has been made or a bankruptcy petition filed against the transferor and it is even advisable in such circumstances to delay a transfer if notice has been received of an act of bankruptcy committed by the transferor within the previous three months.

If a transfer, duly signed by a transferor, is received for registration after the death of the transferor, registration may not on that account be refused, unless probate or letters of administration have previously been registered, in which case the shares should be registered in the name of the executor or administrator.

Refusal of transfer

In the absence of contrary provisions in the Articles, a shareholder is entitled to transfer his shares to whomsoever he pleases, and even to transfer partly paid shares to a pauper on the eve of liquidation (*Parker's Case* (1867) 2 Ch App 685); but the directors may be given power to refuse transfers at their discretion. Table A, for example, empowers directors to refuse any transfer of shares which are not fully paid if they disapprove of the transferee or if the company has a lien on the shares (reg 24), and similar provisions appear in most Articles. Fully paid listed shares, however, must be free from any restriction on the right of transfer.

Where such a power to refuse a transfer is given, it must be exercised by the directors in good faith, in the interests of the company and not through purely personal motives, but the burden of proving lack of good faith lies upon the person disputing their decision (*Re Coalport China Co* [1895] 2 Ch 404).

Articles often give the directors power to refuse to register a transfer without assigning reasons for the refusal. If such a power is exercised, the secretary should in reply to inquiries asking why the transfer has been rejected call attention to the provisions of the Articles and steadfastly refrain from giving the reasons for the rejection, for the court will not draw unfavourable inferences from such refusal but if reasons are given will consider them.

The exercise of the power necessitates the passing of a resolution at a board meeting, so that where one of three directors died and only one of the surviving directors objected to the person to whom the deceased director's shares had been transferred, registration was permitted as, the voting at the board meeting having been equal, no resolution refusing the transfer had been passed (*Re Hackney Pavilion* [1924] 1 Ch 276). The right to exercise the power may be lost by undue delay (*Re Swaledale Cleaners Ltd* [1968] 1 WLR 432).

If a receiving order or charging order is made, or an injunction issued against the transferor, any transfer must, of course, be refused, and if a stop notice is formally served on the company a transfer should not be registered until at least eight days after notice of its lodgment has been given to the person who issued the stop notice (see p 56).

Notice of a refusal to register a transfer must be given to the transferee within two months after the date on which the transfer is lodged with the company (1948 s 78).

Stamp duty

The secretary should check that transfers are properly stamped since under s 17 of the Stamp Act 1891 any person whose office it is to enrol, register or enter in any rolls, books or records any instrument and who enters one which is not duly stamped is liable to a fine of £10.

The consideration being stated on the form of transfer, it is not difficult to ascertain whether the stamp is adequate in most cases, but if the amount of the consideration is considerably less than the market value of the shares, the secretary should request the person lodging the transfer to obtain an adjudication of the duty by the Commissioners of Inland Revenue. In any case of doubt, the stamping of the document with an adjudication stamp relieves the secretary of liability. In the case of a transfer of shares by way of gift inter vivos, an adjudication stamp is essential.

The following are the rates of duty on transfers (Finance Act 1974, s 49 and Sched 11):

Consideration or (in the case of gifts inter vivos) value of shares		
Exceeding £	*Not Exceeding* £	*Duty* £
–	5	0·10
5	10	0·20
10	20	0·40
20	30	0·60
30	40	0·80
40	50	1·00
50	60	1·20
60	70	1·40
70	80	1·60
80	90	1·80
90	100	2·00
100	120	2·40
120	140	2·80
140	160	3·20
160	180	3·60
180	200	4·00

*Consideration or (in the case of gifts
inter vivos) value of shares*

Exceeding	Not Exceeding	Duty
£	£	£
200	220	4·40
220	240	4·80
240	260	5·20
260	280	5·60
280	300	6·00
300	–	£1·00 per £50 or part

Where the person who is becoming the beneficial owner of the shares by virtue of the transfer (whether or not he is the transferee) is resident outside the Scheduled Territories and the transfer is for full consideration in money or money's worth, stamp duty is payable at the rate of 1% (ibid). The Scheduled Territories are now the United Kingdom, the Channel Islands, the Isle of Man, the Republic of Ireland and Gibraltar (SI 1972 No 2040).

A fixed duty of 50p is, however, payable on transfers falling within certain categories which are roughly listed on the reverse of stock transfer forms. This list should not be regarded as exhaustive and the certificate appearing on the reverse of the forms can be amended to fit the circumstances in cases where, as a matter of law, only the fixed duty is payable. Such transfers are often submitted to a marking officer before being lodged for registration, in which case, if the explanation is marked by the officer 'Transfer passed for fifty pence', the secretary need not question the adequacy of the stamp. Section 44 of the Finance Act 1942 provides, in effect, that such transfers do not need adjudication.

Circulars setting out the requirements of the Stamp Acts for the guidance of secretaries may be obtained on application to the Board of Inland Revenue.

Transmission of shares, which is the vesting of shares in a new holder otherwise than by execution of an instrument of transfer, occurs on the death or bankruptcy of the registered holder. As to bankruptcy see p 59.

TRANSMISSION OF SHARES ON DEATH

On the death of a sole shareholder his shares vest in his personal representatives (ie his executors or administrators), who are usually the only persons to be recognised by the company as entitled to the shares and who become entitled to all dividends payable and will be liable for all sums due in respect of the shares to the extent of the deceased holder's assets.

If the shares of the company are not listed on The Stock Exchange, the secretary may first learn of the death of a member from a request for a valuation of the shares at the date of death. The secretary should write stating the price or prices at which the last transactions, at arm's length, before the date of death, were recorded, and that this is the only indication he has of their value, if this is the case.

A personal representative may either (a) allow the shares to remain registered in the name of a deceased, or (b) apply to have his own name entered as registered holder, or (c) transfer the shares (1948 s 76 and reg 30, Table A). In private companies, Articles frequently include special provisions regarding the disposal of shares passing by transmission.

Whichever course is adopted, evidence of the title of the personal representative must be produced to the company. Production of a grant of probate, letters of administration or any document which is in law sufficient evidence thereof (eg an office copy of a grant of probate or letters of administration) must be accepted as evidence of title notwithstanding anything in the Articles to the contrary (1948 s 82). A note of the death, the name and address of the executor or administrator, and of the production should be entered in the register and on the share certificate. The Yellow Book provides that a listed company may not charge a fee for registering a death; other companies may charge such a fee if authorised by the Articles, although the practice of doing so is falling into disuse. It is usual for the secretary to signify the fact that the relevant document has been produced to him by placing a rubber stamp on it with his signature or initials and the date.

If the personal representative's application for the shares to be placed in his own name is accepted, a new account should be opened in the register in his name, without reference to his representative capacity, for the fiduciary nature of his title should not appear on the register. See p 242 for a form of request. This need not be stamped, and is applicable only where the shares are to be placed in the name of the sole personal representative or the names of all of them where more than one. Where this course is adopted, the personal representative on registration becomes fully liable, even beyond the extent of the deceased's assets, for all sums due in respect of the shares. On such registration a new share certificate must be issued to the personal representative. The directors may refuse to comply with the request where the Articles give them power to refuse a transfer; but if the Articles contain no power of veto, the directors cannot refuse to register an executor as a member (*Scott* v *Frank F Scott* (*London*) *Ltd* [1940] Ch 794; but see reg 30, Table A). Where the company takes power to limit the number of shareholders in a joint account, The Stock Exchange require in the case of listed shares that up to four persons may be registered.

A personal representative has power to transfer shares notwithstanding that he is not a member of the company (1948 s 76), but unless the shares have been placed in his own name, his description on the transfer should indicate the capacity in which he signs, eg James Smith, of 1 Brown Street, London, Grocer, executor of Sam Smart. A personal representative can also notwithstanding that he is not a member institute an application to the court under 1981 s 75 for relief on the grounds of unfairly prejudicial conduct (1981 s 75(9)) (see p 193).

Where Table A applies, the directors may give notice requiring the personal representative to elect either to register himself or to transfer the shares and if the notice is not complied with within ninety days they may withhold dividends and bonuses (reg 32).

CALLS ON SHARES

Where the conditions of issue provide that moneys payable for shares are to be paid by fixed instalments on fixed dates, such instalments are not calls since no call is made by the company.

Where there are partly paid shares, it may be necessary to call on the holders from time to time to pay the whole or a portion of the amount unpaid on their shares. Although partly paid shares are now rare, in such a case the provisions in the Articles must be observed, and usually the board will need to pass a resolution authorising the call to be made, though sometimes a resolution of the company in general meeting is required. Whichever form of resolution is employed, the sum to be called up and the date of payment should be specified. Unless the Articles provide to the contrary, a call should not be made on certain members of a class to the exclusion of others (but see reg 20).

The amount which may be called up from time to time may be limited by the Articles (see reg 15) or by the terms of issue.

Notice of the call should be given to shareholders and care must be taken to give the notice specified in the Articles and to state the time and place for making payment, as failure to do this may render the call unenforceable (*Re Cawley & Co* (1889) 42 Ch D 209 at p 236 per Lord Esher MR).

The Articles sometimes provide for interest on calls not paid by the appointed day (reg 18).

The Articles may allow the directors, at their discretion, to accept in advance of calls amounts unpaid on shares, and to pay interest on such amounts out of capital (*Lock* v *Queensland Investment & Land Mortgage Co* [1896] AC 461) (see 1948 s 59(*b*) and reg 21). Such interest must be paid from distributable profits (1980 ss 39 and 45(2)). Dividends must not be payable on amounts paid in advance of calls if a Stock Exchange listing is desired, and amounts so paid cannot subsequently be refunded to the shareholder except on a winding-up (*Re Wakefield Rolling Stock Co* [1892] 3 Ch 165). Where some consideration other than cash is accepted in settlement of a call, the court may subsequently challenge the validity of the consideration (*Re White Star Line Ltd* [1938] Ch 458).

Non-payment of calls

The effect of non-payment of a call will depend on the Articles. In any case action for the amount may be taken against the holder, or his personal representative should he be dead, but additional rights may be exercised if the Articles permit. Thus, Articles usually empower the directors to refuse a transfer of shares on which calls remain unpaid; or to forfeit the shares; or to prohibit the holder from attending or voting at meetings.

Unpaid calls are debts in the nature of specialty debts (1948 s 20) which are not statute-barred until after twelve years.

In proceedings against shareholders for unpaid calls, difficulty may arise in the following cases on account of the status of the holder:

(1) *Minors* may be able to repudiate all liability during minority or within a reasonable time of attaining full age (eighteen years—Family Law Reform Act 1969, s 1).

(2) *Mentally disordered persons* may repudiate liability if it can be shown that they took the shares while of unsound mind and that the company was aware of the insanity at the time.

(3) *Bankrupts* cannot be sued, but a proof for unpaid calls may be made in the bankruptcy.

Forfeiture

Articles invariably provide that, in the event of non-payment of a call, any share in respect of which the call is unpaid may be forfeited by resolution of the directors (see regs 33 to 39). Forfeiture cannot usually be carried out until the member has been warned of the consequences of the call remaining unpaid and the provisions of the Articles must be strictly observed.

In such cases it is usual for the board to instruct the secretary to write to the holder of the shares concerned, before a resolution for forfeiture is passed, warning him that if the call is not paid by a certain date the shares will be liable to forfeiture. If no satisfactory reply to this letter is received, the board may resolve that the shares be forfeited and a letter will be sent notifying the holder of the forfeiture. The following form of letter warning a holder of forfeiture may be employed:

> Dear Sir,
>
> I am directed by the Board to remind you that the call on shares held by you in this company made on the ..... day of ...., and amounting to £....., has not yet been received.
>
> The Board hereby require you to pay this call in accordance with Article ..... of the Articles of Association together with interest at the rate of £..... per cent per annum on or before ...., 19.....
>
> I hereby give you notice that in the event of non-payment within the time specified, the shares in respect of which the above call is made will be liable to forfeiture in accordance with Article .... of the Articles of Association, together with all dividends declared in respect of such shares. [In addition, you will remain liable to pay any sums due in respect of such shares notwithstanding the forfeiture.]
>
> By order of the Board,
> .... *Secretary*

Forfeited shares may be cancelled, sold or re-allotted, but the Articles normally provide that the former holder remains liable for the unpaid calls until the amount has been paid. In the case of a resale, the purchaser also becomes liable for the amount of the call outstanding, and cannot vote until the liability has been extinguished, but it is advisable to call upon him specifically for the sum due.

Articles sometimes empower directors to accept a surrender of shares, but it appears that this power can only be exercised where the shares surrendered are subject to forfeiture (or perhaps where a surrender of fully paid shares is accepted in exchange for shares of the same nominal value), for an unlawful reduction of capital might otherwise be effected (*Bellerby v Rowland & Marwood's Steamship Co Ltd* [1902] 2 Ch 14).

In disposing of forfeited or surrendered shares the purchaser may be credited with the amount paid up at the time of the forfeiture, but the shares cannot be credited as fully paid if the sum paid on reissue is less than the amount unpaid at the time of the forfeiture, for this would amount to the issue of shares at a discount.

In order to safeguard the purchasers of forfeited shares, Articles frequently provide that a statutory declaration by an officer of the company as to the propriety of the forfeiture shall, together with the receipt for the purchase consideration, constitute the purchaser's title and be deemed conclusive evidence of the facts therein stated as against all persons claiming to be entitled to the shares. This declaration should be supplied if required. As, however, under 1948 s 75, an instrument of transfer must be deposited with the company, the alternative method by which the board authorises one of their number to execute a transfer to the purchaser is to be preferred.

If shares in a public company are forfeited or surrendered in lieu of forfeiture, the company:

(*a*) must, if they are not disposed of within three years, at the end of that period cancel them, reducing the company's allotted share capital accordingly, and if such reduction brings its allotted share capital below the minimum for a public company re-register as a private one;

(*b*) must not vote in respect of those shares; and

(*c*) must, if it shows those shares as an asset in its balance sheet, transfer an amount equal to their value out of profits available for dividend to a non-distributable reserve fund.

LIEN

In addition to the right of forfeiture and accompanying power of sale, a private company often has under its Articles a right of lien over the shares of its members in respect of any debts due from them to the company, which is enforceable by sale of the shares (see regs 11 to 14, Table A, but in the case of companies registered since 21 December 1980, Table A confines the lien to moneys due in respect of the shares). The right often differs from the right of forfeiture in that any surplus proceeds of sale, after the payment of the debt and expenses, must be refunded to the shareholder, but the methods employed in exercising the right are usually similar. The Articles *must* be observed carefully in every case. For example if Table A applies, the company was registered before 22 December 1980 and the moneys are due otherwise than in respect of the shares concerned, the right of lien does not extend to shares registered in the names of two or more holders jointly if the moneys are due from one only.

A public company may similarly be given by its Articles a lien over members' shares but, unless its ordinary business includes lending money or certain similar activities and the lien arises in the ordinary course of its business, only for amounts payable on those shares (1980 s 38). The Stock Exchange will allow listed shares to be subject to a right of lien only if they are partly paid.

A right of lien is usually extended to dividends due on the shares concerned.

REDEMPTION OR PURCHASE BY A COMPANY OF OWN SHARES

This is governed in the case of limited companies having a share capital by 1980 s 35 (see p 57) and ss 45 to 62 in Part III of the 1981 Act. The law restricts such a company's ability to issue redeemable shares or buy its own shares to prevent funds passing out of the company to shareholders to the detriment of those who deal with it, since if the company is unable to meet its obligations they will, because it is a limited company, have no recourse to the shareholders. An unlimited company may, subject to its Memorandum and Articles, freely issue redeemable shares or buy its own shares, but the rest of this heading is concerned with limited companies.

1981 s 45 enables a company to issue redeemable shares, if authorised by its Articles, including shares redeemable at the option of the company or the holder. A company must always have some irredeemable shares in issue: otherwise it might be left without any members or issued shares. Redeemable shares may not be redeemed unless they are fully paid: thus redemption cannot relieve a holder of partly paid shares of his uncalled liability. There must be payment on redemption. The terms and manner of redemption must be specified in the Articles. A share which is redeemed is thereby cancelled and the amount of the company's issued share capital is thereby reduced accordingly: there is no consequent reduction in the company's authorised share capital. If a company is about to redeem shares it can issue further shares up to the same nominal amount as if those to be redeemed had never been issued: in other words, it can temporarily have the same amount of its authorised share capital issued twice.

Where a redemption precedes a new issue of shares or occurs within a month after it, capital duty is payable only on any net contribution to the company's assets (1981 s 45(10) to (12)).

Appendix 2 contains a diagram to illustrate the rules in 1981 s 45(5) and (6) relating to the accounts from which the moneys payable on redemption can be drawn.

1981 s 46 enables a company, if authorised by its Articles, to purchase its own shares, including redeemable shares, and applies the rules summarised above as if the purchase were a redemption save that the terms and manner of purchase need not be specified in the Articles. The procedure is outlined below under 'Procedure on purchase of own shares'. In the remainder of this heading references to redemption include purchase by a company of its own shares.

To maintain a company's capital for the protection of those dealing with it 1981 s 53 requires, when a redemption takes place, certain transfers to a capital redemption reserve (that expression having replaced the former capital redemption reserve fund): distribution of this is restricted in the same way as distribution of a company's share capital save that the capital redemption reserve may be used to pay up a fully paid bonus issue.

1981 s 54 enables private companies to redeem shares from capital (ie otherwise than from distributable profits or the proceeds of a fresh issue). Complex rules ensure that so far as possible distributable profits are, however, used first and that the undistributable accounts and reserves are maintained at the highest possible figure. For the protection of shareholders and those dealing with a company a procedure with tight time limits (for which reference should be made to the legislation) is prescribed for redemptions (or purchases) out of capital as summarised below in tabular form (such procedure being in the case of purchases additional to the procedure set out below under 'Procedure on purchase of own shares'):

(a) The directors make a statutory declaration in Form 65 relating to the company's ability to pay its debts immediately after the payment out of capital and for the ensuing year. To this declaration there must be annexed a report by the company's auditors stating, inter alia, that they have inquired into the company's state of affairs and are not aware of anything to indicate that the opinion expressed by the directors in the declaration is unreasonable.

(b) Next follows a special resolution approving the proposed payment out of capital.

(c) Copies of the statutory declaration and of the auditors' report must be filed at the Companies Registry.

(*d*) Notice of the proposed payment out of capital, stating certain matters, must (i) be published in the *London Gazette* if the company is registered in England and Wales or in the *Edinburgh Gazette* if the company is registered in Scotland and (ii) be published in a national newspaper or given to individual creditors.

(*e*) The statutory declaration and auditors' report must be open to inspection.

(*f*) Within five weeks of the special resolution a creditor or non-consenting member can apply to the court for cancellation of the resolution approving payment out of capital.

(*g*) Finally the payment out of capital can be made between five and seven weeks after the special resolution (1981 ss 55 to 57).

If a company is wound up within a year after a payment out of capital any deficiency in the winding-up can be recovered from the recipients of the payment and, unless he shows that he had reasonable grounds for the opinion expressed in the statutory declaration, any director who signed it (1981 s 58).

Procedure on purchase of own shares

If the purchase is a 'market purchase' (basically one on The Stock Exchange or its Unlisted Securities Market) it must be authorised by a resolution in general meeting, which may be an ordinary resolution. The authority may be general or limited, conditional or unconditional. It must specify the maximum number of shares which may be acquired, the maximum and minimum prices (which may be expressed by formulae) and an expiry date for the authority not more than eighteen months ahead. The shares to which the authority relates can be voted on the resolution (1981 s 49).

An 'off-market purchase' (one which is not a market purchase) must, however, be authorised by a *special* resolution which must authorise the *terms of the contract of purchase*, not merely purchases. Again, the authority must have an expiry date not more than eighteen months ahead. The shares to which the authority relates may *not* be voted on the special resolution. The proposed purchase contract or a memorandum of it if it is not in writing must be available for inspection by members at the meeting and at the registered office for at least fifteen days before the meeting (1981 s 47).

A resolution to authorise market purchases or the terms of off-market purchases must be filed at the Companies Registry (1948 s 143(1) and (4)(*a*) and 1981 s 49(10)).

A return of purchases must be made to the Companies Registry (Form 64) (1981 s 52(1),(2) and (3)): public companies have to give extra details relating to prices paid.

Copies of purchase contracts or memoranda of them if they are not written must be kept at the registered office for ten years and be open to inspection by any member and, if the company is a public one, anyone else (1981 s 52(4) and (5)).

There are provisions relating to contingent purchase contracts, the assignment or release by a company of a right to buy its own shares and payments apart from the purchase price (1981 ss 48, 50 and 51).

DIVIDENDS

Profits available for dividends

The Acts contain certain provisions, particularly Part III of the 1980 Act, governing what may be regarded as profits available for distribution, eg as dividend. Any provision of the Memorandum or Articles must also be observed. Dividends may not be paid out of share capital, share premium account (1948 s 56) or capital redemption reserve (1981 s 53) (see p 77).

The rules of Part III of the 1980 Act are complex. The following are the most basic rules and there are exceptions even to these. A company's profits available for distribution are its accumulated, realised profits, so far as not previously utilised by distribution or capitalisation, less its accumulated, realised losses, so far as not previously written off in a reduction or reorganisation of capital (1980 s 39(2)). (Thus by the 1980 Act it is no longer possible to distribute an unrealised profit on a fixed asset.) Realised profits mean such profits as fall to be treated as realised profits in accordance with generally accepted accounting principles (1948 Sched 8 (as substituted by the 1981 Act) para 90 and 1981 s 21(1)). A public company may pay a dividend only if:

(a) the amount of its net assets equals or exceeds the aggregate of its called-up share capital and its undistributable reserves; and

(b) payment of the dividend will not reduce those assets to less than that aggregate (1980 s 40).

There are elaborate rules for determining by what figures taken from what accounts these questions are determined (1980 s 43).

A company is not bound to distribute its profits among its members in the form of dividends unless the Articles so provide, and profits are frequently used for other purposes. Thus, the directors may set aside as a reserve the whole or a portion of the profits, to make provision for future contingencies or to expand the business; and this may be done unless the Articles forbid. Such a reserve does not lose its nature as profit and may subsequently be used to pay dividends.

Basis of payment

Where the Articles are silent, and the relevant regulation of Table A (eg reg 118 of the 1948 Table A) is excluded, dividends must be divided among shareholders in proportion to the nominal value of their shares. That is however rare: usually in accordance with Table A or an express provision in the Articles they will be divisible in proportion to the amount paid up on the shares. If the Articles provide that payment is to be made 'according to the value of the shares', the nominal value should be taken as the basis of calculation (*Oakbank Oil Co* v *Crum* (1882) 8 App Cas 65). In addition, the respective rights of the various classes of shares, as fixed by the Memorandum or Articles, must be considered, eg the rights of the holders of preference shares. In the absence of provision to the contrary in the Memorandum or Articles, preference shares are presumed to be cumulative.

Declaration of dividends

The Articles usually empower the directors to declare an interim dividend but this will not become a debt due to the members until the date of payment and accordingly the declaration can be revoked at any time prior to that date.

A final dividend is normally recommended by the directors but is subject to the approval of the company in general meeting. Following the resolution of the board which recommends the dividend, warrants should be prepared by the secretary in readiness for despatch as soon as the general meeting has given its approval, unless, of course, the general meeting is likely to vary the amount declared by the board or the dividend is payable at a future date.

Variation by the company is, however, extremely unusual, and, where Table A applies, by reg 114 the company has no power to *increase* a dividend recommended by the directors.

Reference should be made to regs 114 to 122 of Table A or the corresponding Articles.

Dividend warrants

Prior to April 1973 dividends were paid net after deduction of income tax. As a result of the Finance Act 1972 dividends no longer have income tax deducted but instead carry a tax credit for the recipient. A voucher or statement (see p 240) should accompany the dividend warrant (or cheque) and should state the actual dividend payment and the amount of tax credit; it should also certify that an amount of advance corporation tax equal to the tax credit will be paid to the Collector of Taxes.

With the aid of a dividend list, the correctness of the warrants may be checked before despatch and a record maintained of payments made and dividends unclaimed.

Forms similar to that referred to above will be employed in the case of an interim dividend.

In the case of joint holders, the warrant is usually made payable to the first named alone, provided the Articles state that any one of such holders can give an effectual receipt (see reg 121).

Lost dividend warrants

If a dividend warrant is lost in transit or by the shareholder to whom it is addressed, a new warrant may be issued after it has been ascertained that the warrant has not been paid by the bank, the bank has been instructed to stop payment of the lost warrant and the shareholder has provided the company with an indemnity.

Dividend mandate forms

Where a shareholder desires payment of a dividend to be made to a bank or some person other than himself a dividend mandate form (see p 241) should be lodged with the company. In the case of a joint holding, such a request must be signed by all the holders.

BONUS SHARES

If the Articles permit, profits may be distributed among the existing members in the form of bonus shares in the proportions in which they would share dividends, profits equivalent to the paid-up value of the shares being capitalised. Such an issue will often involve an increase of the authorised capital. A return of allotments must be made upon the issue (Form PUC 7) and, unless a mere writing up in the nominal value of their shares is involved, allotment letters or share certificates should be sent to the members who are entitled to the new shares. No capital duty is payable on a bonus issue because there is no contribution to the assets of the company.

Part X of the Income and Corporation Taxes Act 1970 should be considered in relation to bonus issues of share capital.

As to use of share premium account or capital redemption reserve for paying up bonus shares, see pp 43 and 77.

RESTRICTIONS ON DEALING IN SHARES

Under the Prevention of Fraud (Investments) Act 1958 as amended it is unlawful to deal in securities, whether as principal or as servant or agent, except under licence issued by the Department of Trade (ibid, s 1). For this purpose 'servant' includes a director or officer (ibid, s 26(4)). Dealing in securities (in which term are included not only shares and debentures, but also rights or interests in shares or debentures) is defined as 'making or offering to make with any person, or inducing or attempting to induce any person to enter into or offer to enter into:

(a) any agreement for, or with a view to, acquiring, disposing of, subscribing for or underwriting securities . . ., or

(b) any agreement the purpose or pretended purpose of which is to secure a profit to any of the parties from the yield of securities or by reference to fluctuations in the value of securities'.

Members of The Stock Exchange and recognised dealers' associations are exempted from the licensing requirements (ibid, ss 2 and 15), and certain other dealers (eg underwriters and issuing houses) may be exempted by Department of Trade order (ibid, ss 2 and 16). A licence is not needed if a transaction is effected with or through a person who is exempt under any of the aforesaid categories or with or through the holder of a licence (ibid, s 2(2)(a)), but this provision does not authorise a person to hold himself out as carrying on the business of dealing in securities.

Nor is a licence required *merely* because a prospectus is issued complying with 1948 s 38 or exempt therefrom under 1948 s 39, or *merely* because an application for shares or debentures is issued together with such a prospectus (ibid s 2(2)(b) and (d)).

By s 14 of the 1958 Act, restrictions are imposed on the distribution of circulars, etc, relating to investments (other than, inter alia, prospectuses, or application forms accompanied by prospectuses, complying with 1948 s 38 or exempt therefrom under 1948 s 39). It is an offence to distribute or possess for distribution circulars containing, inter alia:

(i) an invitation to enter into or offer to enter into any agreement of the type mentioned in (a) or (b) above; *or*

(ii) information calculated to lead directly or indirectly to the recipient's doing any such thing;

unless, inter alia:

(*a*) the distribution or intended distribution is to persons whose business involves the acquisition and disposal, or the holding, of securities; *or*

(*b*) the invitation or information contained in the document is made or given by or on behalf of a member of The Stock Exchange or of a recognised dealers' association or a licensed or exempted dealer, or by or on behalf of a company to holders of securities of, or to employees or creditors of, itself or its subsidiary with respect to securities of itself or the same or another subsidiary; *or*

(*c*) the invitation or information in the document is made or given with respect only to a sale or proposed sale of the securities by auction.

Penalties are imposed by s 13 of the 1958 Act (as amended) on a person who induces other persons to invest money by any statement which he knows to be misleading, false or deceptive, by making recklessly (dishonestly or otherwise) any statement which is misleading, false or deceptive or by any dishonest concealment of material facts.

If an offence under the 1958 Act is committed by a company with the consent or connivance of a director, manager, secretary or other officer, he is also personally liable (ibid, s 19). Offences under the Act may carry terms of imprisonment or fines or both.

CHAPTER 5

MEETINGS

As a general rule a valid meeting of a company cannot be held unless
the meeting was summoned by the proper summoning authority, and
this proper authority is primarily the board of directors (*Re Wyoming
State Syndicate* [1901] 2 Ch 431). In other words, a meeting
summoned by some of the members or some of the directors without
the sanction of the board (or ratification by the board prior to the
meeting) is not a properly constituted meeting and any decisions it
may make will not bind the company. The first step to be taken
towards the effective summoning of a meeting is, therefore, to obtain
from the board of directors authority to summon the meeting. This
should be done by placing a proposal for the summoning of the
meeting before a properly constituted meeting of directors (see
p 105).

The general principle stated above is subject to the following
modifications:

(1) The directors must convene an extraordinary general meeting
on the requisition either of members holding at least one-tenth
of paid-up capital carrying voting rights (1948 s 132—see p 87)
or of an auditor whose notice of resignation contains a
statement of circumstances which he considers should be
brought to the notice of members or creditors of the company
(1976 s 17).

(2) If a public company's net assets are half or less of its called-up
share capital the directors must within 28 days of the earliest
day on which any of them knows this convene an extraordinary
general meeting for a date not less than 56 days from that day to
consider whether any, and if so what, measures should be taken
to deal with the situation (1980 s 34).

(3) If the Articles do not make other provision in that behalf, a
valid meeting may be summoned by any two or more members
holding not less than one-tenth of the issued share capital (1948
s 134).

(4) Where Table A applies, if at any time there are not within the United Kingdom sufficient directors to form a quorum at a board meeting, any one director or any two members may convene an *extraordinary* general meeting (reg 49).

(5) If the annual general meeting is not held within the prescribed period, the Department of Trade may call or direct the calling of the meeting on the application of any member (1948 s 131(2)).

(6) In any case in which it is impossible to convene a meeting in the manner prescribed by the 1948 Act or the Articles, the court may give directions (1948 s 135).

THE ANNUAL GENERAL MEETING

Every company, public or private, must hold an annual general meeting in each year; but the first of these meetings need not be held in the year in which the company is incorporated or in the following year, provided that it is held within eighteen months after the date of incorporation (1948 s 131(1)). If, therefore, a company is incorporated on 1 December 1982, no meeting need be held in 1982 or in 1983, but one must be held not later than 31 May. Not more than fifteen months may elapse between two consecutive annual general meetings (ibid) and companies listed on The Stock Exchange are required to issue their report and accounts, which will normally be circulated with the notice of annual general meeting, within six months of the end of the relevant financial period.

If default is made in complying with the statutory requirements, any member of the company may apply to the Department of Trade, which may direct the meeting to be called. In this event, subject to any directions by the Department, the meeting, if not held in the year in which it should have been held, will not be deemed to be the annual general meeting for the year in which it is held, unless a resolution that it shall be so treated is passed by the meeting (1948 s 131(3)). A copy of any such resolution must be filed within fifteen days.

The normal or 'ordinary' business of annual general meetings includes:

(1) To consider and adopt the accounts. This item of business is usually so described although 1976 s 1(6) merely requires the directors to lay the accounts before the company in general meeting and does not require them to be adopted or approved. The accounts laid by the directors are still the company's statutory accounts even if the company in general meeting

votes not to approve them. The laying of the accounts is usually
done at the annual general meeting, but it can be done at an
extraordinary general meeting and may have to be as 1976 s 6
generally requires the accounts to be laid before the company in
general meeting within seven months if it is a public company,
or within ten months, if it is a private company of the end of the
relevant accounting reference period.

(2) To adopt the auditors' report. Again adoption is unnecessary.
The auditors' report must however be read at the meeting
before which the relevant accounts are laid (1967 s 14(2)): this
means read aloud, not 'taken as read'.

(3) To consider and adopt the directors' report. This report is to be
attached to the balance sheet and accordingly is included in the
documents to be laid before the company in general meeting
under 1976 s 1. Again adoption is unnecessary.

(4) To declare a dividend. This is usually done in general meeting
because the Articles normally provide that dividends, apart
from interim dividends, must be declared in general meeting
(see regs 114 and 115). This item is not an obligatory part of the
business of an annual general meeting and may be done at an
extraordinary general meeting.

(5) To elect or re-elect directors. This item is usually included in the
business of an annual general meeting because the Articles
normally provide that some of the directors shall retire at each
annual general meeting and that the company may then re-elect
them or elect new directors (see regs 89 to 92).

(6) To appoint auditors. At each general meeting at which the
statutory requirements as to the laying of accounts are
complied with, auditors must be appointed to hold office from
the conclusion of that meeting until the conclusion of the next
such general meeting (1976 s 14(1)).

(7) To fix the auditors' remuneration or determine the manner in
which it shall be fixed. This must be done in general meeting
(1976 s 14(8)). Often the general meeting merely resolves that
the auditors' remuneration shall be fixed by the directors.

Special business may also be conducted (see p 90). As to special
notice, see p 89.

Typical procedure at an annual general meeting would therefore be
as follows:

(1) The secretary reads the notice convening the meeting (see
pp 232 and 233), though often this notice is taken as read on the
motion of the chairman.

(2) The auditors or secretary read the report of the auditors, which must be on the table for inspection by any member.

(3) The chairman proposes that the directors' report be taken as read. If the motion is rejected he should then read the report.

(4) The chairman makes his statement and invites and answers questions.

(5) The adoption of the directors' and auditors' reports and the accounts is proposed.

(6) The declaration of the dividend recommended by the directors is proposed.

(7) Directors are appointed or re-appointed.

(8) Auditors are appointed or re-appointed (see p 159).

(9) Special business mentioned in the notice is transacted.

(10) The chairman declares the meeting closed.

The register of directors' holdings (see p 142) must be produced at the beginning of the annual general meeting and must remain open and accessible to any person attending the meeting (1967 s 29(11)).

EXTRAORDINARY GENERAL MEETINGS

The directors are invariably empowered by the Articles to convene an extraordinary general meeting of the company whenever they think fit.

Such a meeting will be summoned in the same manner as an annual general meeting (see p 234), but the period of notice will depend on the type of resolution to be passed (see p 89).

1948 s 132, however, provides that directors must convene an extraordinary meeting if so required by the holders of not less than one-tenth of such of the paid-up capital of the company as carries the right of voting, or, where there is no share capital, by members representing not less than one-tenth of the voting rights.

A requisition under this section must be in writing signed by the requisitionists and must state the objects of the meeting. It may consist of one document signed by all the requisitionists or of several similar documents signed by one or more of them, and must be deposited at the company's registered office.

If the directors do not proceed to convene a meeting within twenty-one days after the deposit of the requisition, the requisitionists or any of them representing more than one-half of the voting rights of all of them may convene a meeting which must, however, be held within three months after the deposit.

Any reasonable expenses of the requisitionists are repayable by the company which may retain sums so repaid out of any fees due or to become due to the directors who were at fault, but no other penalty is imposed on directors who fail to convene a meeting when required by requisition.

As to the requisitioning of an extraordinary general meeting by a resigning auditor pursuant to 1976 s 17, see p 161.

NOTICE

Persons entitled to receive notice

Care must be taken to give notice of a meeting to all persons entitled to receive such notice, for failure to do this may render the meeting invalid; though if all persons entitled to attend do so and unanimously waive the irregularity, the failure to give the necessary notice can be overcome (*Re Express Engineering Works Ltd* [1920] 1 Ch 466 and see further p 100); and see also reg 51 and *Re West Canadian Collieries Ltd* [1962] Ch 370 and *Musselwhite* v *Musselwhite* (*CH*) & *Son Ltd* [1962] Ch 964.

The basic principle is that every member of the company is entitled to notice of a meeting, but the Articles may take away this basic right from certain classes of members, eg from holders of preference shares in certain circumstances, or from holders of shares on which calls have not been paid, or from members who have given no address within the United Kingdom.

Notice of all general meetings must be given to the company's auditors (1967 s 14(7)).

Table A provides that notice shall be given to every member except those members who (having no registered address within the United Kingdom) have not supplied to the company an address within the United Kingdom for the giving of notices to them, and to every person entitled to a share in consequence of the death or bankruptcy of a member, who, but for his death or bankruptcy, would be entitled to notice, and to the auditor for the time being of the company; but adds that no other person shall be entitled to receive notices (reg 134).

In the case of a meeting at which the company's objects are to be altered, notice must be given to certain holders of debentures (see p 182).

Period of notice

(1) In the case of an *annual general meeting*, not less than twenty-one days' notice in writing must be given; and this is so even where the

Articles purport to allow a shorter period (1948 s 133(1)). Regulation 50 of Table A prescribes twenty-one days' notice in writing at the least. An adjourned meeting may be summoned by a lesser period of notice, however, if the Articles so provide, and in any case if all the persons entitled to attend and vote at the meeting so agree, the meeting can be held even where less than twenty-one days' notice has been given (1948 s 133(3)). This agreement need not be obtained at the meeting, so that if, for any reason, it is desired to summon an annual general meeting within twenty-one days, this can be done, provided that all persons entitled to attend and vote agree in advance (see p 235).

(2) In the case of *meetings other than the annual general meeting*, not less than fourteen days' notice in writing is necessary, except in the case of an unlimited company, when seven days' notice will suffice (1948 s 133(1)), or of a meeting at which a special resolution is to be passed, when twenty-one days' notice is needed (1948 s 141(2)). By agreement of a majority in number of members having the right to attend and vote, being a majority holding not less than 95 per cent in nominal value of shares giving the right to attend and vote, a valid meeting (not being an annual general meeting) can be summoned by a lesser period of notice (1948 s 133(3); see p 235).

(3) In construing the above rules, both the day on which the notice is served or deemed to be served, and the day on which the meeting is held will usually be excluded from the period required (reg 50, Table A). Where Table A applies, if notice is posted to members on the first day of a month by first class post, both the first and second days of that month must be excluded since Table A provides that notice shall be deemed to be effected twenty-four hours after it is posted (reg 131). The third day of the month is, therefore, the first of the twenty-one days' notice required for summoning an annual general meeting. The 23rd is the last of the twenty-one days; and, since the day on which the meeting is to be held must also be excluded, the meeting cannot properly be held before the 24th. (It is not clear whether an extra day should be allowed if second class post is used but in principle it seems correct to do so.)

(4) The periods of twenty-one and fourteen days specified in 1948 s 133 are statutory minimum periods. Articles may require longer periods of notice, but cannot authorise shorter periods.

Special notice

'Special notice' is required for a resolution for (i) appointing as auditor a person other than a retiring auditor; filling a casual vacancy in the office of auditor; re-appointing an auditor appointed by the directors to fill a casual vacancy; or removing an auditor before the expiration of his term of office (1976 s 15, see p 160); (ii) the removal of a director (1948 s 184(2), see p 137); and the appointment or re-appointment of a director who is over the age limit (1948 s 185(5), see p 136).

Notice of the intention to move such a resolution must be given *to* the company not less than twenty-eight days before the meeting at which it is to be moved. But if, after such notice is given, a meeting is held within twenty-eight days, the notice is deemed to have been properly given (1948 s 142).

Notice of the resolution must be given by the company at the same time and in the same manner as the notice of the meeting; but if this is not practicable the notice may be given by newspaper advertisement or in any other mode allowed by the Articles not less than twenty-one days before the meeting (ibid).

Contents of notice

The Articles will usually contain certain provisions as to the contents of the notice. Under reg 50 the notice must specify the date, time and place for the meeting and, in the case of special business, its general nature. This last requirement means giving sufficient detail to enable members to determine whether or not it is desirable for them to attend.

In addition, the following detailed information must be given:

(*a*) In the case of an annual general meeting, the notice must state specifically that the meeting is to be the annual general meeting (1948 s 131(1)).

(*b*) If extraordinary or special resolutions are to be passed, the notice must state specifically that they are to be proposed as extraordinary or special resolutions (1948 s 141). Such resolutions should be set out in full.

(*c*) If the company has a share capital, the notice must state with reasonable prominence that a member entitled to attend and vote is entitled to appoint a proxy or, where that is allowed (see 1948 s 136(1)), one or more proxies to attend and vote instead of him, and that a proxy need not also be a member of the company (1948 s 136(2), see p 92).

(*d*) If 'special business' is to be transacted at the annual general meeting, notice must be given. The phrase 'special business' may be defined by the Articles. Table A defines it as all business to be transacted at an extraordinary general meeting, and all business to be transacted at an annual general meeting except the declaring of a dividend, the consideration of the accounts, balance sheets, and the reports of the directors and auditors, the election of directors in the place of those retiring and the appointment of, and the fixing of the remuneration of, the auditors (reg 52).

In drafting notices, it is always wise to err on the side of caution and to give rather more than less information than may be absolutely necessary, for the inadequacy of the notice may invalidate the proceedings at the meeting, and any interests of directors must be clearly disclosed (*Kaye* v *Croydon Tramways Co Ltd* [1898] 1 Ch 358). Thus, notice of intention to alter the company's Articles should always state the nature of the contemplated alterations (*Normandy* v *Ind Coope & Co Ltd* [1908] 1 Ch 84); a notice of intention to increase capital must specify the amount of the proposed increase (*MacConnell* v *Prill (E) & Co Ltd* [1916] 2 Ch 57). A notice 'to elect directors' is sufficient notice to permit the election of directors up to the maximum permitted by the Articles (*Choppington Collieries Ltd* v *Johnson* [1944] 1 All ER 762) but is not good practice.

In the case of listed companies, proofs of all notices of meetings, circulars, proxy forms and other documents to be sent to shareholders must be submitted to the Quotations Department of The Stock Exchange and copies submitted when issued.

Members' notices and statements

Although, in general, it is for the directors to determine what business is to be put before a meeting, the members of a company have power to require the directors to give notice of certain resolutions which they desire to have put to the *annual general meeting*.

The members who desire to exercise this right must deposit at the company's registered office a requisition signed by the requisitionists, or two or more copies which between them contain the signatures of all the requisitionists. This requisition must be deposited not less than six weeks before the meeting; and with it must be deposited or tendered a sum reasonably sufficient to meet the company's expenses in giving effect thereto. It must be supported by members representing not less than one-twentieth of the total voting rights of all the members having at the date of the requisition the right to vote at the meeting, or by not less than one hundred members holding shares in the company on which there has been paid up an average sum, per member, of not less than £100 (1948 s 140).

On receiving such a requisition, the company must give notice of the desired resolution to members of the company entitled to have notice of the meeting by serving them with a copy of the resolution in any manner permitted for service of notice of the meeting, and in the same manner and, as far as practicable, at the same time as notice of the meeting; but, where it is not practicable to serve the notice at the same time as the notice of the meeting, it must be served as soon as practicable thereafter.

The requirement that the requisition must be deposited with the company not less than six weeks before the meeting might give rise to the possibility that its effect might be avoided by summoning a meeting to be held within six weeks of the deposit; but 1948 s 140(4) provides that if, after a copy of a requisition is received, an annual general meeting is called for a date six weeks or less after the copy has been deposited, the copy shall be deemed to have been properly deposited for the purposes of that meeting.

Notice of the desired resolution must be given also to members not entitled to notice of the meeting by giving notice of the general effect of the resolution in any manner permitted for giving such members notice of meetings of the company (1948 s 140(3)).

In addition to requisitioning notices of resolutions to be put before the annual general meeting, members may require the company to circulate to members entitled to have notice of *any general meeting* a statement of not more than one thousand words with respect to the matter referred to in any proposed resolution or the business to be dealt with at the meeting. The requisition for this purpose must be deposited in the same manner as that for a notice and must be supported by the same number of members; and the statement must be circulated by the company in the same manner in which notice of a requisitioned resolution is served, except that it need not be notified to members who are not entitled to notice of the meeting. But the deposit of the requisition must be made at least one week instead of six weeks before the meeting (1948 s 140). The company is not bound to circulate a statement which the court is satisfied is designed to obtain 'needless publicity for defamatory matter' (1948 s 140(5)).

PROCEEDINGS

Proxies

Every member of a company having a share capital who is entitled to attend and vote at meetings is entitled to appoint a person, not necessarily a member of the company, as his proxy to attend and vote instead of him (1948 s 136(1)); any clause in the Articles purporting to take away this right is void. Unless the Articles otherwise provide, a member of a public company (but not of a private company in the absence of provision in the Articles) may appoint two or more proxies (ibid). The donee of a proxy given by a member of a private company may speak at the meeting, notwithstanding anything to the contrary in the Articles (ibid). But a public company proxy may not speak unless authorised by the Articles. A proxy is entitled to vote only on a poll (see p 97) unless the Articles provide otherwise. As to representatives of companies which hold shares, see p 58. A proxy may be (i) special, appointing a person to vote (normally as the appointor directs in the proxy) on the specific resolution(s) set out in the notice of the meeting, or (ii) general, appointing a person to vote as he thinks fit on all business coming before the meeting. Proxies can authorise a person to attend a number of meetings or any meetings held while the proxy remains in force. In this case they should be stamped 50p (Stamp Act 1891, Sched 1; *Marx v Estates and General Investments Ltd* [1976] 1 WLR 380): a proxy for a single meeting (including any adjournment thereof) is free of stamp duty (Finance Act 1949, s 35 and Sched 8).

The form of proxy will normally be regulated by the Articles (see eg regs 70 and 71): see also p 236 for a specimen form.

The Articles may state that proxies to be used at a meeting must be deposited at the registered office of the company or some other place a certain period before the meeting (see, eg, reg 69); but any provision in the Articles which prports to require a proxy or any other document necessary to show the validity of the appointment to be deposited more than forty-eight hours before the meeting or adjourned meeting is void (1948 s 136(3)) and the period prescribed by Articles is normally forty-eight hours, although occasionally a shorter period is found.

Where the Articles do contain such a requirement for the deposit of proxies before the meeting, and the meeting is adjourned, the question whether a proxy deposited after the first holding of the meeting, but not less than the requisite period before it reassembles after adjournment, can be used is a question of construction. If the Articles require the proxy to be deposited not less than forty-eight hours before 'the meeting or an adjournment thereof', the proxy can be used at the adjournment; but if the Articles require the deposit to be made not less than forty-eight hours before 'the meeting', a proxy deposited after the first holding of the meeting cannot be used at the adjournment (*McLaren v Thomson* [1917] 2 Ch 261). A misprint or other palpable mistake in a proxy does not entitle a company to reject the proxy (*Oliver* v *Dalgleish* [1963] 1 WLR 1274).

The Articles may authorise the directors to send out with notices of meetings proxy forms with or without the names of suggested donees inserted therein; and, even in the absence of specific power in the Articles, the directors may do this if they believe it to be in the interests of the company (*Peel* v *LNWR* [1907] 1 Ch 5). But if invitations in this or any other form to appoint as proxy a person or one of a number of persons are issued at the company's expense to some only of the members entitled to be sent notice of and to vote at the meeting by proxy, a fine may be incurred by the company's officers, though the penalty will not be incurred by reason only of the issue to a member at his request in writing of a form of appointment naming the proxy or a list of persons willing to act as proxies, if the form or list is available on request in writing to every member entitled to vote by proxy (1948 s 136(4)). Companies whose securities are listed on The Stock Exchange are required to send out two-way proxy forms to shareholders and debenture holders entitled to attend and vote in the case of all resolutions other than resolutions relating to the procedure of the meeting or to the remuneration of the auditors. A proxy can cast in favour of a resolution the votes of shareholders who do not indicate how their votes should be cast (*Oliver* v *Dalgleish* [1963] 1 WLR 1274).

A proxy may usually be withdrawn or revoked by the donor at any time before the donee has cast his vote (but see *Holman* v *Clegg* (1957) 101 SJ 216). It may be revoked by the donor attending the meeting in person or by depositing at the registered office of the company a written revocation (reg 73), although some Articles provide that a vote given in accordance with a proxy shall be valid notwithstanding revocation provided that no notice of such revocation shall have been received at the registered office, say, one hour before the meeting. If the donor attends the meeting in person, his vote must be accepted even if the Articles state that a proxy shall be revocable only by the deposit of a written revocation (*Cousins* v *International Brick Co Ltd* [1931] 2 Ch 90).

The quorum

Even where a meeting has been properly summoned, its activities may be ineffective if, when it assembles, it is not properly constituted.

In the first place, its acts can have no effect unless the necessary *quorum* is present. The number of members required to be present in order to constitute a quorum is usually fixed by the Articles. Table A requires, in the case of companies formed since 21 December 1980, two members to be present in person or by proxy or, in the case of companies formed previously, three members present in person (reg 53). If the Articles do not provide for the quorum, two members must be personally present (1948 s 134 as amended). Donees of proxies are not members personally present, unless they hold shares in their own right; but the representative of another company, which is a shareholder, is a member personally present. Regulation 53 provides that the quorum must be present 'at the time when the meeting proceeds to business'. If this or similar wording applies, a reduction in numbers below a quorum before a vote is taken will not invalidate the resolution (*Re Hartley Baird Ltd* [1955] Ch 143). Otherwise however a meeting cannot continue if members withdraw leaving no quorum (*Henderson* v *Louttit* [1894] 21 Rettie (Ct of Sess) 674).

Table A provides that if no quorum is present within half an hour of the time fixed for a meeting it shall if convened on the requisition of members be dissolved, but otherwise shall stand adjourned to the same day in the next week and at the same time and place or to such other day, time and place as the directors determine (reg 54). (In the case of companies formed before 22 December 1980 reg 54 goes on to provide that if a quorum is not present within half an hour of the time for the adjourned meeting the members present shall be a quorum.) As a general rule a single person cannot constitute a meeting (see eg *Re London Flats* [1969] 1 WLR 711 and *Jarvis Motors (Harrow) Ltd* v *Carabott* [1964] 1 WLR 1101). It has been held that by 1948 s 134(*c*) a member present in an individual capacity and as trustee can be counted as two members personally present (*McLeod (Neil) & Sons Ltd, Petitioners* [1967] SC 16); and that one member can constitute a class meeting (*East* v *Bennett Bros Ltd* [1911] 1 Ch 163).

A meeting called by the Department of Trade or the court may certainly consist of one person only (1948 ss 131(2) and 135(1)). The court may order a meeting to be held if the quorum provisions would give the minority shareholders a veto disproportionate to their shareholding (*Re HR Paul & Son Ltd* (1973) 118 SJ 166).

The chairman of a meeting

Where the Articles contain provisions for the appointment of a chairman of a meeting, they must be complied with if the meeting is to be properly constituted (see eg regs 55 and 56). If the Articles do not contain any provisions as to who shall act as a chairman of a meeting and if regs 55 and 56 of Table A do not apply, any member elected by the members present may be the chairman (1948 s 134(*d*)); and, where the chairman stops or improperly adjourns a meeting contrary to the wishes of a majority, the meeting may elect a new chairman in his place for the purpose of continuing the proceedings (*National Dwellings Society* v *Sykes* [1894] 3 Ch 159).

It is the duty of the chairman to preserve order and to see that the proceedings are properly conducted in accordance with the provisions of the Acts and the Articles and otherwise in accordance with the wishes of the meeting. He will (subject to any resolution passed by the meeting) decide all incidental questions arising at the meeting which require immediate decision, and in particular ascertain the sense of the meeting on any resolution coming before it (*Second Consolidated Trust Ltd* v *Ceylon AT & R Estates Ltd* [1943] 2 All ER 567). He has the power of deciding when there has been sufficient discussion of a matter, and may move that the question be now put (*Wall* v *London & Northern Assets Corporation* [1898] 2 Ch 469).

Adjourned meetings

Where Table A (reg 57) applies, the meeting can only be adjourned with the consent of the members present and must be adjourned if they so decide. In the absence of such a regulation, any meeting may be adjourned at the discretion of the chairman, but in exercising this discretion the chairman must act in good faith (see *John* v *Rees* [1970] Ch 345—adjournment in case of disorder). The chairman should adjourn only for the purpose of enabling the meeting to conduct its business more efficiently. Unless the Articles provide to the contrary, the chairman is not bound to adjourn a meeting if he considers it unnecessary.

Where a meeting is adjourned, the Articles must be consulted to ascertain whether or not notice of the adjourned meeting must be given. Table A requires notice to be given only where the meeting is adjourned for thirty days or more (reg 57). If the Articles are silent on the point, no notice is necessary (*Kerr* v *Wilkie* (1860) 1 LT 501). Where the Articles prescribe that notice shall be given, the notice need not state the purpose for which the original meeting was called (*Scadding* v *Lorant* (1851) 3 HL Cas 418).

An adjourned meeting is a continuation of the original meeting, and proxies given for the original meeting may be used at the adjournment, unless they are revoked before they are used. As to whether proxies filed between the original and the adjourned meeting can be used, see p 93. As to whether a meeting which breaks up is adjourned, see *Jackson* v *Hamlyn* [1953] Ch 577.

A resolution passed at an adjourned meeting is deemed to have been passed on the date on which it is, in fact, passed (1948 s 144).

Persons entitled to vote

The Articles may determine who shall and who shall not be entitled to attend and vote at meetings of the company (see eg *Bushell* v *Faith* [1970] AC 1099); but, if they contain no provision to the contrary, in the case of a company originally having a share capital every member has one vote in respect of each share or each £10 of stock he holds (1948 s 134). Where Table A applies, the personal representative of a deceased shareholder who has not had himself registered as the holder of the shares (see p 71) may not vote at a meeting (reg 32); though he is entitled to receive notice of the meeting (reg 134). In addition, no member may vote unless all calls in respect of his shares have been paid (reg 65). The receiver, committee or curator bonis of a member of unsound mind may vote (reg 64).

Articles usually provide that in the case of joint holders the vote of the senior who tenders a vote, in person or by proxy, shall be accepted to the exclusion of the others, seniority being determined by the order of the holders' names in the register (reg 63).

The chairman does not have a casting vote unless one is given to him by the Articles (see reg 60).

Generally a subsidiary may not exercise voting rights in respect of shares which it holds in its holding company (see 1948 s 27 and p 57).

Care should be taken to ensure that only those entitled to attend and vote do so and for this reason officials of the company should be posted at the door of the meeting room. Those attending should be asked their names and these should be checked against the register of members and a list of persons appointed as proxies. It is usual for members and proxies attending a general meeting to be asked to sign their names in a book kept for the purpose.

Voting by show of hands

Primarily the voting on a resolution is by show of hands, in which event each person entitled to vote has one vote irrespective of the number of shares he may hold. A donee of a proxy may not vote on a show of hands unless he is a member in his own right or the Articles state that he may (1948 s 136(1)).

Voting by poll

Except on the question of the election of a chairman or an adjournment of the meeting, the members of a company have a statutory right to demand that a poll be taken (1948 s 137). This right may be exercised after a vote by show of hands has been taken (and the Articles may permit a demand for a poll before a vote by show of hands—*Holmes* v *Keyes* [1959] Ch 199). Any provision in the Articles which purports to take away this right to demand a poll is void.

The demand for a poll may be made:

(*a*) by at least five members having the right to vote at the meeting; or

(*b*) by a member or members representing at least one-tenth of the total voting rights of all the members having the right to vote at the meeting; or

(*c*) by a member or members holding shares in the company conferring a right to vote at the meeting, being shares on which an aggregate sum has been paid up equal to at least one-tenth of the total sum paid up on all the shares conferring that right (1948 s 137(1)).

If the Articles contain provision whereby a poll may be demanded by a smaller proportion of the members than those listed above, a demand made by such smaller proportion is effective; but no larger proportion may be required by the Articles. Where Table A applies, a poll may be demanded by two members present in person or by proxy, unless the company was registered before 22 December 1980 in which case the requirement is three such members (reg 58).

The donee of a proxy has the same right as his donor to join in a demand for a poll (1948 s 137(2)).

The Articles may provide for the manner in which the poll shall be taken. Table A provides that it shall be taken in such manner as the chairman directs (reg 59) and that except on the election of a chairman or a question of adjournment the chairman may direct at what time the poll shall be taken (reg 61), ie forthwith, later on the same day or on another day. Unless the Articles otherwise provide, however, the voters must attend and record their votes and the chairman cannot direct that voting cards shall be sent out to them (*McMillan* v *Le Roi Mining Co Ltd* [1906] 1 Ch 331). Where a future day for the poll is fixed, the chairman should specify the hours during which voting shall take place. If this is not done, the lists cannot be closed until midnight, unless all possible votes are previously recorded.

On a poll a member entitled to more than one vote need not use all his votes or cast all the votes he uses in the same way (1948 s 138).

The secretary should make preparations for a poll. Proxies deposited should be carefully scrutinised and a list of members and their proxies made out in a form such as the following:

Name of member	Name of proxy	No of shares	Remarks	Votes	
				For	Against

It is the practice to require the voting cards to express the number of shares held by the voter or the person or persons on whose behalf he is acting as proxy. Scrutineers should be appointed to watch the counting of the votes and in particular to ensure that votes of a member lodging a valid proxy who attends and votes in person are not counted twice.

RESOLUTIONS

The cases in which the different types of resolution are required are summarised in Appendix 4.

Ordinary resolutions

Except where the Acts or the Memorandum or Articles require something to be done by extraordinary resolution or by special resolution, a meeting may express its will by ordinary resolution. This is a resolution in favour of which a majority of members entitled to vote and voting either in person or by proxy cast their votes. If the voting is by show of hands, a majority in number of those present in person and voting will suffice; but where a poll has been demanded the votes to which shareholders are entitled must be established from the Articles (normally one vote per share).

Extraordinary and special resolutions

A resolution is an *extraordinary resolution* when it has been passed by a majority of not less than three-fourths of such members as, being entitled so to do, vote in person or by proxy at a general meeting of which notice specifying the intention to propose the resolution as an extraordinary resolution has been duly given (1948 s 141(1)).

A resolution is a *special resolution* when it has been passed by such majority as is required for the passing of an extraordinary resolution and at a general meeting of which not less than twenty-one days' notice specifying the intention to propose the resolution as a special resolution has been duly given (1948 s 141(2)).

The main differences between these two types of resolutions are therefore that a meeting to pass an extraordinary resolution (provided that it is not the annual general meeting) may be summoned by fourteen days' notice (or seven days' if the company is unlimited) (see p 89), whereas a meeting to pass a special resolution

must be summoned by twenty-one days' notice, whether or not it is
the annual general meeting.

Short notice, written resolutions and agreements

Where, however, it is so agreed by a majority in number of the
members having the right to attend and vote, being a majority
together holding not less than 95 per cent in nominal value of the
shares giving that right, a resolution may be passed as a special
resolution at a meeting of which less than twenty-one days' notice has
been given (1948 s 141(2)) (see p 235), and if all the members of the
company are present and agree, any defect in the notice may be
waived (*Re Oxted Motor Co* [1921] 3 KB 32; *Re Bailey, Hay & Co*
[1971] 1 WLR 1357). (See however 1948 s 293 as amended in relation
to a minimum period of notice of seveɳ days for a resolution for a
voluntary winding-up.)

If all the shareholders agree that a resolution passed on short notice
shall be treated as valid, the court will not be ready to hear a
shareholder say that the resolution is not valid (*Re Pearce, Duff & Co
Ltd* [1960] 1 WLR 1014). In *Parker & Cooper Ltd* v *Reading* [1926] Ch
975 and *Re Duomatic Ltd* [1969] 2 Ch 365, it was held that ratification
of directors' acts given by all members entitled to attend and vote at
general meetings, but without a meeting being held, is as binding as a
resolution in general meeting. In *Cane* v *Jones* [1980] 1 WLR 1451 it
was held that an agreement between all members was effective to vary
a company's Articles although there was no meeting or written
resolution. If the Articles permit (eg reg 73A of Table A for
companies registered after 21 December 1980) a written resolution
signed by all members entitled to notice of and to attend and vote at
general meetings will (subject to any provision of the Acts requiring a
meeting to be held – see eg 1948 s 131, 1980 s 34) be as valid as a
resolution passed at a general meeting.

In every case the notice of an extraordinary or a special resolution
should state the actual wording of the resolution to be passed. (In
theory a notice giving the *full* substance of such a resolution might
suffice, but it is difficult to see how one can be sure of doing this
without giving the actual wording.) Notice of a particular resolution
having been given no amendment of substance, however small, is
possible (*Re Moorgate Mercantile Holdings Ltd* [1980] 1 All ER 40).

Filing of resolutions at the Companies Registry

Within fifteen days of the passing of any of the following
resolutions, a printed copy, signed by an officer of the company, must
be filed with the Registrar, who will record it:

(1) Special resolutions (1948 s 143(4)).

(2) Extraordinary resolutions (ibid).

(3) Resolutions agreed to by all the members of a company which, but for such agreement, would have had to be passed as special or extraordinary resolutions (ibid).

(4) Resolutions which bind all members of a class of shareholders (ibid).

(5) Resolutions and agreements agreed to by all members of a class of shareholders which, but for the agreement, would have had to be passed in a particular manner (ibid).

(6) Resolutions to wind up voluntarily (ibid).

(7) Resolutions of directors to re-register old public companies as public companies or by reason of a public company's acquisition of its own shares to re-register it as a private company (ibid).

(8) Resolutions increasing the authorised capital (1948 s 63(2) and 1967 s 51(1)).

(9) Resolutions in respect of authority to allot relevant securities (1980 s 14(6)).

(10) A resolution by a public company under 1980 s 26 to approve an agreement to acquire non-cash assets from founders within its first two years as a public company (1980 s 27(2)).

(11) A directors' resolution under 1981, s 25 to change a company's name which previously did not have to include 'Limited' so that it ends with 'Limited'.

(12) A resolution to authorise market purchases by a company of its own shares (1981 s 49(10)).

The Companies Registry have issued a leaflet specifying the various forms of 'printing', eg typewritten or produced in durable and reliable form by photocopying, approved by the Registrar.

Where Articles have been registered a copy of every resolution or agreement which must be registered under 1948 s 143 (which includes all the types of resolution listed above except (10)) and which is in force must be embodied in or annexed to every copy of the Articles issued subsequently (1948 s 143(2)).

Where the company is operating under Table A and no Articles have been registered, a copy of every such resolution or agreement must be forwarded to any member on request, but a fee of not more than 5p may be charged (1948 s 143(3)).

Where, in any case other than a special resolution altering the objects clause in a company's Memorandum of Association (the filing requirements in relation to which are regulated by 1948 s 5), a company is required to send to the Registrar a document making or

evidencing any alteration in its Memorandum or Articles, there must
be sent with such document a printed copy of the Memorandum or
Articles as altered (which should have endorsed thereon a certificate
signed by, for example, a director or the secretary that it is a true copy
of the altered Memorandum or Articles (European Communities Act
1972, s 9(5)).

MINUTES

Minute books

1948 s 145 provides that minutes of all proceedings at general and
board meetings must be entered in books kept for the purpose.

Any minute of such a meeting purporting to be signed by the
chairman of that meeting or the next one is evidence of the
proceedings.

The minutes do not provide conclusive evidence, however, unless
the Articles so provide (*Kerr* v *Mottram (John) Ltd* [1940] Ch 657) but
the burden of disproving the truth of their contents is on those who
dispute their correctness. Until the contrary is proved, every meeting
whereof minutes have been properly made and signed is deemed to
have been duly convened, and all proceedings had thereat to have
been duly had (1948 s 145).

The use of loose-leaf books for minutes, though permitted, is
inadvisable, unless adequate safeguards against substitution of leaves
are adopted (1948 s 436). The following precautions have been
suggested by the Institute of Chartered Secretaries and Administrators:

(i) The minute book should be provided with a lock which, for
preference, should be on the spine of the book rather than on
the covers, to permit reference to the book without having to
undo the lock.
(ii) The key to the lock should be in the hands of the secretary or
other responsible official, with a duplicate key kept in a safe
place, eg at the bank.
(iii) The loose-leaf pages should be numbered serially as inserted.
(iv) The minutes should be serially numbered throughout the
book and not in a separate series for each meeting.

The last page relating to each meeting should be signed by the
chairman and all other pages initialled (or signed) by him.

In *Hearts of Oak Assurance Co Ltd* v *James Flower & Sons* [1936]
Ch 76, the court refused to accept a loose-leaf minute book as
evidence but this was before 1948 s 436 was enacted.

It is permissible to keep a record of the minutes in non-legible form provided that they are capable of being reproduced in legible form (Stock Exchange (Completion of Bargains) Act 1976, s 3).

Keeping of minutes

Care and accuracy should be observed in recording the proceedings of both general and board meetings, for it is reasonable to assume that proceedings not mentioned in the minutes did not occur.

Careful notes should be taken during the meeting and the full minutes prepared and written into the minute book as soon as possible after it.

In writing up minutes the secretary should endeavour to include every detail of a material nature, without overburdening his statements with unnecessary matter.

Thus a minute of a resolution at a board meeting approving transfers of shares might be worded as follows:

'Resolved that transfers numbered 84 to 97 be registered and that the seal be affixed to the new certificates needed, numbered 153 to 166.'

A draft of the minutes of the first meeting of the directors of a company is given at p 220.

Minutes of a resolution passed at a general meeting should state the nature of the resolution, ie whether it is an ordinary, extraordinary or a special resolution, and *the number of votes for and against* where these are announced by the chairman. Where figures are not announced it should be recorded that a resolution was passed unanimously, or by the requisite majority, as the case may be. In addition it should be stated whether the voting was by poll or show of hands. It is not usual to state the number of votes at a board meeting, but directors voting against a resolution may ask for their dissent to be recorded.

If minutes are not kept, the company and every officer in default is liable to a fine (1948 s 145(4)).

Reading of minutes

In practice, minutes of a board meeting are usually signed by the chairman of the next meeting. They are usually circulated to board members a reasonable period before the next meeting rather than read aloud at that next meeting. Any alterations should be made before the minutes are signed and should be initialled by the chairman. A resolution should be passed authorising any alterations. Before signing, the chairman should put the minutes to the meeting for confirmation.

The minutes of general meetings are usually read and signed at the next succeeding *board* meeting, it being neither necessary nor advisable to wait for the next general meeting which may not be held for a year or more.

Inspection of minutes

1948 s 146 provides that the minute book of proceedings at general meetings must be kept at the registered office, and that any member may:

(*a*) inspect the same without charge during business hours; and

(*b*) require a copy to be supplied within seven days of request at a charge of not more than 2½p per hundred words.

The Articles or the company in general meeting may restrict the time at which the minutes are open for inspection, but at least two hours must be allowed in each business day.

When a general meeting is held at some place other than the registered office strict compliance with the above section will prevent the secretary from having the minute book with him at the meeting. In such a case he would be well advised to have at hand copies of the minutes of recent general meetings.

Members are not entitled to inspect the minutes of directors' meetings, but reports made to the directors by accountants or solicitors for the purposes of the company may be inspected (see *Gouraud* v *Edison Gower Bell Telephone Co of Europe* (1888) 57 LJ Ch 498, and *Dennis & Sons Ltd* v *West Norfolk Farmers Manure & Chemical Co-operative Co Ltd* [1943] Ch 220).

CLASS AND SECTION 206 MEETINGS

In certain circumstances, it may be necessary to summon a meeting of a class of shareholders. Such meetings are usually summoned either (*a*) where a variation of class rights is involved under the Articles or 1980 s 32, or (*b*) under 1948 s 206.

In the case of a class meeting summoned under 1980 s 32, the provisions of the Articles as to general meetings of the company apply, so far as applicable, subject to the following qualifications:

(i) A quorum shall be two persons holding or representing by proxy at least one-third of the issued shares of the class, except that at an adjournment one holder of shares of the class or his proxy suffices.

(ii) Any holder of shares of the class present in person or by proxy may demand a poll.

Notice of such meetings must be given to all members of the class concerned, whether or not they are entitled to receive notice of a general meeting.

The statutory regulations concerning proxies (see pp 92 to 94) apply to meetings of a class of members of a company (1948 s 136(5)).

Under 1948 s 206, where a compromise or arrangement is proposed between a company and (*a*) its creditors or any class of them, or (*b*) its members or any class of them, the court may on summary application order a meeting of the group concerned to be summoned. The order of the court which authorises the summoning of the meeting will determine the nature of the notice and the form of proxy to be sent out with the notice; but any reasonable form of proxy may be employed if a shareholder thinks fit not to use the form sent out with the notice, and a proxy cannot be rejected on the ground that it has not been deposited at the company's registered office within the time specified in the notice (*Re Dorman Long & Co Ltd* [1934] Ch 635). If the arrangement is approved by a majority in number representing three-fourths in value of those members of the group who, being present personally or by proxy, record their votes, and the sanction of the court is obtained, the compromise or arrangement will become binding on the company and all creditors and members concerned when an office copy of the court order has been delivered to the Registrar.

BOARD MEETINGS

A company's Articles usually contain regulations for the summoning, constitution and conduct of board meetings. Table A and most special Articles leave such matters largely to the discretion of the directors by providing that they may regulate their meetings as they think fit (reg 98). This gives the board the power to issue standing orders for the conduct of their meetings.

Regulations 98 to 106 of Table A or the relevant Articles should be studied.

Table A gives the directors the power of delegating any of their powers to committees (reg 102). This enables the work of the board to be done by some of its members only. But any act of a committee must have behind it the sanction of a properly constituted board meeting. In other words, the acts of a committee will not have the effect of an act of the board unless the committee was appointed by a properly constituted board meeting. If Table A is excluded and the Articles do not authorise the directors to delegate their powers to committees, they may not do so (*Re Leeds Banking Co, Howard's Case* (1866) 1 Ch App 561).

An attendance book may be signed by all directors present at each meeting of the board. Where the meeting is attended by other officials of the company, such as the auditors, they may also sign.

Agenda papers should be prepared by the secretary for both general and board meetings, setting out briefly the matters with which the meeting is to deal.

CHAPTER 6

ANNUAL RETURN, ACCOUNTS AND REPORTS

ANNUAL RETURN

At least once in every year a company having a share capital must make a return (Form 6A) to the Registrar of Companies containing the particulars set out in 1948 Sched 6 Part I (1948 s 124). These particulars are as follows:

(1) The address of the registered office.

(2) (a) The address at which the register of members is kept if this is not the same as the registered office.

(b) The address at which a register of holders of debentures is kept if this is not the same as the registered office.

(3) A summary, distinguishing between shares issued for cash and shares issued as fully or partly paid-up otherwise than in cash, specifying—

(a) the amount of the share capital and the number of shares into which it is divided;

(b) the number of shares taken from the commencement of the company up to the date of the return;

(c) the amount called up on each share;

(d) the total amount of calls received;

(e) the total amount of calls unpaid;

(f) the total amount of the sums (if any) paid by way of commission in respect of any shares or debentures;

(g) the discount allowed on any shares issued at a discount in so far as it has not been written off at the date of the return;

(h) the total amount of the sums (if any) allowed by way of discount on any debentures since the date of the last return;

(i) the total number of shares forfeited;

(j) the total amount of shares for which share warrants are outstanding at the date of the return and of warrants issued and surrendered since the date of the last return and the number of shares comprised in each warrant.

(4) Particulars of the total amount of the company's indebtedness in respect of mortgages and charges which require to be registered with the Registrar of Companies.

(5) A list containing the names and addresses of all persons who, on the fourteenth day after the annual general meeting for the year, are members of the company, and of persons who have ceased to be members since the date of the last return (or since the date of the incorporation of the company in the case of the first return), stating the number of shares held by each of the existing members at the date of the return, specifying shares transferred since the date of the last return (or incorporation in the case of the first return) by persons who are still members and have ceased to be members respectively, and the dates of the registration of the transfers; and, if the names are not arranged in alphabetical order, having an index annexed.

(6) Particulars of directors and the secretary at the date of the return required to be stated in the register of directors and secretaries.

Although in general this return must be made in every year, it need not be made in any year in which the company is not required to hold an annual general meeting (see p 85). Moreover, if the return for either of the two preceding years has given the full particulars required by para 5 above, it is necessary to give only such of the particulars as relate to persons ceasing to be or becoming members since the date of the last return and to shares transferred since that date (1948 s 124(1)).

Where a dominion register is kept 1948 s 124(2) applies.

Annual return of company with no share capital

A company which has no share capital is not required to file the above return but must once in every calendar year make a return (Form 7) stating (1948 s 125):

(a) the address of the registered office;
(b) the addresses at which the registers of members and debenture holders are kept, if elsewhere than at that office;
(c) particulars of the directors and the secretary;
(d) a statement showing the total indebtedness of the company in respect of mortgages and charges requiring registration.

Date for making annual return

The annual return must be made up to the fourteenth day after the annual general meeting for the year. It must be completed within forty-two days of the meeting and a copy signed by a director and the secretary must be forthwith forwarded to the Registrar of Companies (1948 s 126).

PREPARATION, PRESENTATION AND REGISTRATION OF ACCOUNTS

The considerable volume of legislation which deals with a company's accounts can be divided into three topics: (i) the keeping of accounting records; (ii) the presentation of accounts to the members; and (iii) the registration of accounts.

Keeping of accounting records

1976 s 12 provides that every company shall cause to be kept accounting records sufficient to show and explain the company's transactions. The accounting records must disclose with reasonable accuracy at any time the financial position of the company at that time and enable the directors to ensure that any balance sheet and profit and loss account prepared by them gives a true and fair view of the company's state of affairs or, as the case may be, profit or loss; and must in particular contain (*a*) daily entries of all receipts and expenditures of money, (*b*) a record of the assets and liabilities of the company and (*c*) where the company's business involves dealing in goods, statements of (i) stock held by the company at the end of each financial year, (ii) stocktakings used or to be used to prepare any statement of stock referred to in (i), and (iii) all goods (except goods sold in ordinary retail trade) sold and purchased including details of buyers and sellers.

The accounting records must be kept at the registered office or at such other place as the directors think fit and must at all times be open to inspection by the officers of the company; but if they are kept at a place outside Great Britain, there must be sent to and kept in a place in Great Britain such accounts and returns with respect to the business dealt with in the books outside Great Britain as will disclose with reasonable accuracy the financial position of the business at intervals not exceeding six months and enable the company's balance sheet and profit and loss account to be prepared in accordance with the relevant statutory requirements.

A private company must keep such accounting records for three years and a public company for six from the date on which they are made (1976 s 12(9)). Severe penalties, including imprisonment, are laid down for a defaulting officer where a company fails to comply with the requirements of the 1976 Act for the keeping of accounting records.

Duty to prepare, lay and deliver accounts by reference to accounting reference periods

The expression 'laying and delivering' is used in the 1976 Act and herein as referring to the laying of accounts before the company in general meeting and delivering a signed copy thereof to the Registrar.

By 1976 s 1, the directors of every company are under a duty periodically to prepare, lay and deliver accounts containing the information required by the Acts. The documents required to be comprised in the accounts of a company in respect of any accounting reference period are the profit and loss account, balance sheet, report of the auditors and the report of the directors (1976 s 1(5)). The profit and loss account must be prepared in respect of the period beginning with the day after that to which the previous profit and loss account was made up (or in the case of the profit and loss account for the company's first accounting period beginning with the first day of that period) and ending not more than seven days before or after the end of the relevant accounting reference period; and a balance sheet must be prepared as at the date to which the profit or loss account is made up.

The period for which a profit and loss account is prepared is called a 'financial year' whether it is a year or not (1948 s 455(1)).

See however p 117 below for exemptions for small and medium-sized companies from the obligation to deliver full accounts to the Registrar.

The directors of an unlimited company are not normally required to deliver accounts to the Registrar (see p 196).

Determination of accounting reference period

The 1976 Act contains complex provisions for determining and altering a company's accounting reference period. The following summarises briefly the relevant provisions (ss 2 and 3).

In each calendar year the date on which a company's accounting reference period comes to an end is its 'accounting reference date' which shall (1976 s 2(2)) be 31 March unless (i) before 1 October 1977 (the date when 1976 s 1 came into operation) or, as the case may be, within six months of incorporation of the company, notice is given to the Registrar on Form 2 specifying a different accounting reference date, (ii) the Registrar with the consent of the company and before 1 October 1979 determined some other date or (iii) the company gives to the Registrar notice on Form 3 of the alteration of the date to which the current and subsequent accounting reference periods are to run (1976 s 3); but the relevant accounting reference period cannot be extended to exceed eighteen months (1976 s 3(5)). Such notice may relate back to a previous accounting reference period in the case of a company which is a subsidiary or holding company of another company provided that the new accounting reference date coincides with the accounting reference date of that other company and that the notice is given before the period allowed for laying and delivering the accounts in relation to the previous accounting reference period has not expired (1976 s 3(3)); such notice of alteration of previous and subsequent accounting reference periods must be given on Form 3a. If the effect of the notice is to extend an accounting reference period, it must not, unless otherwise directed by the Secretary of State, be given within five years of a previous extension of an accounting reference period under 1976 s 3. This restriction does not apply if the effect of the notice is to shorten an accounting reference period, nor if the company is a subsidiary or holding company of another and the new accounting reference date coincides with the other's accounting reference date.

Period allowed for laying and delivering accounts

The period allowed for laying and delivering accounts in relation to any accounting reference period of a company is, in the case of a private company, ten months or, in the case of a public company, seven months after the end of the relevant accounting reference period (1976 s 6). Where, however, a company carries on business or has interests outside the United Kingdom, the Channel Islands and the Isle of Man and notice to that effect claiming an extension of the period for laying and delivering accounts is given to the Registrar on Form 5 then the period can be extended by three months. A separate notice is needed for each period for which the claim is made. Special provisions apply in respect of the first accounting reference period commencing from the date of incorporation (if longer than twelve months) and where the effect of a notice given under 1976 s 3 is to shorten an accounting reference period. The Secretary of State may extend the period for laying and delivering accounts if for any special reason he thinks fit to do so (1976 s 6(3) to (7)).

Penalties and default orders

If the requirements of the 1976 Act as to the laying and delivering of accounts are not complied with before the end of the period allowed then each director of the company is guilty of an offence and liable to be fined unless he can prove that he took all reasonable steps for securing that those requirements would be fulfilled within that time (1976 s 4). The company itself may also be liable to a penalty for failure to deliver the accounts. For such failure the court may make a default order, on application by any member or creditor of the company or by the Registrar, requiring the directors to make good the default within such time as may be specified in the order (1976 s 5).

Duty to supply copies of accounts

A copy of every balance sheet, including every document required by law to be annexed thereto, of which a copy is to be laid before the company in general meeting, together with a copy of the auditors' and directors' reports, must, not less than twenty-one days before the date of the meeting, be sent to every member of the company (whether or not he is entitled to notices of meetings) and to every holder of debentures of the company (whether or not he is so entitled) and to all other persons so entitled, eg the auditors (1948 s 158 and 1967 s 24).

This general rule is subject to the following modifications:

(a) Copies need not be sent (i) to a member or debenture holder who is not entitled to notices of meetings if the company is unaware of his address; (ii) to more than one of the joint holders of shares or debentures none of whom is entitled to notices of meetings; (iii) in the case of joint holders of shares or debentures some of whom are and some of whom are not entitled to receive notices of meetings, to those who are not so entitled (1948 s 158).

(b) If copies are sent less than twenty-one days before the meeting, they shall nevertheless be deemed to have been duly sent if it is so agreed by all the members entitled to attend and vote at the meeting (ibid).

(c) Where a company has no share capital, copies need not be sent to members or debenture holders who are not entitled to notice of the meeting.

Any member of a company and any holder of debentures (whether or not he is entitled to have a copy of the balance sheet sent to him) is entitled to be furnished on demand, within seven days and without charge, with a copy of the last balance sheet of the company, including every document required by law to be annexed thereto, together with a copy of the auditors' and directors' reports (1948 s 158(2) and (3), and 1967 s 24).

Listed companies are also required to circularise to shareholders or insert as paid advertisements in two leading daily newspapers half-yearly interim reports.

GROUP ACCOUNTS

In general, where at the end of its financial year a company has subsidiaries the profit and loss account and balance sheet required under the 1976 Act to be prepared in respect of the relevant accounting reference period shall include accounts or statements (referred to as 'group accounts') dealing with the state of affairs and profit and loss of the company and its subsidiaries; and any such group accounts shall accordingly be included among the documents required to be comprised in the accounts of the company for the purposes of the requirements of 1976 s 1 as to laying and delivering accounts (1948 s 150). Group accounts are, however, not necessary where the company is at the end of its financial year the wholly-owned subsidiary of another body corporate incorporated in Great Britain, ie where it has no members except that other body corporate and its wholly-owned subsidiaries or its or their nominees (1948 s 150(2)(a) and (4)).

Moreover, group accounts need not deal with a subsidiary if the directors are of the opinion that it is impracticable, or would be of no real value to members of the company, in view of the insignificant amounts involved, or would involve expense or delay out of proportion to the value to members of the company or that the result would be misleading (1948 s 150(2)(b)). In addition, provided that the approval of the Department of Trade is obtained, group accounts need not deal with a subsidiary if the directors are of the opinion that the result would be harmful to the business of the company or any of its subsidiaries, or that the business of the holding company and that of the subsidiary are so different that they cannot reasonably be treated as a single undertaking (ibid). If such exceptions apply to all a company's subsidiaries group accounts are not needed.

However, where group accounts are not submitted or any subsidiaries are excluded from them, the particulars prescribed in 1948 Sched 8 para 69 must be given in a note to the accounts.

Form of group accounts

Where group accounts are required, they must consist of a consolidated balance sheet dealing with the state of affairs of the company and all the subsidiaries which must be dealt with and a consolidated profit and loss account dealing with the profit or loss of the company and those subsidiaries (1948 s 151); but the directors may depart from this form if they think that it is better to do so in order to present the same or equivalent information and to present it in such a way that it may be readily appreciated by members. In particular they may publish group accounts consisting of (i) more than one set of consolidated accounts, one dealing with the company and one group of subsidiaries and others with other groups of subsidiaries, or (ii) separate accounts dealing with each of the subsidiaries, or (iii) statements expanding the information about the subsidiaries in the company's own accounts. Moreover, the group accounts may be wholly or partly incorporated in the company's own balance sheet and profit and loss account.

The overriding principles to be borne in mind are that the group accounts, whatever form they take, must (as explained below at p 115) give a true and fair view of the state of affairs and profit or loss of the company and its subsidiaries dealt with as a whole so far as concerns the members of the company (1948 s 152), and must combine the information contained in the separate balance sheets and profit and loss accounts of the holding company and the subsidiaries dealt with, though with such necessary adjustments as the directors think necessary (1948 Sched 8 paras 61 and 68).

Financial year of holding companies and subsidiaries

A holding company's directors must secure that, except where in their opinion there are good reasons against it, the financial year of each of its subsidiaries shall coincide with the company's own financial year (1948 s 153).

Where the financial year of a subsidiary does not coincide with that of its holding company, the group accounts must (unless the Department of Trade otherwise direct) deal with the subsidiary's state of affairs at the end of its financial year ending with or last before that of the holding company, and with the subsidiary's profit or loss for that financial year (1948 s 152(4)).

In this event, whether or not the affairs of the subsidiary are dealt with in the group accounts, a note to the accounts or group accounts must state, in respect of the subsidiaries whose financial years do not coincide with that of the company, the reasons why the company's directors do not think such coincidence necessary and the dates on which such subsidiaries' financial years ended (the earliest and latest such dates being sufficient if there are several) (1948 Sched 8 para 70).

FORM AND CONTENT OF ACCOUNTS

The 1981 Act inserted new ss 149 and 152 and a new Sched 8 into the 1948 Act which together lay down the form and content of the accounts of an individual company and of group accounts, which will each include balance sheet, profit and loss account and information to be given in notes to the accounts. However where a banking, insurance or shipping company is involved or where the relevant financial year began before 15 June 1982 the accounts may instead comply with the previous ss 149 and 152 and Sched 8 which are redesignated as ss 149A and 152A and Sched 8A: where advantage is taken of this option various rules as to, eg accounts and disclosure of certain matters in the directors' report will continue to apply as they did before the 1981 Act (see p 128) (1981 ss 16 and 17 and Sched 2). References to a company's profit and loss account include in the case of a company not trading for profit its income and expenditure account.

The overriding requirement in ss 149 and 152 is that the balance sheet and the profit and loss account of a company give a true and fair view of, respectively, the state of the company's affairs and its profit or loss for the financial year and that group accounts give a true and fair view of the state of affairs and profit or loss of the company and the subsidiaries dealt with by those accounts as a whole so far as concerns members of the company. If compliance with the detailed requirements of Sched 8 and all other requirements of the Acts whether as to the accounts of an individual company or as to group accounts would not provide sufficient information to give a true and fair view, any necessary additional information must be provided in the accounts or notes to them. If, owing to special circumstances, compliance with such requirements would prevent the giving of a true and fair view, even if additional information were provided, the directors may so far as necessary depart from them: if they do so, particulars of the departure, the reasons for it and its effect must be given in a note to the accounts.

A company's profit and loss account need not comply with the above rules if the company has subsidiaries and its profit and loss account is framed as a consolidated profit and loss account dealing with the company and all or any of its subsidiaries, complies with the statutory requirements as to consolidated profit and loss accounts (see p 113) and shows how much of the consolidated profit or loss is dealt with in the accounts of the company. If advantage is taken of this exception the fact must be disclosed in a note to the group accounts.

The Secretary of State may, on the application of or with the consent of a company's directors, modify the requirements of Sched 8 as to group accounts.

Under Sched 8 a balance sheet must be compiled in one of the two formats and a profit and loss account in one of the four formats set out in the Schedule. The detailed provisions of Sched 8 are not listed here. Once one format for the balance sheet or profit and loss account has been adopted, it must be followed in later years unless in the opinion of the directors there are special reasons for a change: any such change and the reasons for it must be explained in a note to the accounts which include it. Certain modification of the format is allowed as specified in Sched 8: for example, when the special nature of the company's business requires the directors shall adapt the arrangements and headings and subheadings in respect of items which are given arabic numbers in the formats. Various notes to the formats must be observed. Preliminary expenses, expenses of and commission on the issue of shares or debentures, and costs of research must not be treated as assets in a balance sheet.

Schedule 8 Part II sets out certain accounting principles and rules, including one set called 'the historical cost accounting rules' and another called 'the alternative accounting rules', which allow departures from the historical cost accounting rules to reflect current cost accounting principles. Part III lists information which, if not given in the accounts, must be provided in notes to them. Part IV contains provisions which apply where the company is a holding company or subsidiary and Part V provisions which apply where it is an investment company. In Part VI there are a number of rules which apply in the interpretation of the previous Parts of the Schedule and which also by 1981 s 21(1) apply to the rest of the Acts.

In the preparation of a company's accounts, due regard should also be had to the recommendations contained in each *Statement of Standard Accounting Practice* which is from time to time prepared by the Accounting Standards Committee and approved by the Committee's constituent accountancy bodies (and to the publications of the International Accounting Standards Committee). A secretary will normally be guided in respect of these by the company's auditors.

Every balance sheet, and every copy laid before the company in general meeting or delivered to the Registrar pursuant to 1976 s 1 must be signed on behalf of the board by two of the directors (or if there is only one director by that one) (1948 s 155). Unless the balance sheet has been signed as required above no copy may be issued, circulated or published; and each copy issued, circulated or published must include a copy of the signature(s). There must be attached to the balance sheet the profit and loss account, any group accounts and the auditors' and directors' reports and the directors must approve the profit and loss account and any group accounts before the balance sheet is signed on their behalf (1948 ss 156 and 157).

Whenever the Acts refer to a document annexed or required to be annexed to the accounts or any of them, the phrase does not include the directors' report (1948 s 163), but note that references in 1976 s 1 to documents *required to be comprised in* the accounts of a company *do* include the auditors' and directors' reports.

Accounting exemptions for small and medium-sized companies

1981 ss 5 and 10 contain 'accounting exemption provisions' (which may be amended by statutory instrument) for small and medium-sized companies under which modified accounts may be delivered to the Registrar. The relaxations extend also to the requirements relating to notes to the accounts and documents to accompany accounts. Full accounts, disregarding the exemptions, must still be prepared, audited, reported on by the auditors and laid before the company in general meeting. The exemptions comprise 'exemptions for individual accounts' and group exemption under s 10. The exemptions for individual accounts enable an individual company to deliver to the Registrar modified accounts as provided in s 6. Under group exemption, if a holding company is entitled to and avails itself of the exemptions for individual accounts it may deliver to the Registrar modified group accounts.

A company qualifies as a small or medium-sized one if in the financial year concerned and the preceding one it satisfies at least two of three qualifying conditions. These conditions are that turnover, 'balance sheet total' (broadly, total assets) and average number of employees must not exceed certain limits. The limits are:

	Small company	*Medium-sized company*
Turnover	£1,400,000	£5,750,000
Balance sheet total	£ 700,000	£2,800,000
Average number of employees	50	250

The exemptions cannot however apply to a company which is:

(a) a public company;

(b) a banking, insurance or shipping company; or

(c) (subject as mentioned below) a member of an 'ineligible group'

(1981 s 5(3)) or to accounts prepared in accordance with 1948 Sched 8A (see p 128) (1981 Sched 2 para 7(2)). A banking company means a company which is a recognised bank or licensed institution under the Banking Act 1979 and an insurance company means a company to which Part II of the Insurance Companies Act 1982 applies. An ineligible group is a group which includes:

(i) a company within (a) or (b) above;

(ii) a body corporate which is not a company but which can lawfully exercise power under its constitution to offer its shares or debentures to the public (ie a body corporate which is not a company but which in its ability to offer its securities to the public is equivalent to a public company); or

(iii) a body corporate which is not a company but is a recognised bank or licensed institution under the Banking Act 1979 or an insurance company within the meaning of the Insurance Companies Act 1982 to which Part II of that Act applies.

However a company which is exempt from the obligation to appoint auditors under the provisions relating to dormant companies (see p 159) is entitled to the benefit of the exemptions for individual accounts notwithstanding that it is a member of an ineligible group (1981 s 12(9)).

Once qualified as a small or medium-sized company, a company will not lose that status by failure in one year alone to satisfy two out of three of the qualifying conditions. Special provision is made for newly incorporated companies and for the first financial year for which a company prepares accounts in accordance with the new Sched 8 to the 1948 Act introduced by the 1981 Act. A holding company required to prepare group accounts qualifies as a small or medium-sized company only if the group would do so if it were a single company.

Modified accounts of an individual company delivered to the Registrar must bear the signature of two directors (or one if there is only one director) on the balance sheet as full accounts would and must set out immediately above such signatures (or signature) a statement that the directors have relied on the exemptions for individual accounts and that they have done so on the ground that the company is entitled to the benefit of those exemptions as a small company or medium-sized one (as the case may be).

Such modified accounts delivered to the Registrar must be accompanied by a special auditors' report and the auditors must have provided the directors with a report stating whether in their opinion the requirements for exemption are satisfied in relation to the documents to be delivered.

The main features of the exemptions for individual accounts for a small company are:

(i) a modified balance sheet showing figures by reference to only the main headings of the full accounts need be delivered (save that certain information about sums due has to be disclosed in the balance sheet or a note);

(ii) the profit and loss account and directors' report need not be delivered;

(iii) the information required to be given in notes to the accounts is reduced;

(iv) the information required by 1948 s 196 and 1967 ss 6, 7 and 8 about the salaries and similar benefits of directors and higher paid employees need not be delivered.

Under the exemptions for individual accounts for a medium-sized company a profit and loss account modified as stated in 1981 s 6(8) may be delivered to the Registrar instead of the full one and the information concerning turnover required by 1948 Sched 8 para 55 need not be given.

Group exemption under s 10 applies the exemptions for individual accounts summarised above to group accounts as if they were the accounts of one actual company. Where modified group accounts are delivered to the Registrar the statement by the directors referred to above must include a statement that the documents delivered include copies of modified group accounts delivered by virtue of s 10 and the auditors' report to the directors stating whether the requirements for exemption are satisfied in relation to the documents to be delivered will extend to the requirements of the group exemption.

Publication of accounts

1981 s 11 contains certain rules relating to the publication of accounts. Publishing a balance sheet or other account means publishing, issuing or circulating it or otherwise making it available for public inspection in a manner calculated to invite members of the public generally or any class of them to read it (1981 s 21). In 1981 s 11 'full individual accounts' means the accounts of an individual company in either their full form as required by 1976 s 1 or the modified form permitted for delivery to the Registrar by the provisions dealt with under the preceding heading. 'Full group accounts' is interpreted similarly. For brevity, full accounts as required by 1976 s 1 are called in this explanation '1976 Act accounts'.

Where a company publishes full individual accounts it must publish with them the relevant auditors' report (ie the normal auditors' report or the special auditors' report referred to under the preceding heading).

Where a company required to prepare group accounts publishes full individual accounts it must also publish with them:

(a) if the individual accounts are 1976 Act accounts, group accounts in their full form as required by the 1976 Act; and

(b) if the individual accounts are modified accounts, modified group accounts.

If a company publishes full group accounts without full individual accounts, it must publish with them the relevant auditors' report.

A company is regarded as publishing 'abridged accounts' if it publishes any balance sheet or profit and loss account relating to any financial year of the company or purporting to deal with any such financial year, otherwise than as part of full individual accounts or full group accounts. Where a company publishes abridged accounts it must publish with them a statement indicating:

(i) that they are not full accounts;

(ii) whether full accounts have been delivered to the Registrar (or, where the company is an unlimited one exempt from doing this, that this is so);

(iii) whether the company's auditors have made an auditors' report in respect of accounts for the financial year in question; and

(iv) whether any such report was an unqualified one (1981 s 11(6)).

Clearly this rule applies to certain types of summary of or extract from a balance sheet or profit and loss account. But where should the line be drawn? It is suggested that to constitute a balance sheet or profit and loss account there must be a series of figures, albeit only a few figures, connected by addition or subtraction and demonstrating the amounts of assets and liabilities or profit or loss. A mere statement of profits cannot therefore be a profit and loss account. A preliminary announcement of the results for a financial year will almost certainly constitute abridged accounts if it includes the information required by The Stock Exchange to be given by listed companies in accordance with the Yellow Book, but an advertisement setting out a summary of the figures included in such a preliminary announcement may or may not constitute abridged accounts depending on its contents.

It is considered that the statement required by 1981 s 11(6) need not deal with comparative figures for a preceding year which are included in any publication of abridged accounts; in other words, although the statement required by s 11(6) must indicate whether the new figures are full accounts, whether they have been audited, etc, the statement need not indicate these matters in respect of the figures for the preceding year. 1976 Act accounts have to include comparative figures for the preceding year but this does not make them accounts for the preceding year: the same principle should apply to abridged accounts.

Financial statements for a past year or series of past years contained in prospectuses, offer documents or other company circulars will often constitute abridged accounts for those years.

1981 s 11(6) does not apply to announcements of interim (half-yearly or quarterly) results as these do not relate to or purport to deal with the financial year of the company, only with part of a financial year.

Where a company publishes abridged accounts it must not publish the auditors' report with them.

Information as to subsidiaries and substantial holdings

(*a*) Subsidiaries

Where at the end of its financial year the company has subsidiaries, a note to the company's accounts must state the information specified in 1967 s 3 and 1981 s 4 in the case of each subsidiary.

The information required by 1967 s 3 is fairly straightforward:

   (i) the subsidiary's name;
  (ii) its country of incorporation (save that an English company need not specify this for a subsidiary incorporated in England or a Scottish company for a subsidiary incorporated in Scotland); and
(iii) the identity of the class of each subsidiary's shares held by the company and the proportion of the nominal value of the allotted shares of that class held by the company, with a statement of the extent to which that proportion is held by the company itself (or its nominees) and of the extent to which it is held by subsidiaries of the company (or their nominees).

For the purposes of (iii) above shares of a body corporate are treated as being held, or as not being held, by another such body if they would, by virtue of 1948 s 154(3) (see p 12) be treated as being held or, as the case may be, as not being held by that other body for the purpose of determining whether the first-mentioned body is its subsidiary.

However if the company's directors are of the opinion that the number of the company's subsidiaries is such that giving the above information would result in particulars of excessive length, that information need not be given except in the case of subsidiaries carrying on the businesses the results of which, in the opinion of the directors, principally affected for the relevant year the amounts of the profit or loss of the company and its subsidiaries or the amount of their assets. But if advantage is taken of this provision the statement required by 1967 s 3 must say that it deals only with subsidiaries carrying on such businesses and the particulars of subsidiaries which are given and those which are omitted must be annexed to the company's annual return and so be available for public scrutiny at the Companies Registry.

The information required by 1981 s 4 is more complicated and is outlined below under 'Information required by 1981 s 4'.

(*b*) Bodies corporate other than subsidiaries

If at the end of its financial year a company holds (1) shares of any class comprised in the equity share capital of another body corporate (not being its subsidiary) exceeding in nominal value one-tenth of the nominal value of the allotted shares of that class; or (2) shares in another body corporate (not being its subsidiary) exceeding in nominal value one-tenth of that other body corporate's allotted share capital; or (3) shares in another body corporate (not being its subsidiary) which are stated or included in its accounts at more than one-tenth of its assets (as so stated), the information specified in 1967 s 4 and in certain circumstances 1981 s 4 must be given in a note to the accounts. Case (2) does not apply where accounts are prepared in accordance with 1948 Sched 8A.

For this purpose, shares of a body corporate are treated as being held, or as not being held, by another such body if they would by virtue of 1948 s 154(3) (but on the assumption that para (*b*)(ii) had been omitted therefrom) be treated as being held or, as the case may be, as not being held by that other body to determine whether the first-mentioned body is its subsidiary.

The information to be given in accordance with 1967 s 4 comprises:

(i) the name of the other body corporate;

(ii) its country of incorporation (save that an English company need not specify this where the other body corporate is incorporated in England or a Scottish company where that other is incorporated in Scotland); and

(iii) the identity of each class of shares of the other body corporate which are held by the company and the proportion of the nominal value of the allotted shares of that class held by the company.

If the number of bodies corporate within case (1) or (2) is such that, in the opinion of the company's directors, giving the above information would result in particulars of excessive length, an exemption applies similar to the one summarised above under 'Subsidiaries'.

The requirements of 1981 s 4 are outlined below under 'Information required by 1981 s 4'.

Neither (a) nor (b) above requires the disclosure by a company of information with respect to a subsidiary (or, as the case may require, another body corporate) if the subsidiary (or other body corporate) is incorporated outside the United Kingdom or, being incorporated in the United Kingdom, carries on business outside the United Kingdom, if the disclosure would, in the opinion of the directors of the company, be harmful to the business of the company (or any of its subsidiaries in case (a)) or of that other body and the Department of Trade agrees that the information need not be disclosed.

Information required by 1981 s 4

1981 s 4 requires, subject to many exceptions summarised below, the giving of further information (in a note to the accounts) with respect to:

(i) each subsidiary for which information is given under the above rules relating to subsidiaries; and

(ii) each other body corporate for which information is given in accordance with case (2) of the above rules relating to bodies corporate other than subsidiaries and in which the company holds more than one-fifth in nominal value of the allotted share capital.

In deciding whether shares in a body corporate are or are not held by the company for the purposes of this section one applies the rule explained above under the heading 'Bodies corporate other than subsidiaries'.

The further information is:

(a) the aggregate amount of the capital and reserves of the other body corporate (whether it is a subsidiary or not) at the end of its financial year ending with or last before the company's financial year; and

(b) the profit or loss of that other body corporate for its said financial year.

The further information is not needed where the company's accounts are prepared in accordance with 1948 Sched 8A.

Also, it need not be given in the case of a subsidiary if:

 (i) the company is exempt from preparing group accounts because it is the wholly owned subsidiary of another body corporate incorporated in Great Britain; or

(ii) the company prepares group accounts and either the accounts of the subsidiary are included in them or the company's investment in the subsidiary's shares is included in or in a note to the company's accounts by the equity method of valuation.

It need not be given in respect of a body corporate which is not a subsidiary if the company's investment in its shares is included in or in a note to the company's accounts by the equity method of valuation.

The further information need not be given in respect of a body corporate if that body corporate is not required to deliver a copy of its balance sheet to the Registrar and does not otherwise publish that balance sheet in Great Britain or elsewhere and the company holds under half in nominal value of that body corporate's allotted share capital.

The further information need not be given to the extent that it is not material.

If the company takes advantage of the exceptions relating to the giving of particulars of excessive length which are referred to above under 'Subsidiaries' and 'Bodies corporate other than subsidiaries', then the information which would otherwise require to be given by 1981 s 4 with the similar information which is given in accordance with the section must be annexed to the company's annual return.

Ultimate holding company

Where, at the end of its financial year, a company is the subsidiary of another body corporate, the name of the body corporate regarded by the directors as being the company's ultimate holding company and, if known to them, the country in which it is incorporated must be stated in a note to the company's accounts (1967 s 5). The provision does not, however, require the disclosure by a company which carries on business outside the United Kingdom of information with respect to the company's ultimate holding company if the disclosure would, in the directors' opinion, be harmful to the business of that holding company or of the first-mentioned company or any other of that holding company's subsidiaries and the Department of Trade agrees that the information need not be disclosed.

Remuneration of directors and higher paid employees

The following particulars must be given in a note to the accounts of a company prepared under 1976 s 1:

(1) *The aggregate amount of directors' emoluments*

The amount must include any emoluments paid to or receivable by any person in respect of his services as director of the company or in respect of his services, while a director of the company, as director of any subsidiary, or otherwise in connection with the management of the affairs of the company or any subsidiary; and must distinguish between (a) emoluments for services as a director whether of the company or its subsidiary; and (b) other emoluments (1948 s 196).

The term 'emoluments' in this context includes fees and percentages, sums paid by way of expenses allowance in so far as charged to United Kingdom income tax, any contribution paid in respect of him under any pension scheme, and the estimated money value of any other benefits received by him otherwise than in cash (ibid).

(2) *Particulars of directors' emoluments and waivers*

Subject as mentioned below, the following particulars must be given:

(i) the emoluments of the chairman or, if in a financial year there have been more than one, the emoluments of each of them while chairman (1967 s 6(1)(a));

(ii) the emoluments of the most highly paid director, if more than the chairman (1967 s 6(2));

(iii) the number of directors who had no emoluments or whose several emoluments amounted to £5,000 or less and the number whose emoluments fell within each of the £5,000 brackets above that amount (1967 s 6(1)(b));

(iv) the number of directors who have waived rights to receive emoluments and the aggregate amount of the said emoluments (1967 s 7(1)).

A company which is neither a holding company nor a subsidiary is not subject to the requirements of these sections as respects a financial year in which the amount shown in its accounts under 1948 s 196(1)(*a*) does not exceed £60,000 (SI 1982 No 1698). For the purposes of 1967 s 6, unlike (1) above, one does not include contributions paid in respect of a director under any pension scheme. 1967 s 6 contains exceptions in respect of directors who.discharge their duties wholly or mainly outside the United Kingdom.

(3) *The aggregate amount of directors' or past directors' pensions*

For the purposes of this requirement, the expression 'pension' includes any superannuation allowance or gratuity or similar payment. The amount shown must not include any pension paid or receivable under a pension scheme (as defined below) if the scheme is such that contributions thereunder are substantially adequate for the maintenance of the scheme; but subject to this modification must include any pension paid or receivable in respect of any such services of a director or past director as are mentioned under heading (1) above, to or by him or, on his nomination or by virtue of dependence on or other connection with him, any other person (1948 s 196).

The expression 'pension scheme' mentioned above means a scheme for the provision of pensions in respect of services as director or otherwise which is maintained in whole or in part by means of contributions; and the expression 'contribution' means any payment (including an insurance premium) paid for the purposes of a scheme by or in respect of persons rendering services in respect of which pensions will or may become payable under the scheme, except that it does not include any payment in respect of two or more persons if the amount paid in respect of each of them is not ascertainable.

The amount shown must distinguish between pensions in respect of services as director, whether of the company or its subsidiary, and other pensions (ibid).

(4) *The aggregate amount of any compensation paid to directors or past directors in respect of loss of office*

The figure must include sums paid to or receivable by a director or past director for loss of office as director of the company, or for loss, while a director of the company or in connection with his ceasing to be a director, of any other office in connection with the management of the company's affairs or of any office as director or otherwise in connection with the management of the affairs of a subsidiary. The figures shown must distinguish (*a*) between compensation in respect of the office of director, whether of the company or a subsidiary, and compensation in respect of other offices, and (*b*) between sums paid by or receivable from, respectively, the company, its subsidiaries and others (1948 s 196).

(5) *Higher paid employees*

There must be shown, divided into brackets of £5,000, the number of other persons in the company's employment (other than those working wholly or mainly outside the United Kingdom) whose emoluments in the financial year exceeded £30,000 per annum (1967 s 8; SI 1982 No 1698).

In complying with the requirements of 1948 s 196 (cases (1), (3) and (4) above) the following general propositions must be borne in mind:

(*a*) In each case it is necessary to include all relevant sums paid by or receivable from the company, its subsidiaries and anyone else, except sums to be accounted for to the company, to any subsidiary, or under 1948 s 193 (see p 138) to past or present members.

(*b*) The figures must show the aggregate of the sums receivable in respect of a financial year, whenever paid; or, in the case of sums not receivable in respect of a period, the sums paid during the financial year; save that:

(i) where, as mentioned above, a payment is not included because the person receiving it is liable to account for it, and the liability is subsequently released (in whole or in part), or is not enforced within two years; or

(ii) where any expenses allowances are charged to United Kingdom income tax after the end of the relevant financial year;

such sums must be shown in the first accounts in which it is practicable to show them.

(*c*) Generally the term 'subsidiary' means a subsidiary as defined by 1948 s 154 (see p 11); but, for the above purposes only, if a director of the company was also a director of another body corporate by virtue of the company's nomination, direct or indirect, that other body corporate is to be deemed to be a subsidiary whether or not it falls within the terms of s 154. For the purpose of the requirements concerning emoluments and pensions, only subsidiaries which were such at the time the services were rendered need be taken into account; and as regards compensation for loss of office, only subsidiaries which were such immediately before the loss of office need be considered.

In each of cases (1) to (5) above it is necessary to include the corresponding amount for the immediately preceding financial year (1967 s 11(1)).

It is the duty of any director of the company or any person who is or has within the previous five years been an officer of the company to give notice to the company of any particulars required for the purpose of complying with the above rules (1948 s 198 and 1967 ss 6(5) and 7(3)).

Loans to and transactions with directors, persons connected with directors and officers

Certain details of such matters must be given in a note to a company's accounts or to group accounts prepared by a holding company as explained at p 155.

Schedule 8A accounts

This heading relates to the rules as to accounts (including allied documents such as the directors' report) which apply where accounts are drawn up in accordance with 1948 ss 149A and 152A and Sched 8A rather than the new ss 149 and 152 and Sched 8. Such accounts must state that they are prepared in compliance with s 149A or 152A and Sched 8A. This option is available where the financial year concerned began before 15 June 1982 or where the company is a banking, insurance or shipping company or, if the accounts are group accounts, has such a company as a subsidiary (1981 Sched 2 paras 1 and 2).

The detailed requirements of Sched 8A are not listed here but they are generally less detailed than those of Sched 8. Under Part III of Sched 8A these requirements are further reduced for banking, insurance and shipping companies: where a financial year begins on or after 15 June 1982 the former references to a banking or discount company, which meant a company which satisfied the Department of Trade that it ought to be subject to those reduced requirements, are to be read as references to a banking company (ie a recognised bank or licensed institution) which so satisfies the Department of Trade. Only about one-third of recognised banks receive this special treatment; by SI 1970 No 327 it no longer applies to the English and Scottish clearing banks. A banking company's accounts are not to be treated as failing to give a true and fair view on the grounds that they take advantage of this treatment, eg by maintaining hidden reserves.

Where accounts are prepared in accordance with Sched 8A various rules as to eg accounts and disclosure of certain matters in the directors' report continue to apply as they did before the 1981 Act (1981 s 16 and Sched 2). For example:

(1) in construing the rules in 1980 Part III on the distribution of profits and assets an asset which is not clearly a current one will continue to be treated as fixed (1980 ss 39(8) and 41(11)) whereas the new Sched 8 to the 1948 Act provides the contrary (para 75);

(2) the directors' report must continue to state certain particulars of shares and debentures issued during the year (1967 s 16(1)(*b*));

(3) the accounts need not comply with the additional requirements introduced by the 1981 Act concerning the giving of information about subsidiaries and other bodies corporate in which the company has a substantial holding; and

(4) the duty introduced by the 1981 Act for auditors to consider whether the directors' report is consistent with the information given in the accounts (1967 s 23A) will not apply.

However some requirements which existed before the 1981 Act are abolished for both Sched 8 and Sched 8A accounts, eg the obligation to give particulars of exports in the directors' report (1967 s 20), and some new requirements introduced by the 1981 Act apply to both types of accounts, such as the obligation to state the terms of redemption of any redeemable shares (not just redeemable preference shares) (1948 Sched 8 para 38(2) and Sched 8A para 2(*a*)).

Companies advertising for deposits and insurance companies

Companies which issue advertisements for deposits may be subject to special accounting requirements under the Protection of Depositors Act 1963 and regulations made thereunder (SI 1976 No 1954 as amended by SI 1978 No 1065): note that the repeal of the Protection of Depositors Act 1963 by the Banking Act 1979 has not yet been brought into force and note also 1980 s 83. Insurance companies will in most cases need to observe Part II of the Insurance Companies Act 1982.

THE DIRECTORS' REPORT

The directors' report, which must be attached to the balance sheet prepared in accordance with 1976 s 1 and which is 'comprised in' the accounts laid and delivered by a company under that section, must contain a fair review of the development of the business of the company and its subsidiaries during the financial year and of their position at its end and state the amounts, if any, which the directors recommend shall be paid by way of dividend or carried to reserves (1948 s 157(1)).

It must also state or contain:

(a) the names of the persons who, at any time during the financial year, were directors of the company (1967 s 16(1));

(b) the principal activities of the company and its subsidiaries in the course of that year and any significant change in those activities in that year (1967 s 16(1));

(c) particulars of any significant changes in the fixed assets of the company or any of its subsidiaries which have occurred in the year and of any substantial difference in the market value of any land (as at the end of the year) from the amount at which it is included in the balance sheet which should be brought to the attention of members or holders of debentures (1967 s 16(1)(a));

(d) as respects each person who was a director at the end of the year, particulars of his interests at the end of the year and at the beginning of the year (or, if he was not a director then, when he became a director) according to the register of directors' holdings (see p 142) (1967 s 16(1)(e)) save that these details may be given in a note to the accounts instead of in the directors' report (1967 s 16(4A));

(e) particulars of any important events affecting the company or any of its subsidiaries which have occurred since the end of the year (1967 s 16(1)(f)(i));

(f) indications of likely future developments in the business of the company and its subsidiaries and of their activities (if any) in the field of research and development (1967 s 16(1)(f)(ii) and (iii));

(g) in the case of companies of such classes as may be prescribed in regulations, such information as may be prescribed about the arrangements in force that year for securing the health and safety at work of employees of the company and its subsidiaries, and for protecting other persons against risks to health or safety arising out of or in connection with the activities at work of those employees (1967 s 16(1)(g), added by the Health and Safety at Work etc Act 1974. (As at 1st January 1983, no such regulations had been made.)

(h) in the case of companies employing an average of more than 250 persons during the financial year, a statement describing the action taken during the year to introduce, maintain or develop arrangements to:

(i) provide employees systematically with information on matters of concern to them,

(ii) consult employees or their representatives on a regular basis,

(iii) encourage employees' involvement in the company's performance through an employees' share scheme or otherwise, and

(iv) achieve a common awareness by employees of financial and economic factors affecting the company,

leaving aside persons employed to work wholly or mainly outside the United Kingdom (1967 s 16(1)(h), added as from 1st January 1983 by the Employment Act 1982 s 1);

(i) various particulars concerning any shares in the company bought or otherwise acquired by the company itself or its nominee, or acquired by any other person with financial assistance from the company in circumstances such that the company has a beneficial interest in the shares, or which are made subject to a lien or other charge in favour of the company (1967 s 16A);

(j) if the company (not being a wholly owned subsidiary of a company incorporated in Great Britain) has, or the company and its subsidiaries have between them, in the financial year given more than £200 for political or charitable purposes a statement of the amount given, and, in the case of political purposes, certain additional particulars (1967 s 19, but subject as stated therein, the figure of £200 being substituted by SI 1980 No 1055);

(k) in the case of companies employing more than 250 people, a statement of the company's policy as to certain matters concerning employment of disabled persons (Companies (Directors' Report) (Employment of Disabled Persons) Regulations 1980 (SI 1980 No 1160)).

Listed companies are required by the Listing Agreement to circulate with each annual report certain additional information in relation to themselves and their subsidiary and associated companies (if any). Companies whose shares are traded on the Unlisted Securities Market must similarly circulate with each annual report the information specified in the general undertaking applicable to such companies. By Stock Exchange requirements listed companies and companies whose shares are traded on the Unlisted Securities Market must include in the directors' report particulars of any authority given by shareholders to the board to buy the company's own shares and also of any such purchases or contracts or options for such purchases entered into since the end of the financial year covered by the report. (Particulars of purchases made during the year must be disclosed in accordance with 1967 s 16A.)

THE AUDITORS' REPORT

The company's auditors are required to make a report to the members on the accounts examined by them and on the balance sheet, the profit and loss account and all group accounts prepared under 1976 s 1 of which a copy is, in accordance with s 1(6), laid before the company in general meeting (1967 s 14), but see p 159 in relation to dormant companies. By 1967 s 56(2)(*a*) a report on the balance sheet or profit and loss account extends to any notes to the accounts in question giving information required by the Acts and required or allowed to be given in a note to the accounts.

The auditors' report must be attached to the balance sheet (1948 s 156) and comprised in the accounts to be laid and delivered for the purposes of 1976 s 1. It must be read before the company in general meeting (1967 s 14(2)).

The report must:

(*a*) except in the case of a company that is entitled to, and has availed itself of, the benefit of any of the provisions of 1948 Sched 8A Pt III, state whether in the auditors' opinion the company's balance sheet and profit and loss account and (if it is a holding company submitting group accounts) the group accounts have been properly prepared in accordance with the Acts and whether in their opinion a true and fair view is given—

(i) in the case of the balance sheet, of the state of the company's affairs as at the end of its financial year;

(ii) in the case of the profit and loss account (except a consolidated profit and loss account), of the company's profit or loss for its financial year;

(iii) in the case of group accounts, of the state of affairs and

profit or loss of the company and its subsidiaries dealt with thereby, so far as concerns members of the company;
(b) in that excepted case, state whether in the auditors' opinion the company's balance sheet and profit and loss account and (if it is a holding company submitting group accounts) the group accounts have been properly prepared in accordance with the Companies Acts 1948 to 1981 (1967 s 14(3)(b) as amended by the 1980 Act and the Companies (Accounts and Audit) Regulations 1982 (SI 1982 No 1092)).

It is the duty of the auditors, in preparing their report, to carry out such investigations as will enable them to form an opinion as to the following:
(a) whether proper accounting records have been kept by the company and proper returns adequate for their audit have been received from branches not visited by them; and
(b) whether the company's balance sheet and (unless it is framed as a consolidated profit and loss account) profit and loss account are in agreement with the accounting records and returns;

and if the auditors are of opinion that any of these are answerable in the negative they must state that fact in their report (1967 s 14(4)).

If the auditors fail to obtain all the information and explanations which, to the best of their knowledge and belief, are necessary for the purposes of their audit, they must state that in their report (1967 s 14(6)).

It is also their duty, in preparing their report on the accounts, to consider whether the information given in the directors' report is consistent with the accounts and if they think it is not to state that in their report on the accounts (1967 s 23A, added by the 1981 Act).

Furthermore, if the details required by 1980 ss 54 and 56 concerning loans to and other transactions with directors, persons connected with directors and officers (see p 155) are not duly given in notes to the accounts, the auditors must state them in their report on the balance sheet, so far as they reasonably can (1980 s 59).

CHAPTER 7

DIRECTORS

Appointment of directors

Every company is required to have a director as well as a secretary, and if there is only one director, that sole director cannot also be the secretary (1948 s 177). Moreover, every public company registered since 1 November 1929 must have at least two directors (1948 s 176). A company may be a director (see 1948 s 200(2)(*b*)) but a corporation the sole director of which is secretary to the company may not be a sole director (1948 s 178(*b*)).

The first directors of a company are sometimes named in and appointed by the Articles but, whether or not this is the case, the statement of particulars to be delivered on application for registration of a company (Form 1) must contain the name and relevant particulars of the persons who are to be the first directors of the company (1976 s 21) (and any appointment by the Articles is void unless the person appointed is also named in the statement of particulars (1976 s 21(5)). Table A provides that the number of directors and the names of the first directors shall be determined by a majority of the subscribers to the Memorandum (reg 75).

The appointment of directors other than the first directors is usually provided for in the Articles. Table A gives the power of appointment to the company in general meeting, but allows the existing directors to fill a casual vacancy or to appoint an additional director (reg 95). If a Stock Exchange listing is desired, the Articles must state that a director appointed to fill a casual vacancy or as an addition to the board shall hold office only until the next annual general meeting and shall then be eligible for re-election.

In the case of a public company, a motion for the appointment of two or more directors at a general meeting may not be made by a single resolution unless a resolution that it shall be so made has first been passed by the meeting without any vote being given against it (1948 s 183(1)). If this requirement is not observed, the resolution appointing two or more directors is void, and no provision for the automatic reappointment of retiring directors in default of another appointment will take effect. But a special resolution altering the Articles may be passed in the ordinary way although it involves the appointment of two or more persons as directors (1948 s 183(4)).

The Articles may contain provision for a director to appoint an alternate to act for him in circumstances specified in the Articles. An alternate director will not normally be deemed to be a director for the purposes of the Acts unless he is 'a person in accordance with whose directions or instructions the directors are accustomed to act' (see 1948 ss 124(4) and 455(1), 1967 ss 25(3), 27(11) and 56(3) and 1980 s 63).

Retirement of directors

Table A provides that directors shall retire by rotation (see regs 89 to 97) and similar provisions are usually incorporated in special Articles. Great care must be taken in applying the provisions of the Articles, for considerable difficulties may ensue if these are not strictly observed.

Where there is provision in the Articles for the automatic reappointment of a retiring director if the vacancy caused by his retirement is not filled at the general meeting, this provision will operate even if the meeting resolves that he shall not be reappointed (*Grundt* v *Great Boulder Proprietary Gold Mines Ltd* [1948] Ch 145— though see reg 92 contrary). The provision will not operate where a resolution to appoint directors has been rendered void under 1948 s 183(2) or where the retirement is under 1948 s 185.

Articles may also provide that a director shall vacate office in certain events (see reg 88), and may make provision for resignation; but even if there is no provision for this latter event, it seems that even a verbal resignation may have effect (*Latchford Premier Cinema Ltd* v *Ennion* [1931] 2 Ch 409), though the company may, in such a case, be entitled to damages for breach of a service agreement.

Where Articles give a director the power of assigning his office (in practice this is very unusual) an assignment must be sanctioned by special resolution of the company (1948 s 204). An appointment of a new director by will of a deceased director is an assignment for this purpose.

Managing director

The directors are frequently given power by the Articles to appoint one of their number managing director and to delegate to him such of their powers as they think fit (see regs 107–109).The terms of his appointment and his remuneration will (subject to the Articles) be fixed by the directors, and the latter usually takes the form of a salary with or without a director's fee and with or without a bonus related to profits. A provision contained in the Articles under which a person is appointed managing director does not in itself constitute a contract between him and the company, and he should, for his protection, enter into an agreement with the company after it has been incorporated. The managing director is not a 'clerk' or 'servant' of the company within the meaning of 1948 s 319. He is not usually subject to retirement by rotation or counted in arriving at the number to retire. On ceasing to be a director he automatically ceases to be managing director but it would normally be an implied term of any service agreement entered into that the company would not remove him from his office as a director (*Shindler* v *Northern Raincoat Co Ltd* [1960] 1 WLR 1038).

Age limit for directors

1948 s 185 lays down two general rules, namely: (*a*) that no person can be appointed a director if at the time of his appointment he has attained the age of seventy; and (*b*) that a director shall vacate office at the conclusion of the annual general meeting commencing next after he attains the age of seventy; but these general rules are subject to a number of important modifications:

(i) they do not apply to a private company unless it is a subsidiary of a public company (or a company registered in Northern Ireland as a public company) (1948 s 185(8));

(ii) if the company was first registered after the beginning of the year 1947, the section has effect subject to the provisions of the company's Articles (1948 s 185(7));

(iii) if the company was registered before the beginning of the year 1947, the section has effect subject to any alterations of the company's Articles made after the beginning of 1947; and if at the beginning of the year 1947 the Articles contained provisions for the retirement of directors under the age limit or for restricting the appointment of directors over a given age, the section does not apply to directors to whom such provisions apply (ibid);

(iv) the main rules will not prevent the appointment of a director over seventy years of age or require him to retire on attaining that age if his appointment is or was made or approved by the company in general meeting; but special notice (see p 89) is required for such appointment or approval; and the notice both to and by the company must state or must have stated the age of the person to whom it relates (1948 s 185(5)).

Where a director does retire under the section, no provision for automatic reappointment will operate; and if the meeting at which he retires does not fill the vacancy, it may be filled as a casual vacancy (1948 s 185(3)).

If a director who retires under 1948 s 185(2) is reappointed (as he may be under 1948 s 185(5)) or another director is appointed in the place of a director so retiring, the retiring director or new director must be treated, for the purpose of determining the time at which he or any other director is due to retire, as if he had become a director on the day on which the retiring director was last appointed before his retirement (1948 s 185(6)). Except in this case, however, the retirement of a director out of turn under 1948 s 185(2) is to be disregarded in determining when other directors retire (ibid).

Removal of directors

Notwithstanding anything in the Articles or in any agreement with the director, a company may by ordinary resolution remove a director before the expiration of his period of office, but not a director of a private company who on 18 July 1945 held office for life (1948 s 184): a life director appointed after that date may however be removed.

Special notice (see p 89) must be given of any resolution for the removal of a director or for the appointment of any person in place of a director so removed, and, on receiving notice of an intended resolution to remove a director, the company must forthwith send a copy of the resolution to the director, who is entitled to be heard at the meeting (1948 s 184(2)).

The director may, moreover, make representations in writing and request that they be notified to members of the company, in which event the company must, if it is not too late, state in any notice of the resolution given to members that representations have been made, and send a copy of the representations to every member to whom notice has been sent. If a copy is not sent, because the notice is received too late or because of the company's default, the director may require the representations to be read out at the meeting (1948 s 184(3)). If a vacancy created by the removal of a director is not filled at the meeting by which he is removed, it may be filled as a casual vacancy.

Compensation for loss of office

It is not lawful for a company to make any director any payment by way of compensation for loss of office, or as consideration for or in connection with his retirement from office, unless particulars of the proposed payment (including the amount thereof) are disclosed to the members of the company and the proposal is approved by the company (1948 s 191). Disclosure must be made to all the members while the payment is still a proposal: where no disclosure is made to, eg, preference shareholders, the directors can be liable for misapplication of the company's funds (*Re Duomatic Ltd* [1969] 2 Ch 365).

It is also not lawful for any such payment to be made to any director by the company or by any other person in connection with the transfer of the whole or any part of the undertaking or property of the company unless similar disclosure and approval has taken place (1948 s 192). A sum paid in breach of this rule is held by the recipient on trust for the company.

If any such payment is proposed in connection with a transfer of all or any of the shares in the company, being a transfer resulting from one of four types of offer, it is the duty of the directors to whom payments are to be made to take all reasonable steps to secure that particulars of the proposed payment are included in or sent with any notice of the offer given to any shareholder. The four types of offer are (*a*) an offer made to the general body of the shareholders; (*b*) an offer made by or on behalf of some other body corporate with a view to the company becoming its subsidiary or a subsidiary of its holding company; (*c*) an offer made by or on behalf of an individual with a view to his obtaining the right to exercise or control the exercise of not less than one-third of the voting power at any general meeting of the company; and (*d*) any other offer which is conditional on acceptance to a given extent (1948 s 193).

If a director fails to take such reasonable steps, or if any person, who has been properly required by such director to include particulars in or send them with such notice fails to do so, he is liable to a fine of £200 (1948 s 193(2) as amended by 1980 Sched 2), and if the requirements as to such payments have not been complied with, or if the making of the proposed payment is not approved before the transfer of any shares in pursuance of the offer, any sum received by the directors is deemed to have been received by them in trust for the persons who have sold their shares as a result of the offer (1948 s 193(3)).

The making of the proposed payment must be approved by a meeting summoned for the purpose of the holders of the shares to which the offer relates, and of all other holders of shares of the same class; and if this does not include all members of the company and there are no provisions in the Articles for summoning and regulating such a meeting, the provisions of the 1948 Act and the Articles relating to general meetings shall apply subject to any modification ordered by the Department of Trade (1948 s 193(4)). If at such a meeting a quorum is not present, and after the meeting has been adjourned to a later date, a quorum is again not present, the payment to the director will be deemed to have been approved (1948 s 193(5)).

The application of 1948 ss 191–193 is substantially modified by s 194 which provides that a bona fide payment by way of damages for breach of contract or by way of pension in respect of past services (including any superannuation allowance, superannuation gratuity or similar payment) is not to be treated as compensation for loss of office or as consideration for or in connection with retirement from office.

Payments falling within ss 191–194 will normally be taxable in the hands of the recipient (ss 187 and 188 of and Sched 8 to the Income and Corporation Taxes Act 1970 as amended) to the extent that they exceed £25,000.

Directors' qualification

Articles may provide that a director shall hold a certain number of shares in the company. Where the Articles do require shares to be held, the number of shares so required must be obtained within two months of the director's appointment or such shorter time as may be prescribed by the Articles; and if they be not obtained within such period, or the director ceases at any time to hold the necessary number of shares after appointment, his office is to be vacated. In such an event, the person so vacating office cannot be reappointed until he has acquired the requisite qualifying shares. Any director who continues to act after his office has thus been rendered vacant is liable to a fine which increases daily (1948 s 182 as amended by 1980 Sched 2).

In construing the Articles, attention must be paid to the expressions used, for the acquisition of shares may be made a condition precedent to appointment, eg where the Articles state that no person may be appointed a director unless he 'shall have acquired' a certain number of shares. In this event, an appointment before the shares are acquired is ineffective ab initio, and the statutory two months of grace are not enjoyed. Articles may require the qualifying shares to be held by the director 'as beneficial owner'; but, in the absence of such a requirement, the holding of sufficient shares as trustee for some other person is sufficient (*Howard* v *Sadler* [1893] 1 QB 1). The fact that the director has received the shares as a present

from promoters does not disqualify him (*Re Innes & Co Ltd* [1903] 2
Ch 254). Unless the Articles otherwise provide, it is sufficient if the
shares are held jointly with another person (*Grundy* v *Briggs* [1910] 1
Ch 444). But the holding of a bearer warrant will not qualify (1948
s 182(2)). A provision that qualification shares shall be held by a
director 'in his own right' does not mean that it is necessary for him to
be the beneficial owner.

Disqualification of directors

The Articles may provide for certain circumstances in which
directors become disqualified (see eg reg 88). An undischarged
bankrupt may not act as a director except with the permission of the
court which adjudged him bankrupt (1948 s 187); and the court has
power to make a disqualification order restraining persons convicted
of certain offences (including offences in connection with the
promotion, formation or management of a company) or who has
been persistently in default in filing documents with the Registrar
from so acting for a specified period (1948 s 188 as amended by 1981
s 93).

The period of disqualification for persistent default in filing
documents with the Registrar can be up to five years: and s 9(1A) of
the Insolvency Act 1976 provides for disqualification for up to fifteen
years where a company has gone into insolvent liquidation and the
court considers the director's conduct makes him unfit to be
concerned in the management of a company.

Acts of disqualified directors

The acts of a director are valid notwithstanding any defect that
may afterwards be discovered in his appointment or qualification
(1948 s 180). Similarly, acts done by a person as a director are valid
notwithstanding that it is afterwards discovered that his appointment
has been terminated because he has attained the age of seventy (1948
s 185(2)).

Register of directors and secretaries

Every company is required to keep at its registered office a register
of directors and secretaries containing the following particulars:

(1) *Particulars as to directors*

(*a*) In the case of an individual, his present Christian name and surname, any former Christian name or surname (see 1948 s 200(9)(*d*)), his usual residential address, his nationality, and his business occupation, if any.

(*b*) In the case of a corporation, its corporate name and registered or principal office (1948 s 200).

In addition, where the company is a public company or a subsidiary of a public company (including a Northern Irish one), the dates of birth of directors also must be stated.

Where a director holds or has held directorships in other companies, these must also be recorded in the register; but it is not necessary to record directorships not held during the preceding five years; or in dormant companies; or in companies of which the company is the wholly-owned subsidiary, or which are the wholly-owned subsidiaries either of the company or of another company of which the company is the wholly-owned subsidiary. For this purpose the expression 'company' includes any body corporate incorporated in Great Britian; a body corporate is deemed to be the wholly-owned subsidiary of another if it has no members except that other and that other's wholly-owned subsidiaries and its or their nominees; and a company is dormant during any period in which no significant accounting transaction (see 1981 s 12(6)) occurs (1948 s 200(2) as amended).

(2) *Particulars as to secretaries*

(*a*) In the case of an individual, his present Christian name and surname, any former Christian name and surname (see 1948 s 200(9)(*d*)), and his usual residential address.

(*b*) In the case of a corporation or a Scottish firm, its corporate or firm name and registered or principal office (1948 s 200(3)).

The particulars contained in the register must also be included in the annual return (see p 108).

The register of directors and secretaries must be open for inspection during business hours by any member free of charge, or by any other person on payment of a fee not exceeding 5p; but the Articles or the company in general meeting may restrict the time to not less than two hours a day (1948 s 200(6)).

For the purposes of 1948 s 200, a person in accordance with whose directions or instructions the directors are accustomed to act is deemed to be a director and officer of the company (1948 s 200(9)(*a*)).

Listed companies must notify the Quotations Department of The Stock Exchange without delay of any changes in the directorate.

Registration of particulars relating to directors and secretaries

The statement of particulars to be delivered to the Registrar on application for registration of a company (Form 1) must contain the relevant particulars—the particulars required to be kept in the register discussed under the preceding heading—of the first directors and secretary and their respective written consents to act (1976 s 21). Notification of any changes of directors or secretary, or of any changes in their registered particulars, must be given to the Registrar (on Form 9b) within fourteen days of the change; such notification must specify the date of the change and contain a written consent to act signed by each person named as having become a director or secretary (1948 s 200(4)).

Register of directors' holdings

Every company must keep a register showing as respects each director of the company (1) the number of shares of each class in, and the amount of debentures of each class of, the company or any other body corporate, being the company's subsidiary or holding company, or a subsidiary of the company's holding company, in which he (or his spouse or infant child (1967 s 31)) is interested and (2) particulars of the occurrence of certain events relating to such shares or debentures including any change in the registered interests (1967 s 29). The rules set out in 1967 s 28 have effect for the interpretation of, and otherwise in relation to, this provision (1967 s 27(2)). There are certain exceptions (see SI 1967 No 1594 and SI 1968 Nos 865 and 1533).

The register need not include particulars of shares in any body corporate which is the wholly-owned subsidiary of another body corporate (1967 s 27(13) and SI 1968 No 865).

A director is bound to notify the company in writing of the subsistence of relevant interests and of the occurrence of most of the events requiring to be recorded in the register (1967 s 27(1)), the company itself being bound to insert in the register particulars of the granting to and exercise by a director (or his spouse or infant child) of a right to subscribe for shares or debentures of the company (1967 s 29(2)). Notification must be given within five days of acquisition or of the occurrence of the relevant event (1967 s 27(3)). Inscription must take place within three days after notification or the event as the case may be (1967 s 29(4)).

For the purposes of the above requirements, any person in accordance with whose directions or instructions the directors of the company are accustomed to act (except by reason only of advice given by him in a professional capacity) is deemed to be a director of the company (1967 ss 27(11), s 29(14) and 56(3)). A director may require that the nature and extent of his interest in any shares or debentures shall be indicated in the register (1967 s 29(5)) but nothing done for the purposes of 1967 s 27 affects the company with notice of, or puts the company upon inquiry as to, the rights of any person in relation to any shares or debentures (1967 s 29(6)).

The register must be kept at the place where the company's register of members is kept or at the company's registered office, except during the holding of the annual general meeting, when it must be produced at the commencement of the meeting and must remain open and accessible during the continuance of the meeting to any person attending the meeting (1967 s 29(7) and (11)). Notice of the location of the register, and of any change in such location, must be given to the Registrar unless it has always been kept at the registered office (Form 27) (1967 s 29(8). An index of the names mentioned in the register must be maintained unless the register is in a form which constitutes an index in itself (1967 s 29(9)). The register must be open to the inspection of any member of the company or the general public and copies thereof must be supplied in a similar way as the register of members (see p 48).

Listed companies must notify The Stock Exchange by the end of the following day (weekends and bank holidays being ignored for this purpose) of any matter notified to the company under 1967 s 27 or 31 in respect of its listed shares or debentures, and The Stock Exchange can publish such information in any manner it may determine (1976 s 25).

Restrictions on dealings in listed securities

It is an offence for a director of a company (or his spouse or infant child (1967 s 30)) to deal in options to buy or sell listed shares in, or listed debentures of, the company or its subsidiary or holding company or a subsidiary of its holding company (1967 s 25) but there is an exemption in respect of buying rights to subscribe, and in respect of convertible debentures. If it appears to the Department of Trade that there are circumstances suggesting that 1967 s 25 has been contravened, they may appoint inspectors to establish whether or not contraventions have occurred (1967 s 32).

Insider dealing

Penal sanctions are also imposed by Part V of the 1980 Act (ss 68–73) against certain dealings in the securities of a company by individuals having unpublished price-sensitive information in relation to those securities which was derived either from their present or past connection with the company (or a related company) or from someone so connected. The prohibition extends to dealings in securities of companies other than the one with which the individual (or his informant) is connected if the information relates to a transaction, actual or contemplated, between the two companies and also to dealings in one capacity by an individual contemplating a take-over offer for the company in another capacity.

The 'dealings' to which the prohibition applies are, in outline, dealings on a recognised stock exchange or through an investment exchange (1980 s 73(3) and (5)) and 'off-market dealings' in advertised securities (1980 s 70(3)). Individuals may be connected with a company as a director, officer or employee of the company or by virtue of a business or professional relationship giving rise to a position of confidence with such persons.

The general conditions of liability are:

(i) that the individual knows that he is or was at any time in the preceding six months, or his informant is or was at any time in the six months preceding the obtaining of the information, connected with the relevant company (or is or was concerned in a take-over or other transaction, actual or contemplated, with the company);

(ii) that the individual or his informant obtained the information by virtue of his connection;

(iii) that it would be reasonable to expect the individual or his informant not to disclose the information except for the proper performance of the functions attaching to his position; and

(iv) that the individual or his informant knows the information is unpublished price-sensitive information in relation to the securities in question.

Any individual prohibited from dealing in any securities himself may not 'counsel or procure' any other person to deal in those securities or communicate the information to any other person if he knows or has reasonable cause to believe that that or some other person will make use of the information for such a purpose.

It is a defence to show that the individual acted otherwise than with a view to the making of a profit or the avoidance of a loss (whether for himself or another person) (1980 s 68(8)(a)), and there are also certain savings for liquidators, receivers, trustees and others. No offence is committed by taking advantage of inside information to refrain from dealing or advise another so to do.

Transactions in contravention of Part V of the 1980 Act are not void or voidable for that reason alone (1980 s 72(3)).

Stock Exchange provisions

In relation to dealings in listed securities, the Code on Take-overs and Mergers and The Stock Exchange Rules for Admission of Securities to Listing should also be considered because the requirements they impose in some respects exceed those of the 1980 Act. For example, Rule 30 of the Code imposes additional obligations with regard to secrecy of unpublished information and prohibits dealings of any kind (including option business) in the securities of the offeree company by any person, not being the offeror, who is privy to confidential price-sensitive information concerning an actual or contemplated offer. The Listing Rules state that the Council of The Stock Exchange attach great importance to the observance of the Code.

The Stock Exchange has also issued a Model Code for securities transactions by directors of listed companies which, inter alia, prohibits dealings during the two months preceding the first announcement of annual and half-yearly results or dividends or distributions to be paid or passed. It also regulates dealings by a director's family and funds of which a director is trustee or beneficiary. The Model Code is to be regarded as a minimum standard of good practice, and listed companies are obliged by The Stock Exchange Listing Agreement to adopt their own rules in terms no less exacting.

Publication of directors' names

A company's business documents need not state the names of its directors: but if, in the case of a company registered after 22 November 1916, a business letter contains in any form (except in the text or as a signatory) the name of any director, then the Christian name, or the initials, and the surname of every other individual director and the corporate name of any corporate director must also be stated (1948 s 201 as amended by the 1981 Act).

These requirements apply also to a company incorporated outside Great Britain which has a place of business in Great Britain, unless such place of business was established before 23 November 1916.

Remuneration of directors

A director has no implied or statutory right to remuneration for his services qua director, but invariably the right to remuneration is awarded by the Articles (see eg reg 76); and if it is not awarded by the

Articles it may be granted by resolution of the company. A director will frequently also hold an executive position with the company, eg managing director or finance director, and as such will receive additional remuneration as an employee.

Where a director serves for a part of a year only, it is not clear whether he is entitled to a proportion of any annual remuneration awarded by the Articles (*Moriarty* v *Regent's Garage Co* [1921] 2 KB 766) unless the Articles (or the resolution in cases where the remuneration is fixed by the company in general meeting) provide that he is to be paid "*at the rate of £x* per annum", although it is probable that the Apportionment Act 1870 would be held to apply and the remuneration taken to accrue from day to day (cf reg 76). Where the appointment of a director is invalid ab initio, he is not entitled to remuneration (*Woolf* v *East Nigel Gold Mining Co Ltd* (1905) 21 TLR 660); but it is otherwise where his original appointment is valid and he becomes disqualified subsequently (*Salton* v *New Beeston Cycle Co* [1899] 1 Ch 775).

Directors who are remunerated for their services are not entitled in addition to an allowance for travelling expenses unless the Articles so provide or the company so resolves (*Young* v *Naval, Military and Civil Service Co-operative Society of South Africa Ltd* [1905] 1 KB 687); but out-of-pocket expenses may be reimbursed.

Particulars as to the remuneration of directors must be given in the company's published accounts (see p 125).

It is unlawful to pay a director remuneration (whether as director or otherwise) free of income tax, or otherwise calculated by reference to or varying with the amount of his income tax, or to or with the rate or basic rate of income tax, and any provision in the Articles or in a contract for the payment of remuneration free of tax etc is to have effect as if it provided for payment, as a gross sum subject to tax, of the net sum for which it actually provides (1948 s 189).

Directors' service agreements

A company must keep at an appropriate place (see 1967 s 26(2)) ie its registered office or principal place of business, or the place where its register of members is kept, copies of written service contracts of any director with the company or any subsidiary (and written memoranda of any unwritten ones), unless (*a*) the contract requires him to work wholly or mainly outside the United Kingdom, in which case only a memorandum of its terms as to duration need be made available (1967 s 26(3A)) or (*b*) the unexpired portion is less than twelve months or it can be terminated by the company within the next ensuing twelve months, without payment of compensation. Notice of the place at which they are kept must be sent to the Registrar (Form 26) unless they have at all times been kept at the registered office. The company must allow them to be inspected during business hours by any member free of charge. By resolution of the company passed at a general meeting, the time for inspection may be restricted to not less than two hours in each business day (1967 s 26(4)).

The prior approval of the company in general meeting is needed before a contract is entered into under which a director will have security of employment for more than five years (1980 s 47): an ordinary resolution is sufficient.

The following points should be noted:

(i) in the case of a director of a holding company, the requirement applies to any agreement for employment with the company or any subsidiary;

(ii) it applies not only to contracts of employment in the strict sense but also to contracts for the provision of services by the director;

(iii) it applies whether or not the agreement is in writing;

(iv) in case (i) the approval required is that of the holding company and that of the subsidiary, if partly owned; but no approval is required from a company incorporated abroad, whether it be an employing company or a holding company, or from a company which is a wholly-owned subsidiary of another company wherever incorporated;

(v) in certain circumstances, where a further agreement is entered into before the expiration of an existing agreement, the unexpired period of the existing agreement is to be added to the period of the further agreement in ascertaining whether the further agreement extends beyond five years.

The provisions summarised above apply also to 'shadow directors' (ie any person in accordance with whose directions or instructions the directors of a company are accustomed to act—1980 s 63(1) and (4)).

The Stock Exchange requires that service contracts between a listed company (or any of its subsidiaries) and any of its directors not expiring or determinable within ten years by the employing company without payment of compensation (other than statutory compensation) must be subject to approval by the company in general meeting; and that all service agreements not expiring or determinable within one year without payment of compensation must be available for inspection prior to and at the annual general meeting.

Loans etc to directors

The 1948 Act (s 190) contained provisions prohibiting, with certain limited exceptions, loans by a company to its directors or the directors of its holding company, or the giving by the company of guarantees or security in connection with a loan made to any such person by a third party. These provisions have now been replaced by ss 49 to 53 of the 1980 Act which, taken together, construct an elaborate code of prohibitions and penalties in relation to loans and other financial transactions (under which credit is granted but which could not strictly be classified as loans) involving directors or persons connected with directors. These provisions are complex and difficult, even obscure. A comprehensive analysis of their ramifications would be inappropriate in a work of this nature but it is to be hoped that the following outline of the principal provisions will be of assistance. In any save a straightforward case, company secretaries would be wise to take professional advice; but it is necessary that the breadth of the provisions should be appreciated in order to be alert to the necessity for such advice in widely differing circumstances.

All companies

All companies are prohibited (1980 s 49) from:

(*a*) making a loan to a director of the company or its holding company;

(*b*) entering into a guarantee or providing security in connection with a loan made by any person to such a director;

unless in the case of (*a*) above the aggregate of the 'relevant amounts' (see 'General' below) does not exceed £2,500 (1980 s 50(2A)).

It should be noted that 'company' for this purpose means a company incorporated under the 1948 Act or one of its predecessor Acts (1980 s 87(5) and 1948 s 455(1)) and therefore does not extend to, for example, a wholly owned but overseas incorporated subsidiary of a UK incorporated holding company.

Exceptions to the foregoing are:

(i) The provision for a director of funds to meet business expenditure if the prior approval of the company in general meeting is given (1980 s 50(4)(*c*) and (5)) or, if such approval is not obtained, the relevant loan is to be repaid or any other liability arising under the transaction is to be discharged within six months from the conclusion of the next following annual general meeting;

(ii) in the case of a money-lending company (see 1980 s 65(1)), a loan or guarantee in the ordinary course of business provided *either* the loan *or* guarantee is on an arm's length commercial basis *or* the loan made or guaranteed is a housing loan (ie a loan for the acquisition or improvement of a dwellinghouse for use as the only or main residence of the director, or for replacing a loan made by another for that purpose), such loans are ordinarily made to employees of the company on no less favourable terms and the aggregate of the relevant amounts does not exceed £50,000;

(iii) loans by a company to its holding company or the provision of a guarantee or security by a company in connection with a loan made to its holding company by any other person.

Relevant companies

These are public companies and any company which is a subsidiary of, or has a subsidiary or fellow subsidiary which is, a public company (1980 s 65(1)). In addition to the prohibitions applicable to all companies (see above), relevant companies are prohibited from:

(*a*) making a *quasi-loan* (see 'General' below) to a director of the company or its holding company or a loan or quasi-loan to any person connected with such a director, or entering into any guarantee or providing any security in connection with any such loan or quasi-loan or loan by any other person (1980 s 49(1)(*b*));

(*b*) entering into a *credit transaction* (see 'General' below) for a director of the company or its holding company or any connected person or entering into a guarantee or providing any security in connection with such a credit transaction by any other person (s 49(2)).

Exceptions. The same general exceptions apply to the additional prohibitions imposed on relevant companies as to the prohibitions imposed on companies generally—subject to special provisions and limitations, amongst which the following may be noted:

(i) the exception for busines expenditure applies only if the aggregate of the relevant amounts does not exceed £10,000 (1980 s 50(5));

(ii) loans and quasi-loans under the exception for a money lending company are permitted in the case of a company which is not a recognised bank only if the aggregate of the relevant amounts does not exceed £50,000(1980 s 50(6));

(iii) credit transactions are permitted if (*a*) the aggregate of the relevant amounts at the time of the transaction does not exceed £5,000, or (*b*) the transaction is entered into in the ordinary course of the company's business and the value of the transaction is not greater than, and the terms not more favourable than, would be offered to a person of equal financial standing not connected with the company (1980 s 50(3));

(iv) intra-group loan or quasi-loan guarantee or security arrangements which would otherwise be prohibited by reason only that a director of one member of the group is associated with another are permitted (1980 s 50(1)).

General

The following are the principal definitions applicable to the foregoing sections (insofar as not directly dealt with):

(1) A *quasi-loan* is a transaction under which one party ('the creditor') agrees to pay, or pays otherwise than in pursuance of an agreement, a sum for another ('the borrower'), or agrees to reimburse, or reimburses otherwise than in pursuance of an agreement, expenditure incurred by another party for another ('likewise the borrower'):

(*a*) on terms that the borrower (or a person on his behalf) will reimburse the creditor; or

(*b*) in circumstances giving rise to a liability on the borrower (or any person on his behalf) to reimburse the creditor (1980 s 65(2)).

For example the provision of a credit card which can be used for personal expenditure can constitute a quasi-loan.

(2) A *credit transaction* is a transaction under which one party (a) supplies goods or sells land under a hire-purchase agreement or a conditional sale agreement; (b) leases or hires land or goods in return for periodical payments; or (c) otherwise disposes of land or supplies goods or services on deferred payment terms (1980 s 65(3)).

(3) *Services* means anything other than goods or land (1980 s 65(1)).

(4) *Connected persons.* A person is connected with a director if such person (not being himself a director) is:

(*a*) the spouse or minor child (legitimate or illegitimate) or stepchild of a director;

(*b*) a body corporate with which the director is associated;

(*c*) acting in the capacity of trustee of any trust (other than an employees' share scheme or a pension scheme) of which the director or his spouse or any minor child or stepchild or associated body corporate is a beneficiary or a possible beneficiary under a power conferred on the trustees; or

(*d*) acting in his capacity as a partner of the director or of a person connected with the director by virtue of any of the foregoing subparagraphs.

For the purposes of (*b*) and (*c*) above, a director of a company is associated with another body corporate if he and persons connected with him are together interested in one-fifth of the equity share capital or entitled to exercise or control the exercise of one-fifth of the voting power at any general meetings of that body corporate (1980 s 64).

A whole section of the 1980 Act (s 51) is devoted to the manner in which '*relevant amounts*' are determined. In essence, the value of the proposed transaction and the outstanding value of all existing loans or other relevant arrangements to or with the person in whose favour a transaction is proposed and his connected persons must be aggregated.

Certain transactions which might otherwise enable the pro-hibitions to be evaded (eg the taking over by a company of loans, guarantees etc made or entered into by outside parties, or the company taking part in a collusive arrangement eg a back to back loan arrangement) are themselves prohibited (1980 s 49(3) and (4)).

For the purposes of these restrictions on loans etc for directors and persons connected with them a shadow director is treated as a director (1980 s 63). A shadow director is a person in accordance with whose directions or instructions the directors of a company are accustomed to act (unless by reason only of advice given by him in a professional capacity).

See p 155 for disclosure in a company's accounts of loans to or similar transactions for directors or persons connected with them.

Powers, duties and liabilities of directors

Subject to the provisions of the company's Articles and the Acts, the management of a company's affairs is in the hands of the directors, and they possess all the powers necessary to enable them to carry out their functions, eg to enter into contracts on behalf of the company, to engage or dismiss employees etc. Their powers may, however, be restricted by the Articles. It may, for instance, be provided that certain acts shall not be done by them unless they first obtain the sanction of the company in general meeting; and, where there is such a provision in the Articles, failure to obtain such sanction may render the directors personally liable to the company. However in favour of a third party dealing with a company in good faith the power of the directors to bind the company is deemed to be free of any such limitation under the Memorandum or Articles, and such a third party is not bound to enquire as to any such limitation and is presumed to have acted in good faith unless the contrary is proved (European Communities Act 1972, s 9(1)). Even where there is such a limitation in the Articles, an act done without prior sanction may be ratified subsequently by the company, provided that it is not ultra vires the company (*Irvine* v *Union Bank of Australia* (1877) 2 App Cas 366).

A director's duties to his company are of a fiduciary nature, and are owed to the company itself, not to its shareholders or to creditors. It is the overriding duty of the directors to exercise their powers in good faith ie in the manner in which they consider it best in the interests of the company (see eg *Bamford* v *Bamford* [1970] Ch 212) and for a proper purpose (see eg *Howard Smith Ltd* v *Ampol Petroleum Ltd* [1974] AC 821 (PC)). The interests of the company in this context means the interests of present and future shareholders: but 1980 s 46, whilst recognising that the duty is still owed to the company alone, requires the directors of a company to have regard, in the performance of their functions, to the interests of the company's employees in general as well as to the interests of its members. The 1980 Act further provides (s 74) that the powers of the company shall, if they would not otherwise do so, be deemed to include power to make provision, in connection with the cessation or the transfer to any person of the whole or part of the undertaking of the company or any subsidiary, for the benefit of persons employed or formerly employed by the company or by such subsidiary. This power may be exercised notwithstanding that its exercise is not in the best interests of the company, and, if so authorised by the Memorandum or Articles, may be exercised by a resolution of the directors (failing which provision it must be exercised as may be provided by the Memorandum or Articles, or otherwise by ordinary resolution of the company).

If the Articles do not restrict a power exercisable by the directors, they are not bound to follow directions given them by the company in general meeting, if they honestly believe that the course they themselves desire to adopt is best for the company (*Quin & Axtens Ltd* v *Salmon* [1909] AC 442); but the company can force its will upon them by altering the Articles by special resolution.

The liabilities of directors to the company and to outsiders who have dealings with the company are determined by the common law and the Acts. At common law they may be liable to the company for eg negligence or breach of trust, and to outsiders for breach of warranty of authority; and under the Acts the company is given statutory civil remedies for breaches of certain directors' duties as, for example, in relation to 1980 s 48 (substantial property transactions involving directors) and 1980 s 49 (see p 148), breach of which entitles the company to declare any arrangement thereby entered into void, to reclaim any gains or profits and to be indemnified against any loss or damage. There can also be liability to outsiders under the Acts, as, for example, under the prospectus provisions (see p 33). This area is however too extensive for full treatment here.

Failure by directors to observe many provisions of the Acts and other statutes may give rise to criminal liability, as, for example, the prohibition on loans etc to directors under 1980 s 49 (see p 148). Again this area is too extensive for treatment here but the note that:—

(1) Under 1967 s 113, any officer of a company who destroys, mutilates or falsifies, or is privy to destruction, mutilation or falsification of a document affecting or relating to its property or affairs, or makes or is privy to the making of a false entry in such a document, is, unless he proves that he had no intention to conceal the state of affairs of the company or to defeat the law, guilty of an offence. Further, any such person who fraudulently either parts with, alters, or makes an omission in any such document, is likewise guilty of an offence.

(2) Under s 19(1) of the Theft Act 1968, any officer of a body corporate, or any person purporting to act as such, who publishes or concurs in the publication of any written statement or account which to his knowledge is or may be misleading, false or deceptive in a material particular, with intent to deceive members or creditors of the body corporate about its affairs is guilty of an offence punishable by up to 7 years' imprisonment.

(3) It is an offence for an officer of a company to make a misleading statement to the company's auditor (1976 s 19—see further p 162 below).

Except as provided in 1948 s 205 (and see reg 136), any provision (whether in the Articles or in any contract with the company or otherwise) for exempting any director or officer of the company or any person employed by the company as auditor from, or indemnifying him against, any liability for negligence, default or breach of trust is void. However, 1948 s 448 provides for relief to be given where the court considers that the director acted honestly and reasonably and in all the circumstances ought fairly to be excused.

1948 ss 328 to 334 set out certain liabilities which may be incurred by a director in the event of the company being wound up. Directors should be particularly mindful of 1948 s 332 (personal liability for trading whilst insolvent) and secretaries should note the case of *Re Maidstone Buildings Provisions Ltd* [1971] 1 WLR 1085 (see p 5).

A person dealing with a company is not generally obliged to satisfy himself that internal formalities have been complied with (*Royal British Bank* v *Turquand* (1856) 6 E & B 327). This rule does not apply in certain cases, eg where the person dealing with the company has actual notice of non-compliance, or where there are circumstances which should have put him on inquiry. The position of a third party dealing with the company is also assisted by s 9 of the European Communities Act 1972 (see p 151).

Interests of directors in contracts

A director should not allow his personal interests and his duties as a director to conflict. Accordingly, any interest in a contract with the company must be permitted by the Articles and disclosed in accordance with the Acts. By 1948 s 199 it is the duty of a director, who is in any way, whether directly or indirectly, interested in a contract or proposed contract with the company (or any transaction or arrangement with it, whether or not constituting a contract, entered into after 22 December 1980 (1980 s 60)) to declare the nature of his interest at a meeting of the directors of the company.In the case of a proposed contract, the disclosure must be made at the meeting of the directors at which the question of entering into the contract is first taken into consideration, or if at that date the director was not interested in the proposed contract, at the next meeting of directors after he becomes interested. In the case of a contract in which a director becomes interested after it is made, he must declare his interest at the first meeting of directors held after he becomes interested.

A director may comply with the above requirements by giving general notice either (i) to the effect that he is a member of a specified company or firm and is to be regarded as interested in any contracts made with such company or firm or (ii) that he is to be regarded as interested in any contract made with a specified connected person (1948 s 199(3)).

For the purposes of s 199 a transaction falling within 1980 s 49 (loans etc to directors—see p 148 above) and whether involving a director or a connected person must be treated as a transaction or arrangement in which he is interested (1980 s 60(2)): this provision applies whether or not the transaction is in fact prohibited under s 49. 1948 s 199 also applies to a 'shadow director' (see p 151) who must declare his interest not at a meeting of the directors but by specific or general notice in writing (1980 s 63).

Table A provides that a director may not vote in respect of any contract in which he is interested, and shall not be counted in the quorum present at a meeting which considers such a contract, subject to the exceptions mentioned in reg 84(2) and (4). In some cases Articles prohibit directors from being interested in contracts and from voting, but the usual modern practice is to make provision similar to that in Table A.

Any arrangement under which a director of a company or its holding company (or a person connected with such a director—see 1980 s 64) is to acquire from the company, or dispose of to the company, any property or interest in property other than cash ('non-cash assets' which expression includes the grant, or extinction, of rights over any property—see 1980 s 87(1) and (4)) having a value in excess of 10 per cent of the company's relevant assets (but with a minimum of £1,000) or £50,000 must first be approved in general meeting by the company (unless a wholly-owned subsidiary) and, in the case of a director of a holding company or a person connected with him, the holding company. In the absence of such approval the arrangement is voidable by the company unless inter alia it is affirmed within a reasonable period by the company and (if applicable) its holding company in general meeting (1980 s 48).

Disclosure in accounts of material interests

1967 s 16(1)(c) required the disclosure, in the directors' report, of the material interests, direct or indirect, of any director in any contract which was in force at any time during the year to which the report related and which, in the opinion of the directors, was a contract of significance in relation to the company's business.

1980 s 54 (which replaces 1967 s 16(1)(c)) requires inclusion in notes to the statutory accounts or group accounts prepared by a company in respect of any accounting reference period ending on or after 22 December 1980 of particulars of transactions, agreements or arrangements entered into or subsisting at any time during the relevant period by the company or any subsidiary, being either:

(i) loans or other transactions or arrangements of any of the types described in 1980 s 49 (pp 148–150) above for a person who is or was a director of the company or of its holding company at any time during the relevant period or connected with such a director; or

(ii) other transactions with the company or a subsidiary in which a person who is or was at any time in the relevant period a director of the company had, directly or indirectly, a material interest, but excepting:

(*a*) a service contract;

(*b*) a transaction or arrangement between the company and another company in which a director is interested solely as a director of the other company; and

(*c*) transactions excluded by 1980 s 58 (certain types of transactions etc where the aggregate values do not exceed specified amounts).

Subject to these exceptions, the disclosure requirements apply whether or not the transaction, arrangement or agreement was one prohibited by the Act. They apply to relevant companies (see p 149) and other companies without distinction, and transactions etc with a person connected with a director are treated as ones in which the director is interested (1980 s 54(4)(*a*)), even where not so treated for the purposes of 1980 s 49.

The particulars to be given in the accounts are specified in detail in 1980 s 55.

There are modified requirements for recognised banks and their holding companies in relation to transactions, arrangements or agreements to which the bank is a party.

It should be noted also that:

(1) The aggregate of the amounts outstanding under transactions etc in the nature of or relating to loans, quasi-loans, credit transactions, guarantees etc made by a company or a subsidiary for officers other than directors and the numbers of officers concerned must be disclosed in the accounts of the company or group accounts as the case may require, but the officers need not be identified (1980 s 56). However, if the amount outstanding in respect of any officer does not exceed £2,500 his case can be omitted.

In the case of transactions etc by a recognised bank for officers of the bank or its holding company, no disclosure is required in the accounts of the bank or its holding company, but the bank or holding company must maintain a full record of matters which would otherwise require to be fully disclosed in its accounts and (except in the case of a recognised bank which is a wholly-owned subsidiary of a company incorporated in the United Kingdom) to make such record available for inspection (1980 ss 56(3) and 57).

(2) For the purposes of the disclaimer requirements summarised above, shadow directors are treated as directors.

(3) No machinery is provided whereby a company or its directors

can ascertain whether any person is connected with a director of the company or its holding company or is a shadow director; but nonetheless liabilities, including penal liabilities, may fall on the company and its directors for infringements of the substantive prohibitions and of the disclosure requirements; and it cannot be assumed that ignorance is a good defence.

Information to be given by directors

In order that the company may be in a position to comply with the various statutory requirements, it is the duty of directors to supply the company with certain information concerning themselves and their activities as follows:—

1 Any person who is appointed or proposed to be appointed director of a company subject to 1948 s 185 (see p 136) at a time when he has attained any retiring age applicable to him under the Act or the company's Articles must give notice of his age to the company (1948 s 186). But this section does not apply on re-appointment on the termination of a previous appointment as director.

Since the register of directors and secretaries must show the ages of directors of companies which are subject to s 185, all such directors may be required to disclose their ages to the company to enable the register to be completed.

(2) It is the duty of a director to give notice to the company of such matters relating to himself as may be necessary to enable the company to comply with the following requirements:

(a) the completion of the register of directors and secretaries (1948 s 200(7)—see p 140);

(b) the completion of the register of directors' holdings (1967 ss 27(1) and 31(2)—see p 142);

(c) the inclusion in accounts of particulars as to directors' salaries, pensions, etc, and waivers of emoluments (1948 s 198 and 1967 ss 6(5) and 7(3)—see p 125).

In the case of the information required by 1967 s 27 the notice must be in writing and be expressed to be given in fulfilment of the obligation imposed by that section (1967 s 27(1) and (9)).

The information needed to enable the company to satisfy the requirements under (c) above must be given also by persons who are or have been at any time during the preceding five years officers of the company (ibid).

(3) Directors and other officers of a company must provide true and accurate information to the auditors of the company in their capacity as such (1976 s 19, and see pp 161 and 162).

CHAPTER 8

AUDITORS

Qualifications of auditors

No person may be a company's auditor unless he is a member of a body of accountants established in the United Kingdom and for the time being recognised by the Department of Trade (1948 s 161(1)). Such bodies are at present the Institute of Chartered Accountants in England and Wales, the Institute of Chartered Accountants of Scotland, the Association of Certified Accountants and the Institute of Chartered Accountants in Ireland (1976 s 13(1)), although the Secretary of State may by statutory instrument add or delete any body (1976 s 13(2)). In addition, the Secretary of State may authorise to be an auditor a person with similar qualifications obtained in a country outside the United Kingdom (1948 s 161(1)(b)), but such authorisation may be refused if corresponding privileges are not conferred by such country on persons qualified in the United Kingdom (1976 s 13(3)).

No person who is an officer or servant of the company, or who is a partner or employee of an officer or servant of the company, may be its auditor (1948 s 161(2)). No body corporate may be a company's auditor (ibid). A person may not be a company's auditor if he is disqualified for appointment as auditor of any other body corporate which is the company's subsidiary or holding company, or a subsidiary of that company's holding company, or if he would be disqualified if the body corporate were a company (1948 s 161(3)).

By 1976 s 13(5), no person shall act as an auditor at a time when he knows that he is disqualified for appointment, and if an auditor to his knowledge becomes disqualified he shall thereupon vacate office and notify the company that he has by reason of such disqualification vacated office.

Appointment of auditors

One or more auditors must be appointed for the purpose of preparing the reports already mentioned (see p 132). The first auditors may be appointed by a resolution of the directors at any time before the first general meeting at which the duty to lay accounts before the company is complied with pursuant to 1976 s 1; and auditors so appointed shall hold office until the conclusion of that meeting (1976 s 14(3)). If the directors fail to make such appointment, the company in general meeting may do so (1976 s 14(4)).

At each general meeting at which accounts are laid before the company pursuant to 1976 s 1 the company in general meeting must appoint an auditor or auditors to hold office from the conclusion of that meeting until the conclusion of the next general meeting at which the requirements as to the laying of accounts are complied with (1976 s 14(1)). If at such general meeting no auditor is appointed or re-appointed then the company is required to give notice of that fact within one week to the Secretary of State who may appoint a person to fill the vacancy (1976 s 14(2)).

The directors, or the company in general meeting, may fill any casual vacancy in the office of auditor, but while any such vacancy continues the surviving or continuing auditor or auditors (if any) may act (1976 s 14(5)). 1981 s 12 enables a company which (i) is not required to prepare group accounts, (ii) falls within the exemption for individual accounts conferred by 1981 s 6 (see p 117) and (iii) is dormant, to dispense by special resolution with the requirement to appoint auditors under 1976 s 14(1). For this purpose a company is to be regarded as dormant for any period during which no significant accounting transaction occurs (1981 s 12(6)).

Duties of auditors

There are a number of reported cases dealing with the general duties of auditors (see eg *Re London and General Bank Ltd (No 2)* [1895] 2 Ch 673, *Re Kingston Cotton Mill Co* (No 2) case [1896] 2 Ch 279 and *Re Thomas Gerrard & Son Ltd* [1968] Ch 455 but discussion of these does not fall within the scope of this work. The new statutory duties imposed by 1980 s 59 (auditors' report to state any non-compliance with 1980 ss 54 and 56; see pp 155 and 156 above) and 1981 s 15 (which adds to the 1967 Act a new s 23A under which the auditors have a duty to check the consistency of the directors' report with the accounts) should however be noted: and see pp 132 and 133.

Removal of auditors

A company may by ordinary resolution remove an auditor before the expiration of his term of office. Notice of the passing of a resolution to remove an auditor must be given to the Registrar on

Form 14 within fourteen days of the meeting at which the resolution was passed (1976 s 14(6)).

Special notice (see p 89) must be given of a resolution proposed to be passed at a general meeting of a company appointing as auditor a person other than a retiring auditor, filling a casual vacancy in the office of auditor, reappointing as auditor a retiring auditor who was appointed by the directors to fill a casual vacancy or removing an auditor before the expiration of his term of office (1976 s 15(1)). On receipt of special notice of such an intended resolution the company shall forthwith send a copy of the resolution to the person proposed to be appointed or removed, or who is retiring or who has resigned. Where notice is given of an intended resolution appointing a person as auditor other than the retiring auditor, or removing an auditor, the retiring auditor or the auditor proposed to be removed has the right to make written representations to the company (not exceeding a reasonable length), and to request that they be notified to the members, in which case, if they are not received too late, the notice to the members must state that such written representations have been received, and a copy thereof must be sent to every member to whom the notice is sent (whether before or after the receipt of the representations); and, if the representations are not so sent, the auditor may (without prejudice to his right to address the meeting) require that they are read at the meeting (1976 s 15(3) and (4)). The representations need not be sent to members or read out at the meeting if, on application by any person claiming to be aggrieved, the court is satisfied that the procedure is being abused to secure needless publicity for defamatory matter (1976 s 15(5)).

An auditor who has been removed is entitled to attend the general meeting at which his term of office would otherwise have expired and any general meeting at which it is proposed to fill the vacancy caused by his removal and to receive all notices and communications relating to any such meeting; he is entitled also to be heard at any such meeting which he attends on any part of the business of the meeting which concerns him as former auditor of the company (1976 s 15(6)).

Resignation of auditors

By 1976 s 16, an auditor may resign by written notice of resignation to the company deposited at the registered office, such notice being effective as from the date of deposit or, if later, the operative date specified in the notice. Such notice will not, however, be effective unless it contains a statement either (a) that there are no circumstances connected with his resignation which he considers

AUDITORS 161

should be brought to the notice of the members or creditors of the company or (*b*) setting out such circumstances. The company must within fourteen days of deposit of the notice send a copy to the Registrar and, if such notice contains a statement of the circumstances referred to in (*b*) above, to every person entitled to receive copies of the company's accounts. The company or any person claiming to be aggrieved may within fourteen days of the receipt by the company of the notice containing such a statement apply to the court. If the court is satisfied that such notice is being used by the auditor to secure needless publicity for defamatory matter, it may order that copies of the notice need not be sent out. The company must within fourteen days of the court's decision, send to the Registrar and to each person entitled to receive copies of the company's accounts a statement setting out the effect of the court order (if such an order is made) or (if no such order is made) a copy of the notice containing the statement of circumstances connected with the auditor's resignation.

Where the auditor's notice of resignation contains such a statement, the auditor is entitled (1976 s 17) to deposit with the notice a requisition calling on the directors of the company forthwith to convene an extraordinary general meeting of the company for the purpose of receiving and considering such explanation of the circumstances connected with his resignation as he may wish to place before the meeting. The auditor may request the company to circulate to the members a statement (not exceeding a reasonable length) of the circumstances connected with his resignation. Unless such statement is received too late (or the court considers that the procedure is being abused to secure needless publicity for defamatory matter), the company must state in every notice of the meeting that the statement has been made and must send a copy to every member to whom the notice is or has been sent. The directors must convene a meeting, to be held not more than twenty-eight days after the date of the notice, calling it within twenty-one days from the date of the deposit of the auditor's requisition. The auditor may, without prejudice to his right to be heard orally, require that his statement be read out at the meeting. Every director who fails to take all reasonable steps to secure the convening of such a meeting is liable to be fined.

Right of auditors to information etc

Every auditor has a right of access at all times to the books and accounts and vouchers of the company, and is entitled to require from the officers of the company such information and explanation as he thinks necessary for the performance of his duties (1967 s 14(5)). The auditors of a company are entitled to attend any general meeting of the company, and to receive all notices of, and other communications relating to, any general meeting which any member of the company is entitled to receive, and to be heard at any general meeting which they attend on any part of the business of the meeting which concerns them as auditors (1967 s 14(7)).

A subsidiary company and its auditors are under a duty to give to the auditors of the holding company such information and explanation as the latter may reasonably require for the purposes of their duty as auditors of the holding company. In the case of a subsidiary which is not a body corporate incorporated in Great Britain, the auditors of the holding company can require the holding company to take such steps as are reasonably open to it to obtain from the subsidiary such information and explanation as the auditors of the holding company may require (1976 s 18).

False statements to auditors

An officer of a company is liable to be fined or imprisoned if he knowingly or recklessly makes a statement which is misleading, false or deceptive in a material particular and such statement is made to the auditors of the company (whether orally or in writing) conveying or purporting to convey any information or explanation which such auditors require or are entitled to require as auditors of the company (1976 s 19).

Remuneration of auditors

Where an auditor is appointed by the directors or the Department of Trade, the body making the appointment may fix his remuneration. In other cases, it is fixed either by the company in general meeting or in such manner as the company in general meeting may determine (1976 s 14(8)). Expenses paid to an auditor are deemed to be part of his remuneration (1976 s 14(8)).

Trade unions and employers' associations

Special provisions apply (under 1976 s 20) to auditors of a body which is both a company and a trade union or employers' association to which s 11 of the Trade Union and Labour Relations Act 1974 applies.

CHAPTER 9

CHARGES AND DEBENTURES

POWER TO BORROW

The Memorandum almost invariably empowers a company to borrow money and to give security for loans, while the Articles usually state the manner in which and the extent to which this power may be exercised (eg reg 79, Table A). Even in the absence of such a provision in the Memorandum, however, a trading company has implied power to borrow and give security (*General Auction Estate and Monetary Co* v *Smith* [1891] 3 Ch 432) although not, normally, to give guarantees, or provide collateral security, for obligations of third parties.

In the majority of cases the power may be exercised by resolution of the board (which must be acting bona fide in the best interests of the company and for a proper purpose), but a limit may be placed upon the power, as in reg 79 of Table A, which prohibits the directors from borrowing more than the nominal amount of the issued share capital, unless they obtain the sanction of the company in general meeting (see p 151).

An express borrowing power in the Memorandum must be exercised for the purposes of authorised objects: it cannot be treated as an independent object even though there is provision in the Memorandum for each sub-clause to be read separately (*Introductions Ltd* v *National Provincial Bank Ltd* [1970] Ch 199).

If a Stock Exchange listing is desired, the borrowing powers of the directors must normally be limited to 'an ascertainable amount.'

Forms of borrowing

All methods of borrowing which are available to individuals may be employed by a company, with the addition of the method involving the issue of a debenture or debentures.

A company which has power to borrow has also implied power to charge its assets as security, unless the power is excluded by the Memorandum or Articles. In general, any of the assets may be charged, including uncalled capital; but in no circumstances may a charge be created over a reserve liability (see p 195) (*Re Mayfair Property Co Ltd, Bartlett* v *Mayfair Property Co Ltd* [1898] 2 Ch 28); or the liability of the members of a company limited by guarantee (*Re Pyle Works Ltd* (1890) 44 Ch D 534).

Types of debentures

Although a number of provisions in the 1948 Act are concerned with debentures, and s 455 contains a definition thereof, it is generally recognised that there is no complete and comprehensive statement of what, in law, constitutes a debenture. However for present purposes it is taken to be a formal written instrument creating or acknowledging loan indebtedness of the company. They can be:

(1) Unsecured or 'naked' debentures, which give no security to the lender but involve merely a promise by the company to repay the indebtedness with or without interest.

(2) Secured debentures, which give security for the indebtedness by way of mortgage or charge on the company's assets. The security in such cases may take either or both of the following forms—

(*a*) a fixed charge on specified assets; or

(*b*) a floating charge on the whole of the assets or on certain classes of assets.

This chapter is principally concerned with secured debentures.

The company cannot dispose of assets which are the subject of a fixed charge except subject to the charge; but, subject to the terms of the debenture creating the charge, it may continue to dispose of assets which are the subject of a floating charge.

Debentures may be either payable to bearer, or payable to the registered holder. Further, they may be either redeemable at a specified date or on demand, or irredeemable, in which case a repayment of the loan can only be claimed in the event of a default or liquidation; but the precise effect of these debentures depends upon the terms of issue (see 1948 s 89).

By s 455 'debenture' includes debenture stock, which is borrowed money consolidated into one amount and constituted and, if applicable, secured, by means of a trust deed. Lenders receive a debenture stock certificate entitling them to repayment of a specific sum, being their entitlement of stock, upon and subject to the terms of the trust deed, which contains the legal contract between the company and the trustees for the stockholders. The use of a trust deed enables action to be taken by the trustees on behalf of all stockholders without delay occurring. The expression 'debenture stock' normally indicates stock secured by a floating charge; where a fixed charge is given as security the stock will normally be called a 'mortgage debenture stock', and where there is no security an 'unsecured loan stock'.

No stamp duty is payable on the issue of debentures and/or charges (Finance Acts 1971 and 1973).

ISSUE, TRANSFER ETC OF DEBENTURES

Issue of debentures

The procedure to be employed on an issue of debentures (including debenture stock) varies with the circumstances.

Where a single debenture is issued to a single creditor, as where a loan is made by the company's bank, there is little to be done beyond the sealing and registration of the necessary documents pursuant to the relevant board resolution. But where a series of debentures is to be issued or an issue of debenture stock is to be made to secure a loan made by a number of persons, a number of other administrative acts must be performed.

If the debentures are to be offered to the public, a copy of the prospectus must be filed (see pp 26 et seq). In such a case applications and allotments will be dealt with much as if an issue of shares were being made; but no return of allotments is required.

Frequently, where a series of debentures is issued, the debentures are supported by a trust deed. This deed appoints trustees in whom are vested the assets which form the debenture-holders' security, and states, inter alia, the circumstances in which a receiver may be appointed. Where a single debenture secured by a floating charge has been issued before the creation of a series of debentures, notice of the creation of the series should be given to the holder, who should be supplied with a copy of the trust deed. As to priority of charges, see p 168.

Except where otherwise provided by the terms of issue, debentures or certificates for debenture stock must be issued within two months after allotment (or lodgement of a transfer) (1948 s 80).

Debentures may be issued at a discount, which must be stated in the next annual return (1948 Sched 6 Pt I para 3(h)) and (under 1948 Sched 8A Pt I para 3) shown in the balance sheet until finally written off. The terms of issue may also provide for a premium on redemption. As to the position under the Control of Borrowing Order 1958 (as amended) see p 44.

Particulars of issues of debentures, and the reasons for the issue, during any financial year, must be stated by way of note to a company's accounts for the financial year (1948 Sched 8 para 41(1)).

A contract to take up and pay for debentures may be enforced by specific performance.

Register of debenture holders

Where a register of debenture holders is kept (ie where debentures payable to the registered holders thereof are issued), the rules laid down for the register of members apply also to the register of debenture holders (see p 47) (1948 s 86, Form 102).

The register may be inspected free of charge by any registered holder of debentures or by any holder of shares, subject to such reasonable restrictions as may be imposed by the company in general meeting; but not less than two hours per business day must be allowed for such inspection. The Articles, the debentures, the relevant trust deed or the debenture stock certificates may provide, however, for the closing of the register for not more than thirty days in any year. Persons other than debenture holders or shareholders may inspect the register on payment of a fee of not more than 5p (1948 s 87(1)).

A copy of the register of debenture holders or of any part thereof may be obtained by any person on payment of a fee of not more than 10p per hundred words or part thereof (1948 s 87(2)). Copies of debenture trust deeds may also be demanded by debenture holders (1948 s 87(3)).

The form of a register of debenture holders is not laid down by the Act, but it usually follows closely that of the register of members. A register in non-legible form is permitted (Companies (Registers and other Records) Regulations (SI 1979 No 53)). It may therefore be in computerised form. Where the debenture instrument provides that the company shall not be obliged to enter in the register notice of any trust to which the debentures are subject, the company is nevertheless not entitled to disregard such notice as it is in the case of shares (*Re Palmer's Decorating & Furnishing Co Ltd* [1904] 2 Ch 743).

Transfer of debentures

A transfer of debentures payable to the registered holder thereof is effected in the manner prescribed by the debenture instrument or by a stock transfer in accordance with the Stock Transfer Act 1963. The procedure prescribed is usually similar to that employed in transferring shares; but the directors do not usually have the right of rejecting a proposed transfer. Basically ad valorem stamp duty (see p 69) is payable on transfers of debentures: however (Finance Act 1976, s 126) exempts transfers of loan capital provided, inter alia, any interest thereon does not exceed a reasonable commercial return and is not calculated by reference to profits.

Debentures are sometimes issued payable to bearer in which case the title warrants issued will be negotiable instruments and should be stamped like share warrants to bearer (see p 54). Such warrants may be transferred by mere delivery of the instrument without the knowledge of the company.

A registered debenture is not a negotiable instrument, and is transferable subject to equities (*Athenæum Life Assurance Society* v *Pooley* (1858) 3 De G & J 294 and *Re Rhodesia Goldfields Ltd* [1910] 1 Ch 239), unless the debenture conditions provide otherwise, as they will normally do.

Reissue of debentures

1948 s 90 allows a company to reissue redeemed debentures, unless:

(1) the Articles or any contract entered into by the company forbid this; or

(2) the company has by resolution or some other act manifested an intention that the debentures shall be cancelled.

As upon the reissue of debentures redeemed on or after 1 November 1929 the holders have the priorities they would have enjoyed if the debentures had not previously been redeemed, the power to reissue may be of considerable value, but it will be lost if a memorandum of satisfaction is registered, or if a clause in any subsequent debenture prohibits the reissue. It is not, however, necessary to keep redeemed debentures alive by transferring them to a nominee pending reissue.

Where debentures have been deposited to secure an overdraft, the fact that the company's account is temporarily in credit is not treated as a redemption of the debentures so deposited.

In the case of a reissue of debentures redeemed before 1 November 1929, the holders on a reissue take priority as if the debentures had not been issued previously (1948 s 91).

Particulars of any debentures which the company has power to reissue must be included in the balance sheet or notes thereto (1948 Sched 8, Pt III, paras 41(2) and Sched 8A, para 2(*d*)).

PRIORITY RIGHTS OF DEBENTURE HOLDERS

Where debentures are issued in a series it is usual to insert a provision that the holders shall rank pari passu for repayment, but, if no such provision is inserted, the debentures rank (*a*) in the order in which they are numbered where they are issued simultaneously, or (*b*) in the order of issue where they are issued at different times (*Gartside* v *Silkstone and Dodsworth Coal and Iron Co* (1882) 21 Ch D 762).

As regards the priorities enjoyed by the holders of two or more single debentures or two or more distinct series of debentures, much depends upon the terms of issue and the nature of the charges created thereby.

In general, fixed charges take priority in the order in which they were created; but a subsequent fixed charge takes priority over a floating charge created previously (*Wheatley* v *Silkstone Haigh Moor Coal Co* (1885) 29 Ch D 715). A clause in a debenture secured by a floating charge prohibiting the creation of subsequent fixed charges does not prevent this rule from operating unless the holder of the fixed charge has notice of the clause (*English and Scottish Mercantile Investment Co* v *Brunton* [1892] 2 QB 700); and, though the registration of the floating charge gives constructive notice of the charge, it does not, in England at any rate, necessarily give constructive notice of the terms thereof (*G & T Earle Ltd* v *Hemsworth Rural District Council* (1928) 140 LT 69). It is common practice, therefore, to register particulars of the relevant prohibition: this is accepted by the Registrar and is assumed to put holders of subsequent fixed charges on constructive notice, but the position has never been tested before the courts.

Where two or more debentures or series of debentures each create a floating charge, they rank, in general, in the order in which they are created, but frequently the first debenture expressly authorises the company to create subsequent debentures with priority over or ranking pari passu with the first debenture. In such a case, power to create a subsequent 'mortgage' with priority does not enable the company to give priority to a subsequent floating charge (*Re Cope* (*Benjamin*) *and Sons Ltd* [1914] 1 Ch 800); but power to create a 'mortgage or charge' will do so (*Re Automatic Bottle Makers Ltd* [1926] Ch 412).

As regards the priority rights attaching to reissued debentures, see above.

The holder of a single debenture can set off a sum owing by him to the company against sums due to him in respect of his debenture; but no such set-off can be made by the holder of one of a series of debentures ranking pari passu inter se (*Re Brown & Gregory Ltd* [1904] 1 Ch 627).

Where in the case of a company registered in England a receiver is appointed on behalf of debenture holders secured by a floating charge, or possession is taken by or on behalf of the debenture holders of any property subject to the charge, then, if the company is not being wound up, the debts which would be entitled to preferential payment were the company being wound up (see p 210) are to be paid out of any assets coming into the hands of the receiver or person taking possession before payments are made to the holders of the debentures, the periods in respect of which preferential treatment can be claimed being calculated from the date of the appointment of the receiver or the taking possession, as the case may be. But any payments so made to the preferential creditors may be recouped out of the assets available for the unsecured creditors (1948 s 94, and see *IRC* v *Goldblatt* [1972] Ch 498).

TRUSTEES FOR DEBENTURE HOLDERS

Where there is a debenture trust deed, this must be consulted for the purposes of determining the rights of the debenture holders inter se and against the trustees appointed under the deed; but as a general rule, any provision in the trust deed or in any contract with debenture holders, where there is such a deed or contract, is void in so far as it would have the effect of exempting a trustee from or indemnifying him against liability for breach of trust where he fails to show the degree of care and diligence required of him as a trustee (1948 s 88). This general rule is subject, however, to the modifications stated in 1948 s 88(2) and (3).

The trustees are not entitled to any remuneration, unless there is provision in the trust deed (*Re Accles Ltd* (1902) 46 SJ 686). Where they are entitled to remuneration, the deed usually provides that their claim thereto shall take priority over the claims of the debenture holders (*Re Locke & Smith Ltd* [1914] 1 Ch 687); but, unless the deed otherwise provides, their right to remuneration ends when a receiver is appointed (ibid).

REGISTRATION OF CHARGES

The provisions relating to registration of charges are contained in ss 95–106K of the 1948 Act. Sections 95–106 (Part III of the 1948 Act) are concerned with the registration of charges created by or over property acquired by English companies or companies incorporated outside Great Britain with a place of business in England. Sections 106A–106K of the 1948 Act (Part IIIA—originally added by the Companies Floating Charges) (Scotland) Act 1961 which was subsequently repealed by the Companies (Floating Charges and Receivers) (Scotland) Act 1972) contain equivalent provisions in relation to Scottish companies or companies incorporated outside Great Britain with a place of business in Scotland.

Registration of charges created by companies

Section 95 of the 1948 Act provides for the registration with the Registrar of Companies in Cardiff of particulars of the following charges if created by a company registered in England:

(a) A charge securing an issue of debentures.
(b) A charge on uncalled capital.
(c) A charge created by an instrument which, if executed by an individual, would require registration as a bill of sale.
(d) A charge on any land (wherever situate) or on any interest therein, but not including a charge for any rent or other periodical sum issuing out of land.
(e) A charge on book debts.
(f) A floating charge on the company's undertaking or property.
(g) A charge on calls made but not paid.
(h) A charge on a ship or aircraft or any share in a ship.
(i) A charge on goodwill, patents, licences under patents, trade marks, copyrights or licences under copyrights.

A 'book debt' means a debt (including a future debt) which would or could be entered in the books of the company in the ordinary course as a debt even if not so entered (*Independent Automatic Sales Ltd* v *Knowles & Foster* [1962] 1 WLR 974). An assignment by way of chage of money when it becomes due at a future date can be registrable as a charge on future book debts (*Re Brush Aggregates Ltd, The Times,* 11 February 1983; cf (*Paul & Frank Ltd* v *Discount Bank (Overseas) Ltd* [1967] Ch 348).

1948 s 106A (as extended by the Companies (Floating Charges and Receivers) (Scotland) Act 1972) provides for the registration with the Registrar of Companies in Edinburgh of particulars of certain charges if created by a company registered in Scotland.

Only the forms of charges mentioned in the appropriate section have to be registered with the Registrar. It is not necessary to register eg an absolute assignment of a book debt (*Ashby, Warner & Co Ltd* v *Simmons* [1936] 2 All ER 697) or an absolute bill of sale (*Stoneleigh Finance Ltd* v *Phillips* [1965] 2 QB 537); nor a deposit of shipping documents; nor an assignment of a hire-purchase agreement (*Re George Inglefield Ltd* [1933] Ch 1).

The charges which do require to be registered must be registered within twenty-one days after the date on which they were created by the company; the Form 47 (England) or Form 47 (Scot) (Scotland) being accompanied by the instrument, if any, by which the charge is created or evidenced. But in the case of a charge created outside the United Kingdom comprising property outside the United Kingdom, a verified copy of the instrument creating or evidencing the charge is sufficient, and the time for registration is within twenty-one days after the date on which such a copy would be received in the United Kingdom in the ordinary course of post assuming that it had been posted with due diligence (1948 ss 95(3) and 106A(3)). As to charges created by a company registered in England on property in Scotland or Northern Ireland, see 1948 s 95(5).

1948 ss 95 and 106A apply only to charges created by the company; but 1948 ss 97 and 106C provide that, where a company acquires property which is subject to any of the charges listed in 1948 s 95 or s 106A respectively, the charge must be registered within twenty-one days after the property has been acquired. For this purpose Form 47b (England) or Form 47b (Scot) (Scotland) should be employed accompanied by a certified copy of the instrument creating or evidencing the charge. But if the property is situated, and the charge was created, outside Great Britain, the time for filing is extended to within twenty-one days of the date on which the copy would be received in the United Kingdom in the ordinary course of post.

1948 s 106 applies the provisions of ss 95 to 105 to charges on property in England wich are created, and to charges on property in England which is acquired, by a company incorporated outside Great Britain which has an established place of business in England. 1948 s 106K applies the provisions of ss 106A to 106J to chages on property in Scotland which are created, and charges on property in Scotland which is acquired, by a company incorporated outside Great Britain which has a place of business in Scotland. It will thus sometimes be necessary to register the same cahrge in both England and Scotland.

An overseas company having a place of business in England or Scotland must file particulars of charges within twenty-one days under 1948 ss 106 and 106K whether or not it has registered under Part X of the 1948 Act (*NV Slavenburg's Bank* v *Intercontinental Natural Resources Ltd* [1980] 1 WLR 1076).

Copies of instruments requiring to be verified or certified under 1948 s 95(3) (or 106A(1)) or s 97 (or 106C) should be verified or certified to be a correct copy under the seal of the company or under the hand of some person interested therein otherwise than on behalf of the company (SI 1979 No 1547 reg 6).

The duty of registering the necessary particulars is imposed on the company, and directors or secretaries who are knowingly parties to a default are liable to be fined; but since, if the registration is not effected within the prescribed period, the charge will become void as against a liquidator or creditors of the company, such registration may be effected on the application of any person interested therein (1948 ss 96 and 106B) and is frequently effected by or on behalf of the chargee. Such a person is entitled to recover from the company the fees paid by him for the registration. It is only a charge created by the company which is rendered void by failure to register within the prescribed period. Non-registration under 1948 s 97 or s 106C of a charge on property acquired by the company will not have this effect.

Particulars to be registered

In the case of a *single mortgage or charge*, the following particulars must be registered (1948 ss 98 and 106D):

(1) The date of creation, if created by the company, or the date of acquisition, if created before the company acquired the property charged.
(2) The amount secured.
(3) Short particulars of the property charged.
(4) The persons entitled to the charge.
(5) In the case of a floating charge created by a company registered in Scotland a statement of the restrictions, if any, on the power of the company to grant further securities ranking in priority to, or pari passu with, the floating charge, or which vary or regulate the order of ranking of floating charges in relation to subsisting securities.

The rate of interest need not be stated.

In the case of a *series of debentures*, the holders of which are entitled pari passu to the benefit of the mortgage or charge, Form 47a (England) or Form 47a (Scot) (Scotland) will be employed including the following particulars (1948 ss 95(8) and 106A(7)):

(1) The total amount secured by the series.
(2) The date of the resolution authorising the issue.
(3) The date of the covering deed (if any) which creates or defines the security.
(4) A general description of the property charged.

(5) The names of the trustees (if any).

(6) In the case of a floating charge created by a company registered in Scotland, a statement of the restrictions, if any, on the power of the company to grant further securities ranking in priority to, or pari passu with, the floating charge or which vary or regulate the order of ranking of floating charges in relation to subsisting securities.

Where more than one issue of debentures in a series is made, particulars of the date and amount of each issue must also be sent to the Registrar, but failure to do this will not invalidate the debentures issued (1948 ss 95(8) and 106A(7)).

In the case of a series of debentures, slight variations exist according to the presence or absence of a trust deed. The following points should be noted:

Where a trust deed is employed (a) registration must be effected within twenty-one days of the execution of the deed; and (b) the deed itself must accompany the registration form.

Where there is no trust deed (a) registration must be effected within twenty-one days of the first execution of any debenture of the series; and (b) one of the debentures of the series must accompany the form.

A trust deed for debenture stock is often executed some weeks after allotment of the stock constituted and secured thereby and, in such cases, an equitable charge is frequently registered against the company to cover the interim period.

If any commission, allowance or discount has been paid or made, whether directly or indirectly, in consideration for a subscription or agreement to subscribe for debentures, or for procuring or agreeing to procure subscriptions, the particulars to be registered must include particulars of the amount or rate per cent of the commission, allowance or discount (1948 ss 95(9) and 106A(8)).

A copy of the certificate of registration issued by the Registrar must, if the company is registered in England, be endorsed on every debenture or certificate of debenture stock secured by the charge so registered which is issued after the creation of the charge (1948 s 99). This is usually printed on the back of the debenture or stock certificate. The certificate of registration is conclusive evidence that the prescribed particulars have been delivered to the Registrar (*Re Mechanisations (Eaglescliffe) Ltd* [1966] Ch 20) and that the requirements of the Act have been complied with (*Re Eric Holmes (Property) Ltd* [1965] Ch 1052 and *Re C L Nye Ltd* [1971] 1 Ch 442).

Registration of memorandum of satisfaction

Since the registration with the Registrar of charges on the company's assets affects the credit of the company, the Act makes provision for enabling the Registrar to record the fact that any registered charge has been satisfied (1948 ss 100 and 106F). Form 49 (England) or Form 49 (Scot) (Scotland) should be employed where the charge has been wholly satisfied. It must be accompanied by a statutory declaration. Where, however, it is desired to keep debentures alive with a view to their reissue, a memorandum of satisfaction must not be registered (see p 167).

A memorandum may be registered to the effect that the charge has been partly satisfied or that part of the assets charged has been released from the charge (Form 49a (England) or Form 49a (Scot) (Scotland)) or has ceased to form part of the company's property (Form 49b (England) or Form 49b (Scot) (Scotland)).

The court may order rectification of the register of charges (1948 ss 101 and 106G) (*Watson* v *Duff, Morgan & Vermont (Holdings) Ltd* [1974] 1 WLR 450).

As to the registration of the appointment of a receiver, see 1948 s 102, p 175.

Register of charges

In addition to the duty of registering certain kinds of charges with the Registrar, every limited company must keep at its registered office a register of charges in which must be entered particulars of all charges specifically affecting the company's property and of all floating charges on the undertaking or any property of the company (1948 ss 104 and 106I). This register must contain a short description of the property charged, the amount of the charge, and the names of the persons entitled thereto (except in the case of securities to bearer) (ibid).

It must be noted that it is necessary to record in this register all charges specifically affecting the company's property and all floating charges, whether or not particulars have to be registered with the Registrar. No time limit is laid down within which entries must be placed in the register; but a penalty is imposed for failing to register.

A copy of every instrument creating a mortgage or charge which requires registration with the Registrar must be kept at the registered office (1948 ss 103 and 106H). These instruments and the register of charges may be inspected free of charge during business hours by any creditor or member of the company (1948 ss 105 and 106J). The register of charges may also be inspected by any other person on payment of a fee of not more than 5p. The company in general meeting may restrict the period during which inspection may be demanded to not less than two hours per day.

RECEIVERS

Appointment of receiver

In the event of a default by the company in complying with the terms on which debentures are issued, various remedies are available to the debenture holders. A simple action for the recovery of any sum due may be commenced; but since more valuable rights are usually given by the debenture instrument, this remedy is rarely employed.

In most cases it will be found that the debenture instrument gives the debenture holders or their trustees power to appoint a receiver or a receiver and manager in writing (see *Cripps* v *Wickenden* [1973] 1 WLR 944) if certain specified events occur.

If the company is registered in England and the debentures are secured by a floating charge (whether or not accompanied by a fixed charge over some of the assets) and a receiver or manager is appointed of the whole or substantially the whole of the company's property, notice of the appointment must be given to the Registrar by the debenture holders or trustees within seven days (1948 s 102) (Form 53) and the following statutory requirements prescribed by 1948 s 372 have to be fulfilled:

(*a*) The receiver must forthwith send notice of his appointment to the company (Form 53c).

(*b*) Within fourteen days after receipt of such notice, or such longer period as may be allowed by the receiver, the company must make out and submit to the receiver a statement of the company's affairs in the prescribed form (Form 109 or 109a).

(*c*) Within two months after receiving this statement of affairs, the receiver must—

(i) send to the Registrar of Companies a copy of the statement and of any comments he thinks fit to make thereon, together with a summary of the statement and his comments, if any;

(ii) send to the company a copy of any such comments, or, if he has none to make, notice to that effect;

(iii) send to any trustees for debenture holders on whose behalf he was appointed, and, in so far as their addresses are known to him, to all debenture holders, a copy of the summary.

The statement of affairs must show as at the date of the receiver's appointment the particulars of the company's assets, debts and liabilities, the names, residences and occupations of its creditors, the securities held by them, the day when the securities were given, and such further and other information as may be prescribed (1948 s 373). The statement must be submitted by, and be verified by statutory declaration of, one or more of the persons who are, at the date of the receiver's appointment, the directors and by the person who is at that date the secretary of the company, or, if the receiver so requires it, by one of the persons mentioned in 1948 s 373(2).

The above provisions, which impose on the receiver the duty of giving the company notice of his appointment and on the company the duty of submitting a statement of affairs, do not apply where a receiver is appointed to act with an existing receiver or to take the place of a receiver dying or ceasing to act, unless the receiver dying or ceasing to act has not fully complied with the requirements (1948 s 372(4)). But the requirements must be complied with where the company is being wound up, notwithstanding that the receiver is also the liquidator of the company (1948 s 372(5)).

Upon the application of a debenture holder or a trustee for debenture holders, a receiver or manager may be appointed by the court whether or not the debenture instrument gives power to make such an appointment in writing without the aid of the court. A receiver appointed by the court has the same duties and must be furnished with a statement of affairs in the same manner as a receiver appointed out of court, subject to the modifications mentioned in 1948 s 372.

A receiver of the whole or substantially the whole of the company's property must file annually (1948 s 372(2)) (and in other cases six monthly—1948 s 374(1)) receipts and payments accounts (Form 57).

When the receiver ceases to act he must file a notice to that effect (1948 s 102(2): Form 57(a)).

Status of receiver

A debenture instrument usually confers extensive powers on a receiver as regards dealing with and disposal of the company's property and management of its business. It also usually provides that a receiver appointed out of court under the power conferred by the instrument shall be deemed to be the agent of the company; but, notwithstanding such a provision, he is, to the same extent as if he had been appointed by the court, personally liable on any contract entered into by him in the performance of his functions, except in so far as the contract otherwise provides (1948 s 369). He is, however, entitled to an indemnity out of the assets in respect of such liability. Any such agency usually ceases on liquidation of the company, though an express power to convey property as agent may continue (*Sowman* v *Samuel (David) Trust Ltd* [1978] 1 WLR 22). Where the agency ceases, personal liability cannot be excluded, but the right of indemnity out of the assets remains available.

A receiver appointed by the court is an officer of the court appointed to assume possession of and, if the order so authorises, to sell the property which forms the debenture holders' security, to collect the rents and profits of such property, and to apply them for the benefit of the debenture holders. Where the debentures are secured by a floating charge, he is usually given power to take over the management of the company's business and undertaking.

Effect of receiver's appointment

The appointment of a receiver with power to take over and manage the company's business may affect adversely the employees of the company. If the appointment is made by the court, or if it is made out of court and the debenture instrument does not provide that the receiver shall be deemed to be the agent of the company, the appointment terminates all contracts of employment; but it will not have this effect if the receiver appointed out of court is deemed to be the company's agent (*Reigate* v *Union Manufacturing Co (Ramsbottom)* [1918] 1 KB 592 and *Griffiths* v *Secretary of State for Social Services* [1974] QB 468). In this latter case, it is usual for the receiver to dismiss those not needed and to inform the others that their employment by the company will be continued on the same terms, the receiver paying their wages as part of the receivership expenses.

Where the appointment does terminate contracts of employment, since their termination usually has the effect of a dismissal without notice, the employees may be entitled to damages for wrongful dismissal against the company; but they will rank only as unsecured creditors in respect of these damages. Certain debts of the company within specified limits, including wages, salary and accrued holiday pay of employees, and advances from a lender used in payment thereof, are required to be paid out of assets comprised in a floating charge (as distinct from a fixed charge) before anything is paid to the debenture holders (see p 211).

Two other important effects of the appointment are that a floating charge crystallises and the assets subject thereto become assigned in equity to the debenture holder. Costs of a subsequent liquidation would therefore not be payable out of the receivership assets (*Re Christionette International Ltd* [1982] 3 All ER 227).

A receiver may be liable to the company or its liquidator or to a surety if he fails to take reasonable steps to obtain a proper price for the assets he sells, and the debenture holder too may be so liable if his interference with the receivership results in such sale (see *Cuckmere Brick Co Ltd* v *Mutual Finance Ltd* [1971] Ch 949; *Standard Chartered Bank Ltd* v *Walker* [1982] 3 All ER Ch 938).

Letters, invoices etc

When a receiver or manager has been appointed, every invoice, order for goods, or business letter bearing the name of the company must disclose the fact that such an appointment has been made (1948 s 370).

Receivers in Scotland

The Companies (Floating Charges and Receivers) (Scotland) Act 1972 introduced the concept of receivership into Scottish law as a remedy available to the holders of a floating charge (see Part II of the 1972 Act).

CHAPTER 10

ALTERATION OF ARTICLES, MEMORANDUM AND SHAREHOLDERS' RIGHTS

ALTERATION OF ARTICLES

Section 10 of the 1948 Act empowers every company to alter or add to its Articles by means of a special resolution.

In exercising this power, the functions of the Articles must be borne in mind. Thus, the Articles cannot be altered so as to permit the company to do what is ultra vires (*Guinness* v *Land Corporation of Ireland Ltd* (1882) 22 Ch D 349); and the court may restrain the company from making an alteration which necessarily causes a breach of contract (*British Murac Syndicate Ltd* v *Alperton Rubber Co Ltd* [1915] 2 Ch 186). The Articles cannot be altered so as to deprive the shareholders of their statutory rights (*Re Peveril Gold Mines Ltd* [1898] 1 Ch 122); or to oppress a minority without benefiting the company (*Menier* v *Hooper's Telegraph Works* (1874) 9 Ch App 350); but it is for the company, and not for the court, to decide what is likely to benefit the company (*Shuttleworth* v *Cox Bros & Co* (*Maidenhead*) *Ltd* [1927] 2 KB 9).

By 1948 s 22, no member of a company is bound by an alteration of the Memorandum or Articles which requires him to increase his holding of shares or increases his liability to pay money to the company, unless (*a*) the alteration is made before he becomes a member, or (*b*) he agrees in writing to be bound. Further a member who considers the alteration unfairly prejudicial may apply to the court (1948 s 23(1) as amended by the 1980 Act, and 1980 s 75). Apart from these provisions, an alteration of the Articles may be retrospective in effect (*Allen* v *Gold Reefs of West Africa Ltd* [1900] 1 Ch 656); but this will not eg enable the company to acquire a lien over shares after they have been transferred for value by a debtor (*M'Arthur* (*W & A*) *Ltd* (*Liquidator*) v *Gulf Line Ltd* [1909] SC 732).

Notice of intention to alter the Articles must indicate the nature of the alteration, and, as in the case of any other special resolution, a copy must be filed with the Registrar (see p 100). If the resolution is for the adoption of new Articles, a print of such Articles identified by the signature of an officer of the company, usually the chairman or secretary, must also be delivered. In any event, by s 9(5) of the European Communities Act 1972, a special resolution altering the Articles which is filed with the Registrar must be accompanied by a printed copy of the Articles as altered which should have endorsed thereon a certificate signed by a director or the secretary that the print is a true copy of the Articles as altered. Small alterations may be dealt with by a rubber stamp or typed or by permanently affixing the new version to a copy of the original in such manner as to obscure the amended words.

ALTERATION OF MEMORANDUM

While the Articles may be altered at will by means of a special resolution, the method of altering the Memorandum will vary according to the nature of the alteration. The following is a summary of the points most likely to be encountered. As to certain general restrictions on amendments under 1948 s 22 and the 1980 Act, see p 179.

Name

Should it be desirable to change the name of a company, it is necessary to obtain the sanction of the shareholders by special resolution. The prior consent of the Registrar to the new name is not required, but the provisions of 1981 s 24 should be borne in mind (and see p 179).

A copy of the resolution must be filed with the Registrar and the fee prescribed by the regulations for the time being in force under 1976 s 37 must be paid.

The Registrar will in due course enter the new name on the register and issue a certificate of incorporation on change of name. The change of name takes effect from the date of issue of this certificate. The Memorandum itself remains unaltered; but since the resolution will 'evidence' a change in the Memorandum the filing requirements of s 9(5) of the European Communities Act 1972 will apply (see p 101).

Registered office

The situation of the registered office may be changed at the will of the company, within the limits of the country named in the Memorandum, without altering that document. Notice of the change must be given to the Registrar within fourteen days (1976 s 23(3)) (Form 4a).

In order to change the country of domicile mentioned in the Memorandum, it would be necessary (except in the case of an alteration by special resolution passed within twelve months after 18 April 1977, pursuant to 1976 s 30(2), to provide that the registered office is to be situated in Wales) to obtain Parliamentary sanction, but, if such a change were decided on, it would probably be found less expensive to reconstruct the company.

Objects

The objects may be altered by a special resolution. The extent of such alteration is, however, restricted by 1948 s 5(1), which provides that the alteration must be required for certain specified purposes.

In effect, no alteration can be made which involves the adoption of some object which is completely foreign to the main object of the company as expressed by the Memorandum. Where, however, a resolution altering the objects is passed, any proceedings taken on the ground that such alteration is not for one of the purposes permitted by 1948 s 5(1) must be commenced within twenty-one days after the resolution is passed, failing which the validity of the alteration cannot be questioned (1948 s 5(9)).

In *Re Parent Tyre Co Ltd* [1923] 2 Ch 222, the court held that the question whether a new object can be conveniently combined with the present business is a matter for the determination of the company itself. But the court has refused to sanction a new object which was manifestly inconsistent with the existing objects (*Re Cyclists' Touring Club* [1907] 1 Ch 269).

An application to the court on the grounds that an alteration of the objects is not for one of the purposes permitted by 1948 s 5(1) must be made by the holders of not less in the aggregate than 15 per cent in nominal value of the company's issued share capital or any class thereof, or by the holders of not less than 15 per cent of any debentures secured by a floating charge which were issued or first issued before 1 December 1947 (1948 s 5(2) and (5)).

Such application must be made within twenty-one days after the date on which the resolution altering the objects was passed; and if it be made, the alteration has no effect, except in so far as it is confirmed by the court (1948 s 5(1)). The application may be made on behalf of the persons entitled to apply by such one or more of their number as they may appoint in writing. It may not be made by any person who has consented to or voted in favour of the alteration.

Notice of any proposed special resolution altering the company's objects must be given to debenture holders entitled to apply to the court as well as to members entitled to notice of meetings (1948 s 5(5)). It is not sufficient to give notice to the trustees for debenture holders (*Re Hampstead Garden Suburb Trust Ltd* [1962] Ch 806). If there are no provisions in the debenture instrument for giving notices to such holders, the provisions of the Articles regulating the giving of notices to members will apply. The debenture holders are not entitled to attend the meeting.

Where a special resolution altering the objects is passed, the following duties have to be carried out:

(*a*) If no application is made to the court, then within fifteen days from the end of the period for making such an application, the company must deliver to the Registrar of Companies a printed copy of the Memorandum as altered, certified by an officer of the company to be a true copy (this is in addition to the usual copy of the special resolution which must be filed within fifteen days of the date on which it is passed) (1948 s 5(7)). This also meets the requirements of s 9(5) of the European Communities Act 1972 (see p 101).

(*b*) If application to the court is made, the company must forthwith give notice of that fact to the Registrar (Form 101), and within fifteen days from the date of any order cancelling or confirming the alteration, must deliver to the Registrar an office copy of the order and, in the case of an order confirming the alteration, a printed copy of the Memorandum as altered (ibid).

Notice of proceedings taken on the ground that an alteration is not for one of the purposes permitted by 1948 s 5(1) must be given to the Registrar by the company as if an application to the court as described above had been made; and thereafter, as regards filing documents with the Registrar, the same rules apply as in the case of such an application.

Where a company desires to sell or dispose of its undertaking to another company, and it is proposed to put the selling company into liquidation, it is not necessary that the Memorandum of the selling company should authorise the sale; but where the selling company is to continue business, such authority is necessary if the result of the sale or disposition is a change in the nature of the company's activities. If, for instance, a manufacturing company sells its undertaking for shares in another company and continues to carry on business as a mere shareholding concern, it would be necessary for the Memorandum to authorise the transaction.

Limited liability

Sections 43 and 44 respectively of the 1967 Act provide for limited companies being re-registered as unlimited and unlimited companies being re-registered as limited. No public company may apply under s 43 to be re-registered as an unlimited company (1980 Sched 3 para 43).

Capital

The alteration of the capital clause in the Memorandum may be necessary where the capital is to be increased or reduced or reorganised, each of which requires detailed consideration.

Increase of capital

If the *issued capital* is less than the *authorised* or *nominal capital*, the issued capital may be increased by the issue of additional shares without any increase in the nominal capital. The procedure in such a case is governed by the Articles, and the exercise of any discretion to issue unissued shares vested in the directors by the Articles is subject to the provisions of 1980 ss 14 and 17 (see pp 23–25).

An increase in the *nominal capital* may be effected by the company in general meeting *if the Articles permit* (1948 s 61). The procedure to be employed as regulated by the Articles must be closely followed (see reg 44 of Table A). If the Articles do not give power to increase the capital, the power may be taken by special resolution, and it appears that by the same resolution the company may exercise the power so obtained (*Campbell's Case* (1874) 9 Ch App 1).

In any event, care must be taken in wording the notice of the meeting, which should state the nature of the resolution required by the Articles and the amount of the increase proposed.

It is not necessary to notify creditors of the alteration, or to obtain the consent of the court, but a notice of increase (Form 10) must be filed with the Registrar together with a copy of the resolution authorising the increase (1948 s 63). Particulars of class rights must be given in the notice. A copy of such resolution must be filed even if the resolution is ordinary (1948 s 63(2)).

Reduction of capital

1948 s 61 provides that, if the Articles permit, unissued shares may be cancelled, which will diminish the amount of the *nominal capital*. The consent of the court is not required, but notice must be given to the Registrar within one month of the resolution.

A reduction of capital in any other form must be carried out in conformity with the provisions of 1948 s 66 which requires:

(1) power to reduce in the Articles;
(2) a special resolution; and
(3) confirmation by the court.

If no power is given by the Articles, it may be taken by special resolution, but a second resolution must be employed to exercise the power. The second resolution may be passed at the meeting at which the first resolution is passed.

After the passing of the necessary resolution, in order to make the reduction of capital effective, it has first to be confirmed by the High Court. Proceedings for this purpose are instituted by petition supported by affidavit evidence, such proceedings being governed by the provisions of Order 102 of the Rules of the Supreme Court.

In all proceedings before the court, the company has to be legally represented. It will therefore be necessary for the company's solicitors, who doubtless will already have been consulted in connection with the preparation of the resolution, to be instructed to make the application to the court for this confirmation. The petition and affidavits in support are all documents of a special nature and will be drafted by the solicitors.

The court has to be satisfied that the meeting at which the resolution was passed, and any other meetings which may be necessary in order to obtain the approval of separate classes of shareholders (unless the company can prove that the reduction of capital is fair and reasonable—see *Re Holders Investment Trust Ltd* [1971] 1 WLR 583) have all been properly convened and requires this to be strictly proved. This requirement is met by affidavit evidence from the secretary or the registrar of the company to establish that a notice of the meeting was sent or delivered to all members entitled pursuant to the provisions of the Articles of Association to receive notice of the particular meeting or meetings. It is therefore essential that a note is kept of the date, time and place of posting or delivery of the notice or notices.

If the reduction involves either a diminution of liability in respect of unpaid share capital or the payment to any shareholder of paid-up capital, the main concern of the court is to see that the creditors of the company will not be prejudiced and, unless the court is satisfied that this is so, it has power under the provisions of 1948 s 67 to direct an inquiry as to creditors. Such an inquiry involves the preparation of a list of creditors at a date fixed by the court, advertising in the Press a notice to creditors of the application and where the list of creditors may be inspected, circularising the known creditors with forms of consent to the reduction, and making provision for the debts of those creditors who do not consent.

Any director or officer who wilfully conceals the name of a creditor or wilfully misrepresents the nature or amount of the debt is guilty of an offence.

If there are special circumstances, the court may rule that the provisions of 1948 s 67(2) shall not apply to any class or classes of creditors in which case the consent of the creditors of that class is not required. The company's solicitors will advise as to what the court regards as a special circumstance; the mere fact that the company is solvent will not be sufficient but normally an inquiry will be dispensed with if the company has adequate cash resources or trustee securities to satisfy the court that creditors are protected or if it can provide an appropriate bank guarantee for this purpose.

When the order of the court has been drawn up and completed, the next and final step to make the reduction effective is to produce the same and deliver a copy thereof to the Registrar (1948 s 69). This section also requires that, in addition to delivering a copy of the order, a copy of a minute approved by the court, showing the amount of the reduced share capital, its division into shares and the amount deemed to be paid up on each share, be delivered to the Registrar. In practice this minute is scheduled to the order and the Registrar regards the delivery to him of a copy of the order as a full compliance with the section. A certificate of registration is issued by him and constitutes evidence of the share capital as stated therein and that the requirements of the 1948 Act have been complied with (1948 s 69(4)).

Notice of the delivery of the order and minute to the Registrar has to be advertised in a newspaper directed by the court usually within twenty-one days of delivery.

Where an order confirming a reduction of capital is made, the court has power to include a direction in the order that the words 'and reduced' be added to the company's name for a certain period and to direct that the reasons for the reduction be published together with any other information in regard thereto which the court may think expedient (1948 s 68). These powers are, however, seldom exercised today, but if the first of these directions is given, then the words 'and reduced' are deemed to be part of the company's name and must therefore be added to the name after the word 'Limited' where it appears on all nameplates, the seal, and all the documents mentioned in 1948 s 108(1)(c).

The minute when registered becomes part of the Memorandum and takes the place of the corresponding part thereof. It must be embodied in every copy of the Memorandum subsequently issued (1948 s 69).

On a reduction of capital, a shareholder shall not be liable for any call or contribution exceeding in amount the difference between the amount of his shares as fixed by the minute and the amount paid or deemed to be paid thereon. But if any creditor entitled to object to the reduction is omitted from the list of creditors and the company cannot pay his debt, a shareholder may be called upon to pay the sum for which he would have been liable had the reduction not taken place (1948 s 70).

The court may provide for the reduction of the company's capital when it makes an order for the purchase by the company of the shares of any member under 1948 s 5(4A) or 1980 s 75 or exercises similar powers under 1980 s 11 and 1981 s 44 or s 57.

As to the redemption or purchase by a company of its own shares, see p 76.

Consolidation and sub-division

If authorised by its Articles, a company may by resolution either:

(1) consolidate its shares into shares of a larger amount; or
(2) sub-divide its shares into shares of a smaller amount (1948 s 61).

In the case of a sub-division, the proportion between the amounts paid and unpaid on the reduced shares must be the same as it was on the old shares. Thus, £1 shares, 75p paid, cannot be divided into two 50p shares, one 50p paid and the other only 25p paid.

Notice must be given to the Registrar, on Form 28 within one month of the resolution authorising the alteration (1948 s 62). The type of resolution to be passed may vary with the Articles of different companies.

Conversion of shares into stock

If the Articles allow, a company may by resolution convert its fully paid shares into stock or reconvert stock into shares. Notice of such a conversion must be given to the Registrar within one month of the resolution on Form 28, as above (1948 s 62). The names of stockholders must be shown as such in the register of members and the annual return.

Alteration of non-essential contents

It was formerly the custom to include in the Memorandum many matters which could lawfully be provided for by the Articles, eg class rights of shareholders; and 1948 s 23 provides that any condition contained in the Memorandum, which could lawfully have been contained in the Articles, may be altered by special resolution. This general rule is subject, however, to the following modifications:

(1) it does not apply where the Memorandum itself provides for or prohibits the alteration of all or any of such conditions;
(2) it does not authorise any variation or abrogation of the special rights of any class of members;
(3) where such a special resolution is passed, application may be made to the court by members (but not debenture holders) as if the resolution altered the objects of the company (see p 181) and in that event the procedure laid down by 1948 s 5 for dealing with such applications will apply. It is not necessary, however, to give notice of a special resolution for this purpose to debenture holders;
(4) no alteration can increase a member's liability to contribute to share capital unless he consents: and all alterations are subject to 1980 s 75 (power of court to grant relief where members unfairly prejudiced).

ALTERATIONS AFFECTING SHAREHOLDERS' RIGHTS

Variation of class rights

Where the company's share capital is divided into shares of different classes, great care must be taken where any valuation of the Memorandum or Articles involves a variation or absorption of the rights attaching to any class of shares eg an alteration in dividend entitlement or voting rights.

The formalities which must be complied with depend primarily upon whether the rights are attached by the Memorandum or otherwise (eg by an ordinary resolution increasing the company's capital by the creation of a new class) and whether the Memorandum or the Articles contain provisions for the variation of those rights:

(i) *Rights otherwise than in Memorandum; provision for variation in Articles*

The Articles of most companies include either reg 4 of Table A or some clause similar to it. Reg 4 provides that class rights may not be varied except with the consent in writing of the holders of three-fourths of the issued shares of the class concerned, or with the sanction of an extraordinary resolution passed at a separate meeting of the holders of the shares of the class (unless, in the case of companies registered before 22 December 1980, the terms of issue otherwise provided).

Any variation must be effected in accordance with the relevant provision(s) of the Articles (1980 s 34(4)) and subject to the following statutory provisions (so far as applicable):

(*a*) 1948 s 72 which provides that, where special provision for varying class rights is given by the Memorandum or the Articles, subject to the consent, as in Table A, of a specified proportion of the holders of the issued shares of the class or the sanction of a resolution passed at a separate meeting, the holders of not less in the aggregate than 15 per cent of the issued shares of the class, being persons who did not consent to or vote in favour of the resolution for the variation, may apply to the court to have the variation cancelled; and that, where such an application is made, the variation shall have no effect unless and until it is confirmed by the courts. Such an application to the court must be made within twenty-one days after the date on which the consent was given or the resolution passed at the separate meeting, as the case may be. Within fifteen days after any order is made by the court, an office copy of the order must be delivered to the Registrar of Companies.

(*b*) Where the rights are to be varied in connection with the giving, variation, revocation or renewal of an authority under 1980 s 14 (see p 23) or with a reduction of capital under 1948 s 66, 1980 s 32(3) prevents any variation unless the holders of three-quarters in nominal value of the issued shares of the class consent in writing or an extraordinary resolution passed at a separate general meeting of the holders of the class sanction the variation (even if the requirements of the Articles are less stringent) and any other requirements under the company's Memorandum or Articles are complied with.

(ii) *Rights otherwise than in Memorandum; no provision for variation in Articles*

1980 s 32(2) provides that the rights may be varied if, but only if, the holders of three-quarters in nominal value of the issued shares of the class consent in writing or an extraordinary resolution passed at a separate general meeting of the holders of the class sanction the variation and any other requirement (however imposed) is complied with.

The rights of dissenting shareholders under 1948 s 72 (see (i) above) are specifically applied (by 1980 s 32(7)) to variations of rights in these circumstances.

(iii) *Rights in Memorandum; provision for variation in Memorandum*

The procedure in the Memorandum must be followed and will be subject to the provision of 1948 s 72 and 1980 s 32(3) (see (i) above)

(iv) *Rights in Memorandum; provision for variation in Articles*

Where the rights are to be varied in connection with the giving, variation, revocation or renewal of an authority under 1980 s 14 (see p 23), or with a reduction in capital under 1948 s 66, 1980 s 32(3) again applies and prevents any variation unless the holders of three-quarters in nominal value of the issued shares of the class consent in writing or an extraordinary resolution passed at a separate general meeting of the holders of the class sanction the variation (even if the requirements of the Articles are less stringent) and any other requirement of the company's Articles is complied with.

In any other case, if the provision for variation was included in the Articles at the time of incorporation the procedure set out in the relevant provision in the Articles should be followed (1980 s 32(4)); but, if the provision for variation was included in the Articles subsequently to incorporation, to effect the variation proceedings must be taken under 1948 s 206 (see p 190).

(v) *Rights in Memorandum; no provision for variation in Memorandum or Articles*

The rights may be varied with the agreement of all the members of the company 1980 s 30(5) or, as was the case prior to the 1980 Act, by a scheme of arrangement under 1948 s 206 (see p 190).

Meetings of holders of shares of a class

1980 s 32 also contains provisions for regulating the convening of and proceedings at class meetings, whether held in compliance with the section or otherwise. The provisions relating to general meetings of the company under 1948 ss 133, 134 and 140 and under its articles are to apply, save that the quorum for a class meeting is two persons at least holding or representing by proxy not less than one-third of the issued shares of the class, but at an adjourned meeting any one holder will form a quorum. Any one such holder present in person or by proxy may demand a poll.

Registration of class rights

1980 s 33 requires that where:

   (i) shares are allotted with class rights which are not stated in the Memorandum or Articles or in any resolution or agreement which has to be filed pursuant to 1948 s 143; or

   (ii) class rights are varied or abrogated otherwise than by alteration of the Memorandum or Articles or by such resolution or agreement as aforesaid; or

   (iii) a new name or designation is assigned to a class of shares in the manner described in (ii) above;

a statement in the appropriate prescribed form (Form 33, 33a or 336) must be delivered to the Registrar of Companies within one month.

Where before 22 December 1980 a company issued shares having such rights as are mentioned in (i) above, a statement in the prescribed form fell to be delivered to the Registrar within three months of the appointed day (1980 s 33(5)).

The mere fact that some shares, otherwise identical with others, rank differently for dividend during the first 12 months after allotment does not involve their being treated for these purposes as a separate class.

Contravention involves the company and every officer who is in default in liability to a fine and for an additional default fine on continued contravention.

Arrangements under section 206

1948 s 206 provides extremely useful machinery for making what it calls a compromise or arrangement between the company and its creditors or any class of them, or between the company and its members or any class of them, and may be used in any case in which it is desired to vary the rights of any class of shareholder and no other means of variation is available or desired to be followed.

The proposals for the compromise or arrangement when formulated are embodied in a document generally known as a scheme of arrangement with a view to placing it before the persons affected for approval. This document is usually prepared by the company's solicitors.

1948 s 206(1) permits the court to order a meeting of the creditors or members affected by the compromise or arrangement and, following the formulation of the scheme, the next step is to apply to the court for an order directing the convening of a meeting of the class of creditors or members affected.

With every notice summoning such a meeting, there must be sent a statement explaining the effect of the proposed compromise or arrangement, and in particular stating any material interests of the directors of the company, whether as directors or as members or as creditors of the company or otherwise, and the effect thereon of the compromise or arrangement, in so far as it is different from the effect on the like interests of other persons; and in every notice summoning the meeting which is given by advertisement must be included either such a statement or a notification of the place at which and the manner in which creditors or members entitled to attend the meeting may obtain copies of the statement (1948 s 207). In the latter case, every such creditor or member must be furnished with a copy of the statement free of charge on application therefor. It is the duty of directors to give notice to the company of such matters relating to themselves as may be necessary to enable the company to prepare the statement.

At the meeting so summoned, the scheme must be approved by a simple majority in number, such majority representing three-fourths in value of the creditors or class of creditors, or members or class of members, as the case may be, present and voting either in person or by proxy at the meeting.

A petition asking the court to sanction the scheme is then presented and the result of the voting at the meeting is reported to the court. On the hearing of the petition by the judge, opponents of the scheme can attend and make their submissions to the court.

If the scheme is sanctioned by the court, to make it effective and binding on the creditors or members concerned and on the company, an office copy of the order made by the court must be delivered to the Registrar; and every copy of the Memorandum of Association of the company issued after the order has been made must have a copy of the order annexed thereto.

The above procedure may be employed also where a company is being wound up, in which event the compromise or arrangement will be binding also on the liquidator and the contributories.

Arrangements under section 209

1948 s 209 provides machinery for compelling a reluctant minority of a class of shareholders to transfer their shares to another company. If an offer to acquire the whole or a particular class of shares is made by another company, and within four months after the making of the offer (or within any shorter period stipulated by the company making the offer: *Re Western Manufacturing (Reading) Ltd* [1956] Ch 436) it has been approved by the holders of not less than nine-tenths in value of the shares affected, the acquiring company may within two months of the expiration of the said four months give notice to any dissenting shareholder that it desires to acquire his shares (Form 100). If such notice is given, the dissenting shareholder may apply to the court within one month from the date of the notice; but if the court does not make an order to the contrary, or no application to the court is made, the acquiring company becomes entitled and bound to acquire the shares of the dissenting shareholder on the terms on which it is to acquire the shares of approving shareholders. The procedure can only be used for a scheme or contract properly so called or contemplated by the section, and not for the purpose of enabling the majority shareholders to evict the minority (*Re Bugle Press, Treby's Application, Re Houses and Estates* [1961] Ch 270 at p 279 CA). As to the application of the section where there is a share exchange offer accompanied by a cash alternative see *Re Carlton Holdings Ltd* [1971] 1 WLR 918.

For the purpose of the above requirements, the phrase 'shares affected' refers only to shares whose transfer is involved, ie it does not include shares already held at the date of the offer by or by a nominee for the acquiring company or its subsidiary. But if the acquiring company or its subsidiary (or a nominee therefor) holds shares of the class concerned to a value greater than one-tenth of the aggregate of all the shares of that class (including the shares held by the acquiring company and its subsidiary), 1948 s 209 applies only if the acquiring company offers the same terms to all holders of the shares affected, and the holders who approve the scheme or contract, besides holding not less than nine-tenths in value of the shares affected, are not less than three-fourths in number of the holders of those shares.

Where notice has been given by the acquiring company to dissenting shareholders and the court has not made an order to the contrary, the acquiring company must on the expiration of one month from the date of the notice or, if an application to the court is then pending, after the application has been disposed of, transmit a copy of the notice, together with an instrument of transfer executed on behalf of the shareholder by any person appointed by the acquiring company, and on its own behalf by the acquiring company (unless a share warrant has been issued in respect of such shares), to the company the shares of which are being acquired, and pay or transfer to that company the amount or other consideration for the dissenting shareholder's shares. Any sums so received must be paid into a separate bank account by the company receiving them and must be held on trust for the dissenting shareholders.

Upon receiving such sums or other consideration, the company whose shares are being acquired must register the acquiring company as holder of the dissenting shareholder's shares.

As a corollary to the above, 1948 s 209(2) provides that where, as a result of an offer to which the section applies, shares are transferred to a company or its nominee, and those shares together with other shares held by the acquiring company or its nominee or the nominee of its subsidiary comprise or include nine-tenths in value of the shares or of any class of those shares, the acquiring company must within one month from the date of the transfer (if it has not already done so) give notice of the fact to the holders of the remaining shares concerned who have not assented to the scheme (Form 100a) and any such holder may within three months from the giving of this notice require by notice (Form 100b) the acquiring company to acquire his shares, either on the terms on which the shares of approving shareholders have been acquired, or on such terms as the court on the application of the acquiring company or the shareholder thinks fit.

Protection of minorities

Where any member of a company (including for this purpose the personal representative(s) of a deceased member) considers that the affairs of the company are being or have been conducted in a manner unfairly prejudicial to the interests of some part of the members (including at least himself) or that any actual or proposed act or omission of the company (including an act or omission on its behalf) is or would be so prejudicial, he can petition the court for an order under 1980 s 75. This section replaced the more restrictive protections previously afforded by 1948 s 210 although it appears that the petitioner must still satisfy the court that the company's affairs are being conducted at the time of the petition in a manner unfairly prejudicial to him *in his capacity as a member* ie as a shareholder and not, for example, as a director.

The Department of Trade may present a petition in the circumstances provided in 1980 s 75(2).

If the petitioner satisfies the court that the affairs of the company are being conducted as aforesaid it may make such order as it thinks fit, including (inter alia) an order regulating the conduct of the company's affairs in future, or requiring it to do or refrain from doing a particular act, or authorising proceedings to be brought in its name, or requiring the members of the company, or the company, to purchase the shares of the prejudiced members. If the company is ordered to purchase such shares, a reduction of capital may be ordered.

Appointment of inspectors by the Department of Trade

The principal provisions in 1948 ss 164–175 as amended and extended by the 1967 Act (principally by ss 35–42 thereof) were further substantially amended by 1981 ss 86–92.

Under 1948 s 164, the members of a company may apply to the Department of Trade to investigate the company's affairs. Such an application must be made by two hundred members or by members holding not less than one-tenth of the issued shares or (where the company has no share capital) on the application of one-fifth of the members. Such application can also be made by the company itself (s 164(1)(c)). Supporting evidence must be provided and security for costs may be required.

Secretaries should note that it is their duty to assist the Department of Trade representatives in making such investigations and to produce for them all books or documents in their custody or power. Past as well as present officers of the company may be called upon to assist in the investigation (1948 s 167 as amended).

The Department of Trade may itself appoint an inspector if there are circumstances suggesting that:

(i) the affairs of the company are being or have been conducted with intent to defraud creditors or for some other fraudulent or unlawful purpose or in a manner unfairly prejudicial to some part of the members or that any actual or proposed act or omission would be so prejudicial or that the company was formed for some fraudulent or unlawful purpose; or

(ii) persons concerned with the formation of the company or the management of its affairs have been guilty of fraud, misfeasance or other misconduct towards the company or its members; or

(iii) the members of the company have not been given all the information with respect to its affairs which they might reasonably expect (1948 s 165(1)(b)).

The above provisions now apply to bodies corporate incorporated outside Great Britain which are carrying on, or have at any time carried on, business in Great Britain (1967 s 42(1)).

Under 1948 s 172 the Department of Trade may appoint inspectors of its own volition if it appears necessary in the public interest to investigate and report on the membership of a company or otherwise with a view to determining the true persons who are or have been financially interested in the success or failure of the company or able to control or influence its policy.

In the event of an appointment being made under this section, the Department of Trade may, in certain circumstances, direct inter alia that transfers of certain shares shall be void, that no voting rights shall be exercisable in respect of such shares, that no further shares shall be issued in right of those shares or in pursuance of any offer made to the holder thereof, and that no dividends shall be paid in respect of such shares.

The Department may also appoint inspectors if it appears that there are circumstances suggesting contravention of 1967 s 25 (see p 143), s 27 (see p 142), or s 31(2) (1967 s 32).

1967 s 109 contains powers for the Department of Trade to require production of a company's books and papers, thus facilitating the work of the Department in relation to its powers to appoint inspectors.

Reserve liability

1948 s 60 allows a company, even in the absence of provision in the Articles, to create a reserve liability by passing a special resolution declaring that a certain portion of its uncalled capital shall not be capable of being called up except in the event and for the purposes of the company being wound up. Once such a resolution has been passed, no call can be made upon the reserve, nor can the reserve be removed.

CHAPTER 11

UNLIMITED, GUARANTEE AND OVERSEA COMPANIES

UNLIMITED COMPANIES

Unlimited company status is normally adopted where the proprietors of a company do not wish it to file accounts (see below) or where corporate status is desired but not limited liability (as where the rules of a professional body eg The Stock Exchange permit its members to incorporate but not to limit their liability).

In the case of unlimited companies, the provisions of the Acts which apply to limited companies having a share capital are modified in certain respects. In particular:

(1) The directors of an unlimited company are not required to deliver accounts to the Registrar in respect of any accounting reference period unless at any time during such accounting reference period the company was a subsidiary or holding company of a limited company or had been carrying on business as the promoter of a trading stamp scheme within the meaning of the Trading Stamps Act 1964 (1976 s 1(8)).

(2) 1948 s 66 does not apply, and an unlimited company may purchase its own shares without restriction.

COMPANIES LIMITED BY GUARANTEE

The 1948 Act defines a company limited by guarantee as 'a company having the liability of the members limited by the Memorandum to such amount as the members respectively thereby undertake to contribute to the assets of the company in the event of its being wound up' (1948 s (1)(2)(b).

In the case of such companies which have no share capital, the provisions of the Acts which apply to companies having a share capital are modified in certain respects including the following:

Memorandum and Articles. Articles must be registered with the

Memorandum (s 6), and must state the number of members with which the company proposes to be registered (1948 s 7(2)). Any provision in the Memorandum or Articles or in any resolution giving any person a right to participate in divisible profits otherwise than as a member is void (1948 s 21).

Annual return. 1948 s 124 (see p 107) applies only to companies having a share capital. Companies not having a share capital must make an annual return in the form prescribed by s 125 (see p 108; Form 7).

Meetings. Where the company has no share capital, subject to any contrary provision in the Articles, not less than 5 per cent in number of the members may call a meeting, and every member has one vote (1948 s 134). 1948 s 136, which gives a statutory right to vote by proxy, does not apply where the company has no share capital.

OVERSEA COMPANIES

Oversea companies are companies incorporated outside Great Britain which have a place of business within Great Britain (1948 s 406). Within one month of the establishment of such a place of business in Great Britain, the oversea company must (1948 s 407(1)) deliver to the Registrar for registration—

(*a*) a certified copy of the charter, statutes or Memorandum and Articles of the company, or other instrument constituting or defining the constitution of the company, and, if the instrument is not in the English language, a certified translation therof;

(*b*) a list of the directors and the secretary of the company containing the particulars detailed in 1948 s 407(2) (Form F2);

(*c*) the names and addresses of some one or more persons resident in Great Britain authorised to accept on behalf of the company service of process and any notices required to be served on the company (1948 s 407(1)) (Form F3);

(*d*) a list of the documents delivered for registration (Form F1); and

(*e*) (by 1948 s 407(2A)) a statutory declaration stating the date on which the place of business was established (Form 14).

Particulars of alterations in the charter, statutes, Memorandum and Articles or other governing instrument (Form F4), the corporate name (Form F4a), the directors or secretary, or the particulars registered in respect thereof (Form F5), or the names or addresses of the persons authorised to accept service on behalf of the company

(Form F6) must be registered with the Registrar (1948 s 409).

Accounts. Every oversea company must in respect of each accounting reference period (determined in accordance with 1976 s 10) prepare accounts similar to those required from companies registered in Great Britain and must deliver copies (accompanied where necessary by a certified translation) to the Registrar (1976 s 9) within thirteen months of the end of the relevant accounting reference period (1976 s 11, which also lays down penalties for non-compliance). Notice to the Registrar of its accounting reference date is given by an oversea company on Form F7. The Secretary of State has power to prescribe for oversea companies exceptions to the strict accounts requirements under the Acts: certain exceptions have been prescribed—see SI 1982 No 676.

Prospectuses. An oversea company which issues a prospectus in Great Britain must comply with the requirements of 1948 ss 417 to 422; and any such prospectus must state the country in which the company is incorporated (1948 s 411).

Name. The name of the company and the country in which it is incorporated must be conspicuously exhibited on every place where it carries on business, and must be stated in legible characters in all billheads, letter-paper, notices and other official publications of the company (1948 s 411).

The Secretary of State has powers, similar to those under 1981 ss 22 et seq (see p 18) in relation to companies incorporated in Great Britain, under which he can prohibit the use of the corporate name as the name under which an oversea company may carry on business in Great Britain (see 1976 s 31 as amended by 1981 s 27). Where use of the corporate name is prohibited, the oversea company may deliver to the Registrar for registration a statement, on Form F13, specifying in place of its corporate name, another name approved by the Secretary of State under which it proposes to carry on business in Great Britain; such name may thereafter be altered by notice to the Registrar, on Form F13a. The name so registered is deemed for all purposes, to be the corporate name of the oversea company (1976 s 31).

Names of directors. Unless the place of business was established in Great Britain before 23 November 1916, the requirements of 1948 s 201 (see p 145) must be complied with (1948 s 201(2)).

Limited liability. If the liability of members is limited, the fact must be stated in legible characters in every prospectus and in all billheads, letter-paper, notices and other official publications in Great Britain, and on every place of business (1948 s 411)).

Charges on property in England. These must be registered with the Registrar of Companies to the same extent as if the company were incorporated in England (1948 s 106) (see p 169).

Branch registers of dominion companies. See 1948 s 123.

Companies incorporated in the Channel Islands or the Isle of Man. All the provisions of the Act as to the filing of documents apply to such companies if they have a place of business in England or Scotland (1948 s 416).

CHAPTER 12

RECONSTRUCTION AND WINDING-UP

RECONSTRUCTION

There are various ways of effecting a corporate reconstruction, but generally they are carried out in either of two ways:

(1) *By a scheme of arrangement pursuant* to 1948 s 206 (see p 190) which, when sanctioned by the court and if provided for by the scheme can be followed by an application to the court for a vesting order pursuant to 1948 s 208 which vests the assets and transfers the liabilities of one comany (the transferor company) to either a new company or an existing company (the transferee company). A vesting order usually provides for the dissolution of the transferor company without a winding-up and directs the Registrar to consolidate the files of the two companies.

(2) *By means of a voluntary winding-up pursuant to* 1948 s 287. Where this method is employed, a company goes into voluntary liquidation and a liquidator is appointed. The liquidator, with the sanction of a special resolution of the company, then contracts to sell the goodwill and assets of the company to a new company, accepting as consideration shares in the new company instead of cash. It is advisable for the resolutions to wind up and to approve the sale to be considered at the same meeting, thus avoiding the situation where the company is in liquidation but the proposed sale does not receive the necessary approval. The shareholders of the company are nominated by the liquidator as allottees of the shares in the new company in accordance with the scheme agreed upon, and arrangements are made with the company's creditors who, if they do not agree to look to the new company, must be paid off. When this has been done, the liquidator summons a final meeting of the old company and makes the necessary returns to the Registrar. This, in due course, brings about the dissolution of the old company.

It is not, however, essential for reconstructions to involve the winding-up or dissolution of an existing company. A reconstruction involving an amalgamation of two or more companies is frequently effected by the formation of a holding company to acquire the shares of the companies to be amalgamated in exchange for shares of the holding company leaving the constituent companies to continue trading as formerly.

In a reconstruction, relief from payment of ad valorem stamp duty and capital duty may under certain circumstances be obtained under s 55 of the Finance Act 1927, as amended by s 31 of the Finance Act 1930, and extended by s 28(5) of the Finance Act 1967 and s 47 of, and Sched 19 to, the Finance Act 1973; but great care must be taken to comply with the technical requirements to enable this relief to be claimed and the company's solicitors should be consulted.

WINDING-UP

Voluntary winding-up

It is not feasible to deal here at length with the many details involved in the winding-up of a company, which may be effected either by order of the court or by the company's own voluntary act. However as, when a company goes into liquidation for the purpose of a reconstruction, the secretary is occasionally appointed liquidator, and as, immediately preceding the commencement of a voluntary winding-up, a number of special duties may devolve upon the secretary, the following summary gives special attention to problems likely to be met within a voluntary winding-up as part of a reconstruction.

The resolution to wind up

A voluntary liquidation is commenced by resolution of the company, the type of resolution required varying with the circumstances (1948 s 278). Thus:

(1) an ordinary resolution will suffice if the liquidation is sought because the period fixed by the Articles for the company's duration has expired, or an event has occurred as a result of which the Articles require the company to be dissolved;

(2) an extraordinary resolution is necessary if liquidation is sought because the company cannot continue its business by reason of its liabilities, and this fact must be stated in the resolution; this is an insolvent, or creditors', voluntary winding-up;

(3) a special resolution is necessary in any other case, ie when the

company is solvent and the members wish to bring its existence to an end, whether as part of a reconstruction or otherwise.

Where the winding-up is for reconstruction purposes, it is advisable at the meeting at which the resolution to wind up is passed to pass resolutions (*a*) appointing the liquidator, and (*b*) (i) authorising the liquidator to sell the business for shares in the new company (see p 200) and (ii) (if the company is solvent and the Articles contain a clause similar to reg 135 of Table A) to divide among the members in specie or kind the whole or any part of the assets of the company (in accordance with that clause). Resolution (a) may be an ordinary resolution but resolution (b)(i) must be a special resolution and resolution (b)(ii) an extraordinary resolution. The various resolutions may be expressed to be interdependent as appropriate but a conditional *winding-up* resolution may not be technically valid. The alternative is to make all the resolutions part of one composite *special* resolution. The notice convening the meeting should provide for these resolutions.

Commencement of a members' winding-up

Before a resolution that a company shall be wound up voluntarily is passed it is necessary, if it is to be a *members'* winding-up, that at a meeting of directors the directors or, in the case of a company having more than two directors, the majority of the directors should make a statutory declaration (Form 108 pp 252 to 254) that in their opinion the company will be able to pay its debts in full within the period (not exceeding twelve months) specified therein. The declaration must be made within the five weeks immediately preceding the date of the passing of the resolution for winding up the company or on that date but before the passing of that resolution, and must embody a statement of the company's assets and liabilities as at the latest practicable date before the making of the declaration. It must be filed with the Registrar not later than 15 days after the day on which the winding-up resolution is passed by the company in general meeting (1948 s 283 as amended in 1981). The declaration should be signed by the directors at their meeting.

Great care should be taken in making such a declaration, for if it be made and the company is not able to pay its debts within the specified period it is presumed, until the contrary is shown, that the directors making it did not have resasonable grounds for their opinion, and if they do not prove the contrary, they may be liable to serious penalties. Moreover the figures shown in the statement of assets and liabilities have later to be compared with the amounts realised as shown in the liquidator's final account. The general meeting of the company which is to pass the winding-up resolution is summoned in the ordinary way in accordance with the rules which govern the summoning of meetings of the company. The company in general meeting must appoint a liquidator (1948 s 285(1)) but it is advisable that this be done at the meeting at which the winding-up resolution is passed. Notice of the meeting need not be given to the creditors.

Commencement of a creditors' winding-up

Where a declaration of solvency cannot be made or filed in accordance with the above requirements, the winding-up commenced by a winding-up resolution will only rank as a creditors' voluntary winding-up. In such a case the resolution is almost invariably an extra-ordinary resolution in the terms of 1948 s 278(1)(c), although it can also be a special resolution in the terms of s 278(1)(b) if the requirement as to the longer period of notice is complied with. In addition to the winding-up resolution, the company may also pass an ordinary resolution appointing a liquidator and members (up to five) of a committee of inspection.

The company must summon a meeting of creditors to be held on the same day as the meeting of the company at which the resolution to wind up is to be proposed, or on the day following (1948 s 293 as amended in 1981). Where this requirement cannot be complied with because the meeting of members is held at a very short notice (as permitted by 1948 ss 133(3)(b) or 141(2)) it is thought that the combined effect of ss 293(1) and (7) (as amended by the 1981 Act) and *Re Centrebind* [1967] 1 WLR 377 (and see also *E. V. Saxton & Sons Ltd* v *R. Miles* (*Confectioner*) *Ltd* The Times 2 March 1983) is that at least seven days' notice of the creditors meeting must be given and that meeting must be convened for not earlier than seven days nor later than eight days after the day on which the members' meeting is held.

Notice of this meeting of creditors must be sent to every creditor by post simultaneously with the sending of the notices to the members, and must be advertised in the *Gazette* and in two local papers circulating in the district in which the company's registered office or principal place of business is situated. The notice must be accompanied by general and special forms of proxy (Forms 80 and 81).

At the meeting of creditors the chair is to be taken by a director appointed by the directors of the company (1948 s 293). A quorum consists of three creditors where the total number exceeds three, or all the creditors where the total is three or less. Resolutions are passed by a majority in number and value of those present personally or by proxy and voting. A secured creditor who does not intend to surrender his security may not vote unless he lodges at the registered office before the meeting a statement giving particulars of the security, the date when it was given and the value at which he assesses it. His vote is limited to the amount by which his debt exceeds the value at which he assesses his security. Minutes and a list of creditors present must be made. The chairman may adjourn the meeting with its consent.

The primary function of the meeting is to enable the creditors, if they so wish, to appoint a liquidator and members (up to five) of a committee of inspection, in either case whether in substitution for or addition to any person or persons appointed by the members. A statement of affairs together with a list of creditors of the company is presented by the directors and the creditors have an opportunity to ask for explanations thereon before they vote on any resolution. If the creditors do not appoint a committee of inspection any appointment of such a committee made by the members lapses.

Appointment of a liquidator

In a *members'* winding-up, the liquidator is appointed by ordinary resolution of the members (1948 s 285). This resolution is usually passed at the meeting at which the company resolves to wind up. The remuneration of the liquidator is also fixed by ordinary resolution (1948 s 285).

In a *creditors'* winding-up, the liquidator may be appointed by resolutions of the company and creditors (1948 s 294). If no person is nominated by the creditors, the nominee of the company is liquidator, but if different persons are nominated, the creditors' nominee is liquidator, subject to the right of any director, member or creditor of the company to appeal to the court. The company's nominee is, however, entitled to act as liquidator until another is appointed by the creditors (*Re Centrebind* (supra)). The remuneration of the liquidator in a creditors' winding-up is fixed by the committee of inspection, or, where there is no committee, by the creditors (1948 s 296).

Within fourteen days after it is passed, notice of a resolution to wind up, whether an ordinary, extraordinary or special resolution, must be advertised in the *Gazette* (1948 s 279), and within fifteen days a copy of the resolution must be filed with the Registrar (1948 s 143). The resolution sent for insertion in the *Gazette* must be signed and, unless the person signing it is a solicitor, accountant or chartered secretary, attested by a person who is (see pp 255 and 256).

Both in a *members'* and a *creditors'* winding-up, the liquidator must give notice of his appointment to the Registrar within fourteen days on Form 39c or 39d, as the case may be (1948 s 305). This form must be filed in addition to the copy of the resolution to wind up, even if the latter resolution also includes the appointment of the liquidator. He must also advertise his appointment in the *Gazette* (ibid) (Form 39e). If a sheriff is in possession, notice should be given to him immediately; he should already have been given notice of the general meeting of the company at which the winding-up resolution is to be proposed.

In a *members'* winding-up, a vacancy in the office of liquidator may be filled by resolution of the company, subject to any arrangement with the creditors (1948 s 286).

In a *creditors'* winding-up, vacancies may be filled by the creditors, unless the original liquidator was appointed by the court (1948 s 304).

In either type of winding-up the court may, on cause shown, remove a liquidator and appoint another liquidator and, where from any cause whatsoever there is no liquidator acting, appoint a liquidator (s 304).

Effect of winding-up resolution

As soon as a resolution to wind up is passed, the company ceases to carry on its business except as required for the beneficial winding-up thereof, and, thereafter, no transfer of shares or alteration in the status of a member may be made except with the sanction of the liquidator (1948 s 282).

The appointment of the liquidator terminates the powers of the directors except in so far as their continuance is sanctioned (*a*) by the company or the liquidator in a *members'* winding-up, or (*b*) by the committee of inspection or the creditors in a *creditors'* winding-up (1948 s 285 and 296). The liquidator becomes agent of the company (*Stead, Hazel & Co Ltd* v *Cooper* [1933] 1 KB 840).

The liquidator has all the powers of a liquidator in a winding-up by the court (1948 s 303), and, subject to one or two exceptions, these may be exercised without obtaining any sanction. The liquidator may, among other things, settle a list of the contributories, make calls, summon meetings of creditors or contributories, carry on the business for the purpose of the winding-up, borrow money, appoint a solicitor, sell the assets of the company for cash, adjust the rights of contributories among themselves, and rectify the register of members. He may also, when necessary, use the company's seal.

The liquidator cannot, however, without sanction (a) pay any class or creditor in full (b) make compromises with creditors, contributories, or debtors or (c) sell the business of the company for shares in another company. Even though the company is solvent, there is no power to pay statute-barred debts without the consent of the contributories (*Re Art Reproduction Co* [1952] Ch 89). The sanctions required are dealt with in the following pages.

The powers of the liquidator may be limited or augmented by proceedings under 1948 s 307, which authorises the liquidator, or any creditor or contributory, to apply to the court to determine any question arising in the winding-up, and empowers the court, where any such application is made, to exercise any of the powers it may exercise in a winding-up by the court.

The following further effects of a winding-up should be noted:

(1) The court may stay actions and proceedings against the company (1948 ss 226, 307 and 308(2)).

(2) Various provisions aimed at setting aside recent execution and distress proceedings become applicable (1948 ss 307, 226, 228, 231, 325, 326, 327).

(3) Certain antecedent transactions entered into by the company can be called into question as can also the past conduct of the company's officers and others in relation to the affairs of the company (see 1948 ss 320, 321 (fraudulent preference) 322 (floating charge), 332 (fraudulent trading) and 333 (misfeasance)).

(4) The period of limitation ceases to run against a creditor in relation to his claim (*Re General Rolling Stock Co* (1872) 7 Ch App 646).

(5) The contracts of employment of employees are automatically terminated, at least where the company is insolvent or the winding-up is followed by cessation of trading (*Measures Bros Ltd* v *Measures* [1910] 2 Ch 248).

(6) The authority of all agents is automatically determined except that a power of attorney expressed to be irrevocable and granted by the company to secure a proprietary interest of or an obligation owed to the donee survives (Powers of Attorney Act 1971 s 4).

(7) All the liabilities of the company, which are notionally discharged, fall to be ascertained as at the date of the winding-up and are replaced by a statutory scheme for the distribution of its assets and a statutory right for the creditor to receive a dividend (see *Lines Bros Ltd* [1982] 2 WLR 1010 CA). The rules

as to distribution among the creditors are mandatory and no contracting out is possible (*British Eagle International Airlines* v *Compagnie Nationale Air France* [1975] 2 All ER 390). In an insolvent liquidation the rights of secured and unsecured creditors are determined in accordance with the provisions applicable to bankruptcies of individuals (s 317). This has the effect of restricting certain types of claim (eg claims for interest or for unliquidated damages in tort or for debts incurred after the creditor became aware of the company's insolvency) and of giving rise to statutory set-offs (see ss 66 and 31 of Bankruptcy Act 1914 and *Re Eros Films Ltd* [1963] Ch 565) which too cannot be contracted out of (*National Westminster Bank Ltd* v *Halesowen Presswork and Assemblies Ltd* [1972] AC 785).

(8) The company ceases to be the beneficial owner of its assets. This may have important tax implications (see *IRC* v *Olive Mill Ltd* [1963] 1 WLR 712; *Ayerst* v *C & K Construction Ltd* [1975] 3 WLR 16).

Making compromises

The creditors of a company in voluntary liquidation are legally entitled to be paid what is owing to them out of the company's assets before any payment is made to the shareholders, and, where a company is being reconstructed, they are not bound to look to the new company for payment. In the majority of cases where the company in liquidation is solvent, there is little difficulty in making arrangements for the discharge of the outstanding liabilities out of cash in hand, but where the liquidator proposes to pay a *class* of creditors in full or to make compromises with any creditors, or with debtors, or with any contributories, he must first obtain sanction.

In a *members'* winding-up, the payment or compromise must be authorised by extraordinary resolution of the company. In a *creditors'* winding-up, it must be authorised by resolution of the committee of inspection (or, if there is no such committee the creditors) or by order of the court (1948 s 303).

A compromise with a class of creditors or contributories may be made under 1948 s 206 (see p 200), or alternatively any arrangement will be binding on the company if sanctioned by extraordinary resolution, and on the creditors if acceded to by three-fourths in number and value of the creditors, subject to the power of the court to amend or vary the arrangement if application is made within three weeks (1948 s 306); but this section can be employed only if the company is in or is about to go into voluntary liquidation.

Selling the company's business for shares

Although, where a company goes into voluntary liquidation for reconstruction purposes, a sale of the business for shares in the new company may be contemplated, the liquidator cannot effect such a sale unless he is authorised to do so by a special resolution of the company (1948 s 287); and, in a creditors' winding-up, he must also obtain sanction from the court or the committee of inspection (1948 s 298).

The special resolution may be passed either before or concurrently with the resolution to wind up, and, when it is passed, all members of the company are bound by the arrangement; but any dissentient member who did not vote in favour of the resolution may, within seven days of the passing of the resolution, serve upon the liquidator written notice of dissent, requiring him either to abstain from carrying the resolution into effect, or to purchase the dissentient's interest in the company at a price to be determined by agreement or by arbitration. This notice must be addressed to the liquidator at the registered office of the company, and nothing in the Articles can take away the dissentient's right to have his interest purchased or the resolution disregarded (*Payne* v *Cork Co Ltd* [1900] 1 Ch 308); and if a price cannot be agreed upon, the dissentient may insist on arbitration, notwithstanding that the Articles make provision for the valuation of his shares (*Baring-Gould* v *Sharpington Pick and Shovel Syndicate* [1899] 2 Ch 80). Finally, where the liquidator elects to purchase the dissentient's interest, he must obtain directions by special resolution of the company as to the manner in which the money is to be raised, and must pay the money to the dissentient before the company is dissolved.

Duties of the liquidator

A winding-up for reconstruction purposes is usually completed within the space of a few weeks; but, where a winding-up is not completed within one year, it is the duty of the liquidator to summon certain meetings and to make returns to the Registrar of Companies.

In a *members'* winding-up, a meeting of the company must be summoned to receive the liquidator's accounts within three months after the expiration of each period of twelve months (1948 s 289). These meetings must be summoned and conducted in accordance with the provisions of the Articles as to general meetings of the company.

In a *creditors'* winding-up, a meeting of creditors must be summoned annually in addition to a meeting of the company (1948 s 299). Seven days' notice of such meetings must be advertised in the *Gazette* and a local paper, and sent by post to every person appearing by the company's books to be a creditor. The chair must be taken by the liquidator or his nominee; but in other respects the procedure at such meetings of creditors is similar to that observed at the first meeting of creditors (see p 203).

In a *members'* winding-up, it is not normally necessary for the liquidator to summon meetings of creditors; but if the liquidator is at any time of the opinion that the company will not be able to pay its debts in full within one year, he must forthwith summon a meeting of creditors and lay before the meeting a statement of the company's assets and liabilities (1948 s 288), and in such a case annual and final meetings of the creditors must be summoned as if it were a *creditors'* winding-up (1948 s 291).

Both in a *members'* and a *creditors'* winding-up which are not completed within one year, the liquidator must make returns to the Registrar of Companies in the prescribed form in duplicate, verified by affidavit (1948 s 342) (Form 92). The first of these returns showing the liquidator's receipts and payments must cover the period from the first appointment of a liquidator to the end of the twelve months following the commencement of the winding-up, and must be sent to the Registrar within thirty days from the date of the relevant meeting of members and (if applicable) creditors (see above). Subsequent returns must be made at intervals of six months, and a final return when the assets of the company have been fully realised and distributed.

The liquidator may apply to the court for directions in relation to any particular matter arising under the winding-up (1948 s 246(3) as read with s 307).

Final meetings and dissolution

In a *members'* winding-up, the liquidator must summon a final meeting of the company as soon as the affairs of the company are fully wound up, to receive and consider an account showing how the winding-up has been conducted and the property of the company disposed of (1948 s 290); and, in a *creditors'* winding-up, a final meeting of the creditors must be summoned also (1948 s 300). A meeting of creditors must also be held in a *members'* winding-up if the liquidator has found the company insolvent (1948 s 291).

It may not strictly be necessary to send notices of these meetings to the members or creditors but such notices are desirable. In any event notice specifying the time, place and object of the meeting must be advertised in the *Gazette* one month at least before the date of the meeting. The procedure is otherwise as in the case of a general meeting of the company or the first meeting of creditors (see p 203).

It is advisable *for the liquidator* before the conclusion of the winding-up to obtain directions as to the disposal of the company's books and papers. In a *members'* winding-up, such directions must be given by extraordinary resolution of the company. As the necessary quorum for passing such a resolution is often not present at the final meeting, it is not unusual for the resolution as to the disposal of books to be brought before the meeting at which the resolution to wind up is passed. Notice of the resolution must, of course, be given. In a *creditors'* winding-up, instructions must be given by the committee of inspection or, if there is no committee, by the creditors (1948 s 341).

Within one week after the date of the final meeting or meetings, the liquidator must file with the Registrar a return of the holding of the meeting (or, if no quorum is present, a return to that effect) and a copy of his account (1948 ss 290 and 300).

The company is deemed to be dissolved at the expiration of three months after the Registrar has registered the liquidator's final account and return of the final meeting (ibid).

Distribution of assets

The assets of the company, after payment of or provision for the costs of the winding-up (including the liquidator's remuneration), fall to be distributed in the following order:

(1) Preferential creditors (s 319).
(2) General creditors, other than (3) and (4) below (s 302).
(3) Claims of creditors which are required to be deferred in an insolvent liquidation eg claims in respect of interest in excess of 5% pa to the date of liquidation (1948 s 317 as read with s 66 of Bankruptcy Act 1914).
(4) Creditors claiming in their character of members eg in respect of pre-liquidation dividends declared but remaining unpaid (s 212(1)(g)).
(5) Members in accordance with their rights unless the articles otherwise provide (s 302).

Claims in each class rank pari passu, and abate rateably, with each other.

Preferential creditors

A list of these is contained in 1948 s 319 (as subsequently amended and expanded). The debts are ascertained by reference to 'the relevant date' ie the date of the winding-up order or resolution or the appointment of a provisional liquidator. Some of the most important types of preferential debts are dealt with below:

(a) The following rates and taxes:

    (i) All local rates due from the company at the relevant date and having become due and payable within twelve months next before that date.

    (ii) All corporation tax, income tax or other taxes (including capital gains tax and development land tax) assessed on the company up to 5 April next before that date and not exceeding in the whole one year's assessment. See also Finance Act 1952, s 30(2), as to sums due as tax deducted under PAYE and Finance Act 1971 s 29(6) for deductions from payments to subcontractors. The Crown is not bound to select the same fiscal year in respect of each of its preferential claims; it can, for example, select a different year for corporation tax from the year which it selects for income tax (*Lord Advocate* v *Kelman & Shirreffs* [1958] CLY 460).

    (iii) The amount of any betting duty, bingo duty, car tax, gaming licence duty, pool betting duty (in certain circumstances) or value added tax due from the company at the relevant date and having become due and payable within twelve months next before that date.

(b) All wages or salary (whether or not earned wholly or in part by way of commission) of any clerk or servant in respect of services rendered to the company during the four months next before the relevant date and all wages whether payable for time or piece work) of any workman or labourer in respect of services so rendered subject normally to a maximum of £800 per person. Under the Employment Protection (Consolidation) Act 1978 s 121, certain entitlements of employees are deemed to be wages for the purposes of s 319.

(c) All accrued holiday remuneration becoming payable to any clerk or servant, workman or labourer (or in the case of his death, to any person in his right) on the termination of his employment before or by the effect of the winding-up order or resolution.

(d) Unless the company is being wound up voluntarily merely for the purposes of reconstruction or amalgamation, all amounts due in respect of contributions payable during the twelve months next before the relevant date by the company as an employer under the Social Security Acts 1973 and 1975.

(e) Contributions under the Redundancy Payments Act 1965 (see s 28 of that Act) but not any claim for redundancy repayment as such or any claim for compensation for loss of office or breach of a contract of employment (but see (b) above).

(f) Subrogated rights

(i) The Secretary of State is subrogated to the rights of an employee against the company in respect of any payments made to the employee pursuant to s 122 of the Employment Protection (Consolidation) Act 1978. To the extent that the employee's rights would have ranked as preferential claims, the Secretary of State is entitled to be paid in the winding-up 'in priority to any unsatisfied claim of the employee' against the company.

(ii) Where any payment has been made to an employee on account of wages, salary or holiday remuneration out of money advanced by some person for that purpose, such person is entitled to a preferential claim in respect of the money so advanced and paid to the extent to which the employee's preferential claim has been diminished by reason of such payment (s 319(4)).

(iii) Preferential debts are a first charge on any assets distrained by a landlord within three months before the date of a winding-up order in a compulsory liquidation. To the extent that such claims are satisfied out of that charge, the landlord steps into the shoes of the claimants (s 319(7)).

Return of capital

Where in a winding-up there are surplus assets after all liabilities to creditors have been discharged in full, this surplus must be applied in accordance with the provisions of the Memorandum and Articles.

In general, it will be used in the first place to repay to the members of the company the amounts paid up on their shares. Where shares preferential as to capital have been issued, the amounts paid up on these must be repaid before a payment is made to ordinary shareholders: and where more has been paid up on some of the ordinary shares than on others, this excess payment must, unless the Articles contain provisions to the contrary, be repaid before a general distribution of the surplus is made (*Ex parte Maude* (1870) 6 Ch App 51). If the realised assets are not enough to repay the preferential capital and such excess payments, the liquidator must make a call on the holders of any partly paid shares (*Re Anglo-Continental Corporation of Western Australia Ltd* [1898] 1 Ch 327) unless the

Articles contain provisions to the contrary (*Re Kinatan (Borneo) Rubber Ltd* [1923] 1 Ch 124). As to the right of holders of preference shares to arrears of cumulative dividends, see p 45.

Where there is a surplus after all the paid-up capital has been refunded, this must be distributed among the shareholders pari passu in proportion to the nominal value of their holdings. But if on the true construction of the Memorandum and Articles the rights of the preference shareholders are exhaustively defined, and no express right to share in surplus assets is thereby given, such shareholders are not entitled to share in surplus assets (*Scottish Insurance Corporation* v *Wilsons and Clyde Coal Co Ltd* [1949] AC 462). The Memorandum or Articles may, moreover, be phrased in such a manner as to exclude a class of shareholder from participation, and great care should be exercised in making such a distribution (see, for example, *Re Fraser & Chalmers Ltd* [1919] 2 Ch 114; *Re National Telephone Co* [1914] 1 Ch 755; and *Dimbula Valley (Ceylon) Tea Co Ltd* v *Laurie* [1961] Ch 353).

APPENDIX 1

SECRETARIAL PROGRAMMES

The following programmes are designed to serve as brief summaries, or check lists, for secretaries in relation to certain of the duties or procedures in the main text. The treatment accorded is not exhaustive and will have to be adapted to the specific circumstances of each case. In particular, the Articles should be consulted upon each point which arises.

In these programmes, as elsewhere in this work, the word 'file' is often used in place of the more cumbersome 'deliver to the Registrar of Companies for registration'.

A draft of the minutes of the first meeting of the directors of a newly incorporated company is given at the end of these programmes.

1a: Formation of a private company

(1) Consider, in relation to proposed name, the provisions of 1981 s 22 (see p 45) and search at Companies Registry to check similar names.

(2) Arrange for the drafting, printing, signing and witnessing by subscribers of the Memorandum and Articles of Association.

(3) Prepare and have signed a statement as to share capital on formation of a limited company with a share capital (Form PUC1).

(4) Prepare and have signed by or on behalf of the subscribers to the Memorandum a statement of particulars to be delivered on application for registration (Form 1) containing the names and relevant particulars of the first directors and secretary and a consent to act signed by each person named as a director or secretary and specifying the intended situation of the company's registered office on incorporation.

(5) Prepare and have signed a declaration of compliance with the requirements of the Acts on application for registration of a company (Form 41).

(6) File the above documents and pay requisite capital duty (if any–see p 15) and registration fee of £50.

(7) A certificate of incorporation will then be issued. *This entitles a private company to commence business.*

(8) File a return of allotments (on the relevant PUC Form) and pay requisite capital duty within one month of each allotment (1948 s 52 and NB 1980 ss 14 and 17/18 see pp 23 to 25).

1b: Urgent duties subsequent to formation

As soon as the above preliminary steps have been taken, the following urgent requirements must be complied with:

(1) The register of members must be opened, and, if it is not kept at the registered office, notice of the place at which it is kept (Form 103) must be filed (1948 s 110).

(2) The register of directors and secretaries must be opened (1948 s 200).

(3) The register of directors' holdings must be opened (1967 ss 27–29 and 31).

(4) The register of charges must be opened (1948 s 104 or s 106I).

   NB In practice in the case of small companies these various registers are frequently contained in a 'combined register'.

(5) If any of the charges listed in 1948 s 95 or s 106A has been created, or property has been acquired subject to such a charge, the prescribed particulars (on Form 47 or 47b) must be filed within twenty-one days of creation or acquisition (see 1948 ss 95, 97 and 106 and p 171).

(6) The important first meeting of directors must be held (see Programme 2).

(7) A return of allotments (on the relevant PUC Form) must be filed within one month of the allotment made at this meeting (1948 s 52 and NB 1980 ss 14 and 17/18 see p 38).

1c: Conversion of a private company to a public company

(1) Convene an Extraordinary General Meeting to pass a Special Resolution:

   (a) altering the Company's Memorandum to state that it is to be a public company; and

   (b) making any other necessary alterations in the Company's Memorandum and Articles of Association.

   NB The relevant capital requirements for a public company must be met at the time when the resolution is passed and the Company's name must be changed so that it ends with the words 'public limited company' or 'plc' (or their Welsh equivalent)—see p 10 and 16.

(2) Prepare and file an application for re-registration in the prescribed form (Form R5) accompanied by the following documents required by 1980 s 5:

   (a) A printed copy of the Memorandum and Articles as amended by the Resolution;

   (b) A copy of a company balance sheet made up to a date not more than seven months previously, with an unqualified auditor's report thereon;

   (c) A written statement from the auditors in relation to the net assets position shown in the balance sheet;

   (d) A valuation report on any shares allotted for a non-cash consideration since the balance sheet date;

   (e) A statutory declaration in the prescribed form (Form R6) as to the passing of the Resolution; the nominal value of the issued

capital and the amount paid up thereon; allotments for non-
cash consideration; and the net assets position as at the date of
application.
(3) Obtain from the Registrar a certificate of incorporation stating that
the Company is a public company.

1d: Conversion of a public company to a private company

(1) Convene an Extraordinary General Meeting to pass a Special
Resolution:
  (a) altering the Company's Memorandum so that it no longer
  states that the Company is to be a public company;
  (b) making any other necessary alterations in the Company's
  Memorandum and Articles of Association. (NB the Company's
  name must be changed so that it no longer ends with the words
  'public limited company' or 'plc' (or their Welsh equivalent)).
(2) Prepare and file an application for re-registration in the prescribed
form (Form R10), signed by a Director or Secretary, together with a
printed copy of the Memorandum and Articles as amended.
(3) Obtain from the registrar after the expiration of twenty-eight days
from the passing of the resolution a new certificate of incorporation:
the Company will become a private company on the issue of the
certificate. NB Dissentient shareholders can apply to the Court for
cancellation of the Special Resolution within twenty-eight days of the
passing thereof (1980 ss 11, 10).

2: Declaring a dividend

(1) Assuming that the board have resolved to recommend a dividend or
declare an interim dividend, the necessary dividend cheques/warrants
should be ordered and stamped.
(2) Where share warrants to bearer have been issued, the declaration
should be advertised in the press.
    Note. As it is usual to close the transfer books for a short time before
the declaration of a dividend, a notice to this effect is usually included
in the advertisement.
(3) Prepare list of dividends and check carefully.
(4) Examine file of requests to pay dividends to persons other than the
registered holder.
(5) Obtain necessary signatures to cheques/warrants.
(6) The company's bankers should be advised of the dividend.
    Note. It will sometimes be found convenient to transfer the net total
of the dividends to a dividend account in which only the numbers of
the warrants need be entered.
(7) Despatch warrants (following passing of Company Resolution, if
applicable).
(8) Collect paid cheques/warrants from bankers and mark off on
dividend lists.
  A form of resolution to be passed by the board for the declaration of an
interim dividend and the closing of the transfer books is given below:

"That an interim dividend of .... per share
in respect of the year ending .... 19...... is
hereby declared, to be payable on .... 19......
to shareholders on the register on .... 19......
That the share transfer books of the company be closed from
.... 19...... to .... 19...... inclusive."

3a: Making a call

(1) Procure passing of requisite board resolution. A form of resolution is given below:
   "That the call of......... per share be made on ....
   shares numbered .... to ...., to be payable on the
   .... day of .... 19...... to the Company at [its
   account with .... Bank Ltd at ....]"
(2) The Articles should be examined in order to ascertain the mode of service of notice, etc.
(3) Prepare and despatch notice to all the members concerned.
(4) Upon receipt of particulars of payments from the bankers, a list of calls unpaid should be prepared.
(5) Letters reminding dilatory members should be despatched.
(6) Payment of the calls must be recorded in the register.
(7) If calls still remain unpaid, the board should be consulted as to the course to be taken.

3b: Forfeiture of shares

(1) Assuming that the board decide to forfeit shares if calls remain unpaid, the Articles should be consulted as to the method to be employed.
(2) Despatch a letter to the shareholder warning him to expect forfeiture if call and interest is not paid by a certain date.
(3) Prepare agenda of forfeiture for next board meeting.
(4) After obtaining resolution of forfeiture from board, despatch letter to the shareholder informing him of the forfeiture.
   A form of resolution for forfeiture is given below:
   "That ...., the holder of
   .... shares of £...... each, upon which......
   per share has been paid, having failed to pay the call authorised by
   the board on .... 19......, due on
   ... 19......, and having failed to comply with the notice served
   upon him on .... 19......, the aforementioned shares are
   hereby declared forfeited."
(5) Make necessary adjustments in the register of members and index (if any).

4: Death of a member

(1) Inspect carefully the copy of probate or letters of administration submitted by the personal representative. If thought necessary, call for the relevant share certificate(s).

   Note. The personal representative cannot be compelled to produce the original grant of probate or letters of administration, notwithstanding anything in the Articles to the contrary (1948 s 82) but the copy should be an official copy.

(2) Note in register name of personal representative, particulars of title, date of grant and date noted.

(3) If the personal representative wishes to be registered as holder of shares, the old certificate must be surrendered, a letter of request for registration obtained, and a new certificate issued.

(4) In this latter case a new account in the name of the personal representative must be opened in the register. In this account he should not be described as a personal representative.

(5) The letter of request should be dealt with as a transfer.

(6) Adjust the index (if any) to the register.

5: Bankruptcy of a member

Upon receiving notice of a receiving order, a note should be made in the register and the name of the trustee entered upon his appointment.

6: Increase of nominal capital

(1) Assuming that the board have resolved to recommend an increase of nominal capital, the Articles should be consulted in order to discover what resolution of the company is necesssary.

(2) Summon meeting of company necessary to pass resolution on appropriate notice. Consider necessity or desirability of resolutions under 1980 ss 14 and 17 (pp 23 to 25) being put to same meeting.

(3) Having obtained the necessary sanction, prepare copy of resolution(s) for filing, with notice of increase on Form 10.

(4) File resolution(s) and notice within fifteen days of resolution (1948 s 63) and comply with the requirements of the European Communities Act 1972 (see p 101–102).

(5) Prepare copies of resolution for supplying to members with copies of Memorandum and Articles or on demand.

   Note. No capital duty is payable on a mere increase in nominal capital.

A form of resolution for an increase of nominal capital to be passed by the company in general meeting is given below:

"That the share capital of the company be increased from £.......... to £............................. by the creation of an additional .... shares of .... each"

7: Reduction of capital

The procedure in the case of a reduction of share capital (other than a reduction of unissued capital–see p 184) will necessitate legal assistance. The following points may, however, require the attention of the secretary:

(1)   Summon general meeting to pass special resolution to amend the Articles (if required) and to reduce capital (1948 s 66).

(2)   File copy of resolution (1948 s 143).

(3)   If an inquiry as to creditors is directed–

   (a)   prepare list of creditors to assist the court in settling a list of those entitled to object (1948 s 67); and

   (b)   prepare to notify creditors of the proposed reduction and the date of the application to the court as directed by the court.

(4)   Upon the making by the court of an order confirming the reduction and approving the minute scheduled thereto, file same with Registrar (1948 s 69).

(5)   See that a copy of the minute is embodied in every copy of the Memorandum subsequently issued (1948 s 69).

(6)   If the words ' and reduced' have to be added to the company's name, attend to alteration of stationery, name plate, seal, etc.

(7)   Amend copies of Memorandum and Articles of Association in hand and particulars of capital on unissued share certificates.

8: Holding the Annual General Meeting

(*Note.* Items referred to in *italics* will be relevant only if the annual general meeting is intended to be the general meeting at which the requirements of the 1976 Act as to the laying of accounts before the company are to be complied with. As to the ordinary business of an annual general meeting see pp 85–86).

(1)   Make certain that the date on which it is intended to hold the meeting is within the statutory period (1948 s 131) *and within the period allowed for laying and delivering accounts for the relevant accounting reference period (1976 s 1).*

(2)   Obtain from a meeting of directors authority to despatch notices to members.

(3)   *See that copies of the statutory accounts are ready for despatching with the notices (1948 s 158 and 1976 s 1(5) and (6)).*

(4)   Prepare and despatch notice of meeting *with copies of accounts* and, if required, proxy forms.

(5)   Remember to send notice to the auditors.

(6)   Prepare agenda for the meeting.

(7)   As and when proxies are lodged, particulars thereof should be entered in a voting list.

(8)   See that the register of members, register of directors' holdings, directors' service agreements, accounts, auditors' report, and minute book are ready to be placed before or, as the case may be, available for the meeting.

   Note. Do not overlook the notice summoning the meeting which is usually read at the meeting.

(9)	Check provisions of Articles relating to polls and prepare a summary of these, and of the procedure to be followed if a poll should be properly demanded, to be available for the chairman at the meeting. Prepare (or ensure that the company's registrars or professional advisers will provide) voting cards for use in the event of a poll.

(10)	Take notes of proceedings at the meeting sufficient to enable the minutes to be written up.

(11)	Within fifteen days after the meeting file with the Registrar copies of any resolutions requiring registration (1948 s 143 and 1967 ss 63(2) and 51(1)).

(12)	Prepare annual return (Form 6a) and file with Registrar within forty-two days after the meeting (1948 s 126).

	Note. In the case of large companies it may be thought advisable to send out admission cards with the notices and to have scrutineers at the doors to see that no unauthroised persons attend the meeting.

9: Draft minutes of first meeting of directors . . . . **Limited**

Minutes of the First Meeting of the Board of Directors held at
on		day, the			day of			, 19 .
	Present: [The first directors appointed pursuant to s 21 of the 1976 Act].
	In attendance: [The first secretary appointed pursuant to s 23 of the 1976 Act]
	[The additional director[s] mentioned in item 1].

(1)	There was laid on the table:
	(*a*)	the Certificate of Incorporation of the company dated . . . . . .
		. . . . . . 19. . . . . . .
	(*b*)	a print of the Memorandum and Articles of Association.
	(*c*)	a copy of the statement (Form 1) required under ss 21 and 23 of the Companies Act 1976 signed by or on behalf of the subscribers to the Memorandum of Association containing:
			(i) particulars of the first Director or Directors of the company and the first Secretary of the company and their respective consents to act in the relevant capacity; and
			(ii) particulars of the intended situation of the registered office of the company.
	(*d*)	[an instrument signed by or on behalf of the subscribers to the Memorandum of Association appointing as first Director or Directors of the company the following person or persons:

		and as first Secretary of the company the following person:
																.]
		[The Directors being of the opinion that the said
		was a person with the necessary knowledge and experience to discharge the duties of Secretary of the company, being [here insert one or more of the qualifications specified in CA 1980 s 79(1)(*a*) to (*e*)]. IT WAS RESOLVED that his appointment as

Secretary be confirmed [on the terms of the [letter] [draft service agreement] produced to the meeting and signed for identification by   and that   be authorised to execute on behalf of the company a service agreement with the said   [embodying the said terms] [on terms to be agreed between him and   on behalf of the company]].

(2) It was resolved that
be appointed as [an] additional director[s] of the company and that the secretary be ordered to obtain the relevant particulars and consent[s] under s 200, Companies Act 1948 (as amended by s 22, Companies Act 1976) and to complete and sign 'Particulars of Directors and Secretaries (Form 9b)' for delivery to the Registrar of Companies.

(3) Each of the directors laid upon the table:
   (a) a list of other directorships held by him and of companies or firms of which he was a member and which might in the future enter into contacts or arrangements with the company and declared in accordance with s 199 of the Companies Act 1948 that he was to be regarded as interested in any contract thereafter made with any such company or firm;
   (b) written particulars of the interests of himself, his wife and children in shares and debentures for inclusion in the Register of Directors' Interests to be kept for the purposes of s 27 of the Companies Act 1967.

(4) It was resolved that
be appointed chairman to hold that office until otherwise resolved.

(5) It was resolved that
of
be appointed auditors of the company to hold office until the conclusion of the first general meeting of the company at which the requirements of the Companies Act 1976 as to the laying of accounts before the company are complied with.

(6) It was resolved that the accounting reference date of the company be   in each year and accordingly that the first accounting reference period of the company be the period ending on   . The secretary was instructed to complete and sign 'Notice of accounting reference date' (Form 2) for delivery to the Registrar of Companies.

(7) It was resolved that the registered office of the company be situated at   and that the Register of Members, Register of Directors' Interests and copies or memoranda of Directors' Service Agreements referred to in s 26 of the Companies Act 1967 be kept thereat. The secretary reported that such address had [not] been specified in the statement referred to above as the intended situation of the company's registered office on incorporation [and accordingly the secretary was instructed to complete and sign 'Notice of change of registered office' (Form 4A) specifying such address as

the situation of the company's registered office for delivery to the Registrar of Companies].

(8) It was resolved that the seal of which an impression is affixed in the margin of these minutes be adopted as the common seal of the company.

(9) It was resolved that, so long as all the issued and fully paid ordinary shares of the company ranked pari passu in all respects, distinguishing numbers for the ordinary shares shall not be maintained.

(10) It was resolved to allot and issue one ordinary share of   to each of the subscribers to the Memorandum of Association (and   further ordinary shares of   each in accordance with applications received), as set out below, payment having been made in cash in full at par:

Name of Allottee   Number of Shares allotted

The sealing of certificates in respect of the shares so allotted was authorised and the secretary was instructed to complete and sign 'Return of allotments of shares issued for cash' (Form PUC 2) for delivery to the Registrar of Companies, together with the appropriate payment of capital duty.

(11) It was resolved that the under-mentioned transfers of ordinary shares be approved and registered [subject to their being duly stamped and presented for registration in accordance with the provisions of the Articles of Association]:

Name of Transferor   Name of Transferee   Number of
                                                      Shares

The sealing of the necessary new certificates, following cancellation of the existing certificates covering the shares concerned, was authorised.

(12) [*Here insert the form of resolution required by the company's bankers for the opening of a bank account.*]

(13) It was agreed:

That the next meeting of the directors shall be held on 19 . . . . . . at . . . . . . m.

[That meetings of the directors be held on the first day in each month.]

[That the chairman [secretary]be authorised to call a meeting of the directors at such time as he thinks fit.]

REDEMPTION AND PURCHASE OF OWN SHARES
PERMISSIBLE CASES UNDER THE 1981 ACT

Moneys payable on redemption	May come from		
	Either	Or	Or
Up to the nominal amount of the shares being redeemed		Fresh issue (s 45(5)(a), second limb)	Fresh issue (s 45(5)(a) second limb)
Premium (if any) on their issue	Distributable profits (s 45(5)(a), first limb, and (b))	Distributable profits (s 45(5)(b))	Fresh issue, but must come from share premium account (including premium on new shares) not from nominal of new shares (s 45(6)(b))
Additional premium (if any) on redemption			Distributable profits (s 45(6)(a))

Notes

(1) References above and in these notes to redemption by a company of its shares include purchase of its own shares.

(2) Fresh issue means a fresh issue of shares made for the purposes of the redemption.

(3) References to the first limb and the second limb of s 45(5)(a) are respectively to the words 'redeemable shares may only be redeemed out of distributable profits of the company . . .' and 'redeemable shares may only be redeemed . . . out of the proceeds of a fresh issue of shares made for the purposes of the redemption'.

(4) In the case of preference shares issued before 15 June 1982 which could have been redeemed under 1948 s 58 any premium on redemption may be paid wholly or partly from share premium account (1981 s 62(2) and (3)).

(5) The diagram does not deal with the provisions of 1981 s 54 which permit private companies to redeem shares out of capital.

APPENDIX 3

REGISTERS TO BE MAINTAINED BY A COMPANY SECRETARY

(1)   Register of members (1948 s 110) with index if necessary (1948 s 111).
(2)   Register of debenture holders (not specifically required by statute but needed if the debentures are to be registered).
(3)   Register of applications and allotments (not obligatory).
(4)   Register of transfers (not obligatory).
(5)   Register of directors and secretaries (1948 s 200).
(6)   Register of interests of directors and their families in the shares and debentures of the company and certain related companies (1967 s 29).
(7)   If a public company, register of information notified in respect of interests in the company's voting shares (1981 s 73) with separate part containing information received pursuant to a request by the company (1981 s 75). Both the basic register and any such separate part must have indexes unless they constitute indexes in themselves.
(8)   If a company has the status of a recognised bank or the holding company of a recognised bank, register of transactions and arrangements described in 1980 s 49 (or agreements therefor) with directors and persons connected with directors which would but for such status have to be disclosed in its accounts (1980 s 57).
(9)   Register of charges (1948 s 104).
(10) Minutes of all proceedings of general meetings, directors' meetings and managers' meetings (1948 s 145).

APPENDIX 4

SPECIAL AND EXTRAORDINARY RESOLUTIONS

The following are the cases in which a special or extraordinary resolution is required. For all other purposes an ordinary resolution suffices. In particular, an ordinary resolution suffices to remove a director from office notwithstanding anything in the company's Articles or in any agreement between it and the director (1948 s 184).

Special resolution

A special resolution is needed to:
(1) Change a company's name (1981 s 24(1)).
(2) Alter the objects in the Memorandum (1948 s 5(1)).
(3) Alter the Articles (1948 s 10).
(4) Alter any provision in the Memorandum which could lawfully have been in the Articles (1948 s 23).
(5) In the case of a company whose registered office is in Wales, alter the Memorandum to provide that the registered office is to be situated in Wales (1976 s 30).
(6) Re-register an unlimited company as limited (1967 s 44).
(7) Re-register a private company as public (1980 s 5).
(8) Re-register a public company as private (1980 s 10).
(9) Disapply the pre-emption rights in respect of allotment of equity securities given by 1980 s 17 (1980 s 18).
(10) Reduce the company's capital (subject to confirmation by the court) (1948 s 66).
(11) Approve the giving of financial assistance by a private company in certain circumstances in connection with the acquisition of shares in itself or its holding company (1981 s 43).
(12) In connection with the purchase of a company's own shares, authorise the terms of:
    (a) a contract for an off-market purchase (1981 s 47);
    (b) a contingent contract (1981 s 48); or
    (c) an agreement for the release by a company of rights of purchase of its own shares (1981 s 50).
(13) Approve the purchase or redemption of a company's own shares out of capital (1981 s 55).

(14)   In the case of a dormant company, resolve that auditors be not appointed (1981 s 12).
(15)   Resolve that a company be wound up by the court (1948 s 222(*a*)) or voluntarily (1948 s 278(1)(*b*)).
(16)   In a voluntary winding-up, sanction the acceptance of shares as consideration for the sale of property (1948 ss 287 and 298).

Rarer matters needing a special resolution are to:
(17)   Determine that uncalled capital shall be called only in a winding-up (1948 s 60).
(18)   Alter Memorandum to render liability of directors or managers or any managing director unlimited (1948 s 203).
(19)   Approve assignment of the office of director (1948 s 204).
(20)   In the case of a company registered under 1948 Part VIII, substitute a Memorandum and Articles for a deed of settlement (1948 s 395).

Extraordinary resolution

An extraordinary resolution is needed to:
 (1)   Resolve that a company cannot by reason of its liabilities continue its business and that it is advisable to wind up (1948 s 278(1)(*c*)).
 (2)   Sanction in a members' voluntary winding-up the exercise of certain powers by the liquidator (1948 s 303(1)(*a*)) or an arrangement with creditors (1948 s 306).
 (3)   Sanction in a winding-up the division of assets among members in specie (reg 135).
 (4)   Direct in a members' voluntary winding-up the way in which the books and papers of the company and of the liquidator may be disposed of (1948 s 341(1)).
 (5)   Do anything else which by a company's Articles requires an extraordinary resolution (other than something for which the Acts require a special resolution or the removal of a director under 1948 s 184 as to which see the introductory wording above at the beginning of this Appendix).

Variation of the rights of a class of shares also usually requires the passing of an extraordinary resolution at a separate meeting of shareholders of that class (1980 s 32 and reg 4).

APPENDIX 5

FORMS

APPENDIX 5

1 Notice of accounting reference date
Form Cos A2

A

THE COMPANIES ACTS 1948 TO 1980

Notice of accounting reference date

Pursuant to section 2(1) of the Companies Act 1976

Form No. 2

2

Please do not write in this binding margin

To the Registrar of Companies

For official use

Company number

Please complete legibly, preferably in black type, or bold block lettering

Name of company

Limited*

*delete if inappropriate

hereby gives you notice in accordance with subsection (1) of section 2 of the Companies Act 1976 that the accounting reference date on which the company's accounting reference period is to be treated as coming to an end in each successive year is as shown below:

Important
The accounting reference date to be entered alongside should be completed as in the following examples:

Please mark X in the box below if a public company

Day   Month

31 March
Day   Month
3 1 0 3

5 April
Day   Month
0 5 0 4

31 December
Day   Month
3 1 1 2

Signed_____[Director][Secretary]† Date_____

Presentor's name, address and reference (if any):

For official use
General section

Post room

oyez The Solicitors' Law Stationery Society, plc, Oyez House, 237 Long Lane, London SE1 4PU   ★ ★ ★ ★ ★   F1692 9-81
Companies A2

2 Form of application for shares

To the Directors,

                     Limited ('the Company')

    I/We hereby apply for   shares of   each in the Company at a price of   each
and enclose a cheque for £

    I/We agree to take such shares subject to the memorandum and articles of association of the
Company and request you to enter my/our name in the Company's register of members as holder
of such shares.

       Dated   19

       Signature:

       Name:

       Address:

Editors' note

This is a simple form of application suitable for use when specific investors
agree to take shares in a company. A form of application used on a public
issue or offer for sale of shares will be much more complex and should be
drafted by the relevant professional advisers.

3 Renounceable letter of allotment

X Limited
(Registered in England No 123456)

To:

Registered Office:

[Date]   19   .

ALLOTMENT LETTER

Dear Sir or Madam,

Issue of   Ordinary Shares of £1 each
at £1.50 per share, credited as fully paid

In response to your application the Directors have allotted to you   Ordinary Shares of £1 each, subject to the memorandum and articles of association of the Company.

The procedure for renouncing all or part of this allotment is explained below. If you wish all the shares comprised in this allotment letter to be registered in your name, you need take no action and a share certificate in respect of them will be sent to you on   19   . The share certificate can be obtained earlier in exchange for this allotment letter on application to me, the Secretary, X Limited, [address].

If you wish to renounce all the shares comprised in this allotment letter in favour of one person (or several persons as joint holders) you should date and sign the form of renunciation below and pass this letter to the person(s) in whose favour you renounce it, who should complete the registration application form below and send it to me, the Secretary, X Limited, [address] to arrive not later than   19   .

If you wish some of the shares comprised in this allotment letter to be registered in your name but to renounce the remainder, or you wish to renounce all such shares but not all to the same person(s), this allotment letter should be split. To do this you should sign the form of renunciation below and send the letter to me, the Secretary, X Limited, [address] stating the number of split letters required and the number of shares to be included in each. I will then send you the split letters.

Surrender of this allotment letter to the Company purporting to have been signed in accordance with these instructions shall be conclusive evidence in favour of the Company of the title of the person(s) surrendering the same to deal with it and to receive a share certificate and/or split letters. Split letters and share certificates will be sent through the post at the risk of the person(s) entitled thereto.

Yours faithfully,

Secretary

Form of Renunciation

To the Directors of X Limited

    I/We hereby renounce my/our right to the shares comprised in the above letter of allotment in favour of the person(s) named in the registration application form below.

Dated   19   .

                          ....

Registration Application Form

To the Directors of X Limited

    I/We hereby request you to register the shares comprised in the above letter of allotment in my/our name(s), subject to the memorandum and articles of association of the Company.

Dated   19   .

Signature(s):   ....

Name(s):   ....

Address(es):   ....

                ....

                ....

Editors' notes

1   This is a simple form of renounceable letter of allotment (in fully paid rather than partly paid form). It is not suitable for use when the shares concerned are to be quoted: a more elaborate, standardised form will then be needed.

2   The period during which the allotment may be renounced should be limited to not more than six months after the issue of the allotment letter: otherwise the allotment letter will be liable to stamp duty.

4 Notice of Annual General Meeting

LIMITED

Notice of Meeting

Notice is hereby given that the Annual General Meeting of   Limited will be held at   on   day,   19   at   am/pm for the following purposes:

1   To consider and adopt the Company's accounts and the reports of the Directors and Auditors for the year ended   19   .

2   To declare a dividend.

3   To [elect] [re-elect] the following as Directors:
        (a) J Smith
        (b) D Jones.

4   To [appoint] [reappoint]   as Auditors of the Company to hold office until the conclusion of the next general meeting at which accounts are laid before the Company.

5   To authorise the Directors to fix the remuneration of the Auditors.

6   As special business, to consider and, if thought fit, pass the following resolutions, which will be proposed as [Special] [Ordinary] Resolutions:

A member entitled to attend and vote is entitled to appoint a proxy (or proxies) to attend and, on a poll, vote instead of him. A proxy need not be a member of the Company.

By order of the Board,

Secretary.

[Date]   19   .

Registered office:

Notes:

1   A form of proxy is enclosed. The appointment of a proxy will not prevent you from subsequently attending and voting at the meeting in person.

2   To be effective the instrument appointing a proxy, and any power of attorney or other authority under which it is executed (or a duly certified copy of any such power or authority), must be deposited at the Company's registered office not less than 48 hours before the time for holding the meeting.

3   [No Director of the Company has a contract of service with the Company or any of its subsidiaries.]
OR
[Copies of all contracts of service under which Directors of the Company are employed by the Company or any of its subsidiaries are available for inspection at the Company's registered office during business hours on any weekday (Saturdays and public holidays excluded) from the date of this notice until the conclusion of the Annual General Meeting and will also be available for inspection at the place of the meeting from fifteen minutes before it is held until its conclusion.]

Editors' notes

1   In the case of a private company a member will not usually be allowed to appoint more than one proxy: in that case delete '(or proxies)' in the last paragraph of the notice.

2   Note 3 above applies to listed companies and is included to comply with a requirement of the Yellow Book.

5 Notice of Extraordinary General Meeting

LIMITED

Notice of Meeting

Notice is hereby given that an Extraordinary General Meeting of   Limited
will be held at   on   day,
19   at   am/pm to consider and, if thought fit, pass the following resolution(s),
which will be proposed as [Ordinary] [Special] [Extraordinary] Resolution(s):

      A member entitled to attend and vote is entitled to appoint a proxy (or proxies) to attend and,
on a poll, vote instead of him. A proxy need not be a member of the Company.

By order of the Board,

Secretary.

[Date]   19   .

Registered office:

Notes:

1   A form of proxy is enclosed. The appointment of a proxy will not prevent you from
subsequently attending and voting at the meeting in person.

2   To be effective the instrument appointing a proxy, and any power of attorney or other
authority under which it is executed (or a duly certified copy of any such power or authority),
must be deposited at the Company's registered office not less than 48 hours before the time for
holding the meeting.

Editors' note

In the case of a private company a member will not usually be allowed to
appoint more than one proxy : in that case delete '(or proxies)' in the last
paragraph of the notice.

6 Form of consent to short notice of a general meeting and/or special resolution

I/We consent to the meeting above-mentioned being held on the date specified in the above notice [and to the resolutions] set out above [numbered 1 and 2] being proposed and passed as special resolutions [at such meeting notwithstanding that the notice given of such meeting] [and resolutions] has been shorter than required by the Companies Act 1948 or the Company's articles.

[Date] . . . .

Editors' notes:

1   The wording of the above form assumes that it will be added at the end of the notice of meeting. If it is to be a separate document alter 'the meeting above-mentioned being held on the date specified in the above notice' to 'the [Annual] [Extraordinary] General Meeting of X Limited called by a notice of meeting dated   being held on   ' and if special resolutions are involved refer to them as 'the resolutions set out in such notice of meeting' or 'the resolutions numbered 1 and 2 in such notice of meeting'.

2   The notice requirements for meetings and those for special resolutions are distinct (see eg 1948 ss 133 and 141 respectively). An extraordinary resolution as such (as distinct from the meeting at which it is to be considered) will not, unless the Articles contain unusual provisions, require a particular period of notice. Although the wording of 1948 s 133 and of most Articles does not stipulate a period of notice for a meeting (as opposed to the resolution) if it is called to consider a special resolution and is not the annual general meeting, the inclusion in the above form of consent of the wording relating to the holding of the meeting does no harm.

3   If required, add at the end of the above form of consent the following wording relating to the sending of balance sheets and documents required to be annexed:

'and I/we agree that copies of the documents referred to in Section 158 of the said Act to be laid before the Company at such meeting shall be deemed to have been duly sent notwithstanding that they were sent less than 21 days before the date of such meeting'.

7 Form of proxy

XYZ LIMITED

I/We

of   being (a) a member(s) of the above-named
Company hereby appoint the chairman of the meeting or
as my/our proxy to vote for me/us and on my/our behalf at the [Annual] [Extraordinary] General
Meeting of the Company to be held on   19   and at every adjournment
thereof. I/We request such proxy to vote on the following resolutions as indicated below:

Resolutions	FOR	AGAINST
1 To adopt the Company's accounts and the reports of the Directors and Auditors for the year ended 19	☐	☐
2 To declare a dividend	☐	☐
3 (a) To elect Mr J Smith a director (b) To re-elect Mr D Jones a director	☐	☐
4 To reappoint Messrs as Auditors of the Company until the conclusion of the next general meeting at which accounts are laid before the Company	☐	☐
5 To authorise the Directors to fix the remuneration of the Auditors	☐	☐
6 [Other resolutions]	☐	☐

etc

Names of joint holders (if any) ....

Signed this .... day of .... 19 ....

Signature ....

Notes:

1   Please indicate with an 'X' in the appropriate boxes how you wish the proxy to vote. The proxy
will exercise his discretion as to how he votes or whether he abstains from voting:

    (a)   on any resolution set out above if no instruction is given in respect of that resolution;
and

    (b)   on any business or resolution considered at the meeting other than the resolutions set
out above.

2   If you wish to appoint someone other than the chairman of the meeting as your proxy please
delete the words 'the chairman of the meeting' and insert the name of the person you wish to
appoint. A proxy need not be a member of the Company.

3   To be effective this form, and any power of attorney or other authority under which it is
executed (or a duly certified copy of any such power or authority), must be deposited at [the
Company's registered office] not less than 48 hours before the time for holding the meeting.

4   Where the member is a corporation this form must be under its common seal or signed by an officer, attorney or other person duly authorised by the corporation.

5   In the case of joint holders only one need sign this form, but the names of the other joint holders should be shown in the space provided. The vote of the senior holder who tenders a vote, whether in person or by proxy, will be accepted to the exclusion of the votes of the other joint holders. Seniority will be determined by the order in which the names of the holders appear in the register of members in respect of the joint holding.

Editors' notes

1   The resolutions included above are of the type likely to appear in the business of an annual general meeting and are included merely by way of example.

2   The exact wording of notes 3 and 4 above will depend on the wording of the company's Articles or (if applicable) regs 68 and 69.

8 Resolutions by a corporation appointing representative(s) to act at meetings of companies

A—Appointment of one representative in relation to a specific company

XYZ INVESTMENTS PLC

Copy of resolution of the Directors passed on   , 19

'IT WAS RESOLVED that John Smith be authorised in accordance with Section 139 of the Companies Act 1948 to act as the representative of XYZ Investments PLC at any meeting of The Eastern Steam Packet Company, Limited.'

I certify that the above is a true copy of a resolution of the Directors of XYZ Investments PLC which was duly passed on the above-mentioned date.

. . . .
Secretary
XYZ Investments PLC

B—Appointment of several representatives to act generally

XYZ INVESTMENTS PLC

Copy of resolution of the Directors passed on   , 19

'IT WAS RESOLVED that John Jones, John Smith, Thomas Green and John Thompson each be authorised in accordance with Section 139 of the Companies Act 1948 to act as the representative of XYZ Investments PLC at any meeting of the members or creditors (or any of them) of any company of which XYZ Investments PLC may from time to time be a member or creditor (the expression creditor herein including a holder of debentures).'

I certify that the above is a true copy of a Resolution of the Directors of XYZ Investments PLC which was duly passed on the above-mentioned date.

. . . .
Secretary
XYZ Investments PLC

9 Copy of resolution for filing

No. . . . .

The Companies Acts 1948 to 1981

COMPANY LIMITED BY SHARES

LIMITED

Special Resolution passed on   19

AT [the Annual] [an Extraordinary] General Meeting of the Company held on
19   the following resolution was duly passed as a Special
Resolution:

. . . .
[Director]   [Secretary]

Editors' Note

If the resolution is an ordinary or extraordinary one rather than a special resolution, alter 'Special' to 'Ordinary' or 'Extraordinary'. Adapt as necessary if more than one resolution is involved.

10 Tax voucher to accompany dividend cheque

THE EASTERN STEAM PACKET COMPANY, LIMITED

Security code
0-123-456

Dividend no   Reference no   TAX VOUCHER   1st April 1984
123   456

[Final] Dividend on Ordinary Shares at 5p per share for year ended 31 December 1983 to shareholders registered on 15 March 1984

I certify that Advance Corporation Tax of an amount equal to that shown below as tax credit will be accounted for to the Collector of Taxes. This voucher should be kept. It will be accepted by the Inland Revenue as evidence of tax credit in respect of which you may be entitled to claim payment or relief.

J SMITH, Secretary

Number of shares	Tax Credit	Dividend Payable
200	£4.29	£10.00

JOHN JONES
1 HIGH STREET
BARCHESTER
BARSET

Notice of any change of address
or any correspondence about this
dividend should be sent, quoting
the reference number given above,
to The Registrar, The Eastern Steam
Packet Company, Limited, 200 Gresham
Street, London EC2A 2AB.

Editors' notes

1   For further details of the way in which a dividend warrant and its accompanying tax voucher should be laid out, see the specification published by the British Standards Institution.

2   The box in the top right corner giving the security code applies only to listed securities; the code is the number given against the name of the security in The Stock Exchange Daily Official List.

11 Request for payment of interest or dividends
Form Cos 5C

REQUEST FOR PAYMENT OF INTEREST OR DIVIDENDS

Above this line for Registrar's use only.

Name of Undertaking	
Please complete in typewriting or in block capitals.	Account Designation (if any)
Full name and address of first named or sole holder. Full name(s) of joint holder(s) (if any).	
Any change of address should be notified by quoting former and present address.	

Full name and address of the Bank Branch, Firm or Person to whom Interest and Dividends are to be sent.

Please forward, until further notice, all Interest and Dividends that may from time to time become due on any Stock or Shares now standing, or which may hereafter stand, in my (our) name(s) or in the name(s) of the survivor(s) of us in the Company's books to:—

or, where payment is to be made to a Bank, to such other Branch of that Bank as the Bank may from time to time request. Your compliance with this request shall discharge the Company's liability in respect of such interest or dividends.

PLEASE SIGN HERE

1 ....   2 ....

3 ....

Date ....   4 ....

NOTES
(i) Executors or administrators must insert the name of the deceased holder.
(ii) This form must be signed by ALL the registered holders.
(iii) A Body Corporate should sign by means of Authorised Signatory(ies) whose capacity must be stated.
(iv) Directions to credit a particular account MUST be given to the bank direct and NOT INCLUDED in this form.
(v) Where instructions are in favour of a Bank, this form should be sent direct to the Bank Branch concerned for completion of the section below.

This form is approved by the Institute of Chartered Secretaries and Administrators and recommended by the Stock Exchange.

Bank's reference number and details:

(1) Sorting code number   —   —

(2) Name of Bank...
Title of Branch...
Please quote all digits including zeros.

(3) Account number (if any)

STAMP OF BANK BRANCH

APPENDIX 5

12 Letter of request
Form Con 41A

LETTER OF REQUEST	
	above this line for Registrar's use only

REQUEST BY EXECUTORS OR ADMINISTRATORS OF A DECEASED HOLDER TO BE PLACED ON THE REGISTER AS HOLDERS IN THEIR OWN RIGHT.

Full name of Undertaking.	TO THE DIRECTORS OF
*Full description of Security. (*See note below*)	

Number or amount of Shares, Stock or other Security and, in figures column only, number and denomination of units if any.	WORDS	FIGURES
		(units of)

Full name of Deceased.	....Deceased

I/We, the undersigned, being the personal representative(s) of the above-named deceased, hereby request you to register me/us in the books of the Company as the holder(s) of the above-mentioned Stock/Shares now registered in the name of the said deceased.

DATED this...day of...19......

Signature(s) of Personal Representative(s)

PLEASE COMPLETE IN TYPE-WRITING OR IN BLOCK CAPITALS.	
Full name(s) and full postal address(es) (including Post Code(s) of the Personal Representative(s)) in the order in which they are to be registered.	
Please state title, if any, or whether Mr., Mrs. or Miss.	

IF AN ACCOUNT ALREADY EXISTS IN THE ABOVE NAME(S) IN THE SAME ORDER THE ABOVE-MENTIONED HOLDING WILL BE ADDED TO THAT ACCOUNT, UNLESS INSTRUCTIONS ARE GIVEN TO THE CONTRARY.

The Certificate(s) in the name of the deceased if not already with the Company's Registrars must accompany this form.	Stamp or name and address of person lodging this form.
No stamp duty is payable on this form in the case of a company registered in England; in the case of a company registered in Scotland stamp duty may be payable.	
*A separate Letter of Request should be used for each class of security.	

This form must be returned to:

The Registrar

....(Name of Company)

....(Address)

....

[Form approved by The Institute of Chartered Secretaries and Administrators]

oyez The Solicitors' Law Stationery Society, plc, Oyez House, 237 Long Lane, London SE1 4PU

Conveyancing 41A

F1314 5/81
★★★★

13 Indemnity for lost certificate
Form Cos 5B

INDEMNITY FOR LOST CERTIFICATE

(above this line for Registrar's use only)

To the Directors of ....

....

The original certificate(s) of title relating to the undermentioned securities of the above-named Company has/have been lost or destroyed.

Neither the securities nor the certificate(s) of title thereto have been transferred, charged, lent or deposited or dealt with in any manner affecting the absolute title thereto and the person(s) named in the said certificate(s) is/are the person(s) entitled to be on the register in respect of such securities.

I/We request you to issue a duplicate certificate(s) of title for such securities and in consideration of your doing so, undertake (jointly and severally) to indemnify you and the Company against all claims and demands (and any expenses thereof) which may be made against you or the Company in consequence of your complying with this request and of the Company permitting at any time hereafter a transfer of the said securities, or any part thereof, without the production of the said original certificate(s).

I/We undertake to deliver to the Company for cancellation the said original certificate(s) should the same ever be recovered.

PARTICULARS OF CERTIFICATE(S) LOST OR DESTROYED

Particulars of Certificate	Amount and Class of Securities	In favour of

Dated this .... day of .... 19 ....

Signature(s) ....

*We ....

hereby join in the above indemnity and undertaking.

*Bank, Insurance Company or Guarantee Society.

oyez The Solicitors' Law Stationery Society, plc, Oyez House, 237 Long Lane, London SE1 4PU   F952   BM29277   9-81
★★★★★

[Form approved by The Institute of Chartered Secretaries and Administrators]
Companies 5B

14 Declaration of trust and power of attorney

DECLARATION OF TRUST AND POWER OF ATTORNEY

To: ....

....

1 I/WE ....

....

HEREBY DECLARE that the share(s) specified in the Schedule hereto, the certificate(s) for which has/have been or will be delivered to you, is/are now and has/have at all times since the said share(s) became registered in my/our name(s) been held in trust for you absolutely.

2 I/WE HEREBY UNDERTAKE to transfer or otherwise deal with the said share(s) as you may from time to time direct and to account to you for all dividends or other moneys paid to me/us on or in respect of the said share(s) and to exercise my/our voting powers and other rights in respect of the said share(s) in such manner as you shall from time to time direct.

3 TO secure the performance of the above undertaking I/WE HEREBY IRREVOCABLY APPOINT YOU my/our Attorney at your cost and expense in all respects:

(a)   to sign in my/our name(s) and on my/our behalf any instrument(s) of transfer of the said share(s) (or to complete any necessary particulars in any instrument(s) of transfer in respect of the said share(s) executed by me/us in blank and delivered to you at any time) and any dividend mandate or form of proxy or consent to short notice of any meeting or resolution in writing or requisition or notice of any resolution or proposal or other document whatsoever (whether of the foregoing description or not) which may in your opinion be necessary or desirable and which as the holder(s) of the said share(s) I/we have power to sign; and

(b)   generally in my/our name(s) and on my/our behalf to execute and do all such instruments and things as you may think fit for the purpose of obtaining or exercising any and all rights and powers of and incidental to the holding or ownership of the said share(s).

[4* [REFERENCE herein to the said shares shall where the subject or context permits or requires include references to any of the said shares.]

THE SCHEDULE above referred to

Name of Company   Particulars of Share(s)

[Insert details]

IN WITNESS whereof these presents have been sealed by me/us this   day of
19   .

†   SIGNED SEALED and DELIVERED by ⎫
    me the said   ⎬
                                        ⎪
    in the presence of: ⎭

‡   THE COMMON SEAL of   ⎫
                                     ⎬
    was hereunto affixed in the presence ⎪
    of: ⎭

---

*   Insert clause 4 if the declaration relates to more than one share.
†   Use this form of words if the declaration is made by an individual.
‡   Use this form of words if the declaration is made by a company.

Editors' Notes
(1)   Stampable 50p.
(2)   This form may be used where, to comply with the requirement that a company has more than one member, one or more shares in a wholly-owned subsidiary are registered in the name of a nominee of the holding company.

15 Resolutions for the purposes of 1980 ss 14 and 17 (allotment of shares)

A—Resolution giving authority to allot relevant securities

THAT the Directors are hereby generally and unconditionally authorised in accordance with Section 14 of the Companies Act 1980 to exercise for a period of [five] year[s] from the date of the passing of this resolution all the powers of the Company to allot relevant securities up to the aggregate nominal amount of £   * and to make offers or agreements which would or might require relevant securities to be allotted after the expiry of the said period (provided that such allotments would fall within the limit aforesaid if made during the said period) and for the purposes of this resolution words and expressions defined in or for the purposes of the said Section shall have the same meaning herein.

*   The amount to be inserted here will generally be the amount of the Company's unissued share capital.

B—Special resolution disapplying 1980 s17 generally

THAT:
(1) Section 17(1) of the Companies Act 1980 shall not apply to the allotment of equity securities which the Directors are authorised to allot pursuant to the authority conferred on them for the purposes of Section 14 of that Act [by the Ordinary Resolution already passed at this meeting];
(2) The Company may before the expiry of the power conferred by this Resolution make an offer or agreement which would or might require equity securities to be allotted after such expiry (provided that such allotments would fall within the limit provided for by the said authority if made before such expiry); and
(3) For the purposes of this resolution words and expressions defined in or for the purposes of the said Section 17 (as amended by the Companies Act 1981) shall have the same meaning herein.

Editors' notes
(1)   An Ordinary Resolution suffices for A above.
(2)   Listed companies will generally require a more complicated version of B above, on which professional advice should be sought, in order to comply with the guidelines of certain bodies of institutional investors while retaining as much flexibility as possible.
(3)   B above is a general disapplication of the pre-emption rules in 1980 s17 pursuant to 1980 s18(1). Such pre-emption rules may also be disapplied (or modified) in relation to a specified allotment pursuant to 1980 s18(2) but subject to the additional requirements in s18(5).

16 Special resolution under 1981 s 47 to approve a contract for off-market purchase by a company of its own shares

---

Special Resolution

THAT the terms of a proposed contract between
                                                                    of the one part and the
Company of the other part providing for the purchase by the Company of certain of its own shares
(a draft of which contract has been produced to this meeting and signed for identification by the
Chairman thereof) are hereby approved and authorised for the purposes of Section 47 of the
Companies Act 1981 and otherwise [but so that such approval and authority shall expire eighteen
months after the date on which this resolution is passed].

Editors' notes

(1)   The words in square brackets are needed only in the case of a public
       company.
(2)   Attention is drawn to the detailed provisions of 1981 s47, eg as to
       voting (subs (9)) and as to the requirement that a copy of a proposed
       contract (or a memorandum of its terms if it is not in writing) must be
       available for inspection (subs (10)).

17 Resolution under 1981 s 49 to authorise market purchases by a company of its own shares

---

Resolution

THAT authority is hereby given for the purposes of Section 49 of the Companies Act 1981
for market purchases (as defined in the said Section) by the Company of any of its [own shares]
[insert class or other description of shares to which authority is to extend] subject to the following
restrictions:

(1) The maximum aggregate number of shares to be so acquired is

(2) The maximum and minimum prices to be paid for shares so acquired shall be respectively
     and

(3) This authority shall expire eighteen months after the date on which this resolution is passed
     but the Company may before such expiry make contracts for such purchases which would
     or might be executed wholly or partly after such expiry.

(4) [Insert any other desired limitations or conditions].

Editors' notes

(1)   An ordinary resolution suffices.
(2)   The maximum and minimum prices may be specified by a formula (but
       without reference to any person's discretion or opinion).

18 Special resolution under 1981 s 55 to approve payment out of capital by a company for the redemption or purchase of its own shares

---

Special Resolution

THAT approval is hereby given for the purposes of Section 55 of the Companies Act 1981 to the payment out of capital (within the meaning of Section 54 of the said Act) by the Company of £   [for] [towards the monies payable on] the [redemption] [purchase] by the Company of [number and brief description of the shares involved] in the Company's share capital.

Editors' note
Attention is drawn to the detailed provisions of 1981 ss 55 and 56, eg as to the timetable to be followed, as to voting (s 55(7)) and as to documents to be available for inspection (s 55(8)).

19 Notice for publication under 1981 s 56 concerning payment out of capital by a company for the redemption or purchase of its own shares

---

[Name of company]

(registered in [England] No 123456)

Proposed payment out of capital pursuant to
Companies Act 1981, Section 54

NOTICE is hereby given pursuant to Section 56 of the Companies Act 1981 that:

(1)   ('the Company') has by a
Special Resolution passed on   19
approved a payment out of capital for the purpose of acquiring by [redemption] [purchase] [number and brief description of shares] in its own share capital.
(2) The permissible capital payment (as defined in Section 54 of the said Act) for such shares is £
(3) The statutory declaration of the Company's directors and the report of the Company's auditors required by Section 55 of the said Act in respect of such payment out of capital are available for inspection by any member or creditor of the Company at the Company's registered office

during business hours on any day (except a Saturday, Sunday or public holiday) up to and including [insert date five weeks after the resolution].
(4) Any creditor of the Company may at any time up to and including [insert date five weeks after the resolution] apply to the [High Court of Justice] under Section 57 of the said Act for an order prohibiting such payment out of capital.

[Date]   ....
                                          Secretary
Registered Office:

Editors' note
A creditor's application to prohibit the payment of capital must be made to 'the court'. By 1981 s 118(3) and 1948 s 455(1) this means the court having jurisdiction to wind up the company. 1948 s 218 specifies which courts have jurisdiction to wind up a company registered in England and s 220 which courts have jurisdiction to wind up a company registered in Scotland.

248 APPENDIX 5

20 Notification under 1981 s 63 or 64 as to an interest in relevant share capital of a public company

TO the Secretary of   Public Limited Company
(hereinafter called 'the Company')

I,   of
hereby give the Company notice [in fulfilment of the obligation imposed by Section [63(1)][64(2)] of the Companies Act 1981][5] that:

(1) This notification relates to, and the expression 'the share capital' used below means, [the Company's whole share capital] [the part of the Company's share capital which is divided into [Ordinary Shares]].[6]

(2) The number of shares comprised in the share capital in which [I know that][7] I was interested[8] immediately after the time when my obligation to make this notification arose is

OR

(2) I no longer have an interest[8] subject to the notification requirement under Section 63 of the [said Act] [Companies Act 1981] in shares comprised in the share capital.[9]

(3) [I am] [of[10]
                     is] the registered holder of all the shares to which this notification relates.

OR

(3) The identities of the registered holders of the shares to which this notification relates and the numbers of those shares held by each of them are [, so far as known to me at the date of this notification,][7] as follows:

           Identity   *Number*

Name   *Address*[10]

[(4) [11]I am a party to an agreement to which Section 67 of the [said Act] [Companies Act 1981] applies. The names and, so far as known to me, the addresses of the other parties to that agreement are as follows:

          Name   *Address*

[Insert number] [None] of the shares to which this notification relates are shares in which I am interested by virtue of the said Section 67.]

[(5) [11][I have] [of
                 has] ceased to be a party to [the agreement referred to in paragraph 4 above] [an agreement to which [the said Section 67] [Section 67 of the said Act] [Section 67 of the Companies Act 1981] applies made between[12]

                                           ].]

Dated   198 .

                      ....

Notes

(1) For the detailed requirements see Part IV of the 1981 Act.

(2) The obligation to make a required notification must be performed within the period of five days following that on which the obligation arises (s 63(6)) but see s 82(3) relating to Saturdays, Sundays and bank holidays and s 64(3) where the notification is required by s 64 (ie, because of a reduction in the prescribed percentage).

(3) The notification must be in writing: s 63(5).

(4) The matters to be specified in a notification are set out in ss 63(5), 65(1) and 72(2).

(5) These words should be included if the person making the notification is a director (s 72(2)) in order to distinguish this notification from a notification under 1967 s 27. Otherwise the words are optional. Where notifications are required by both the 1967 and 1981 Acts they can, if desired, be combined in one document but if this is done care should be taken to follow the distinct requirements of the two Acts.

(6) Note ss 63(10) and 82(2).

(7) These words of qualification may be inserted if desired: see ss 63(5)(*a*) and 65(1).

(8) By ss 66(1) and (2) and 67(6) a person is taken to be interested in shares if certain members of his family, certain bodies corporate or other parties to an agreement to which s 67 applies ('a concert party') and to which he is party are interested in them. Ss 70 and 71 specify certain interests to be taken into account for the purposes of ss 63 to 65 and certain interests to be disregarded. Since therefore:
  (i) a person is taken to be interested in shares in which the ordinary man would probably not regard himself as interested eg (today) shares held by his wife; and
  (ii) there are to be disregarded shares in which the ordinary man would probably regard himself as having an interest, eg shares comprised in a settlement in which he has a life interest (s 71(1)(*e*) and (3));
it may be desired where such deeming provisions apply to insert after 'interested' in the first alternative for paragraph 2 or after 'interest' in the second alternative:
  '(within the meaning of Part IV of the [said Act] [Companies Act 1981]).

(9) If the second alternative for paragraph 2 is used, delete both alternatives of paragraph 3.

(10) Addresses would not seem to be obligatory. S 65 requires only the *identity* of the registered holder. S 72(2) requires a notification to identify the person making it and give his address: from this it would appear that a person's name will normally suffice to identify him.

(11) Paragraphs 4 and 5 should be included only where applicable: see s 67(8) and (9).

(12) Insert names of parties to the agreement in order to identify it: some identification of the agreement would seem necessary as s 67(9) reads 'the notification shall include a statement that he or that other person has ceased to be a party to *the* agreement' rather than '*such an* agreement'. It would not seem necessary to include addresses.

(13) Note the continuing obligations in ss 65(2)(a) and (b) where the person making the notification later becomes aware of particulars of the registered ownership of shares in which he is interested or of any change in such particulars and the obligation to make a further notification if he ceases to have an interest subject to the notification requirement or the percentage level of his interest (rounded down if it is not a whole number to the next whole number) alters.

21 Declaration of solvency (members' voluntary winding-up) Form Cos (WU) 16A

No. 108
(No filing fee payable)

Number of Company } ....

THE COMPANIES ACTS 1948 to 1981

MEMBERS' VOLUNTARY WINDING UP

DECLARATION OF SOLVENCY
embodying a Statement of Assets and Liabilities

Pursuant to Section 283 *of the Companies Act* 1948
as amended by Section 105 *of the Companies Act* 1981

Insert the Name of the Company { ....

....

LIMITED

NOTE.—To be effective the Declaration of Solvency must be made within the five weeks immediately preceding the date of the passing of the resolution for winding up. This declaration must be delivered to the Registrar of Companies before the expiry of the period of 15 days immediately following the date on which the Resolution is passed, otherwise the company and every officer in default is liable to the fines referred to on the last page of this form.

Presented by *Presentor's Reference*..............................

....

....

....

oyez The Solicitors' Law Stationery Society, plc, Oyez House, 237 Long Lane, London SE1 4PU F1894 1/82

★★★★

Companies (W.U.) 16A [P.T.O.

Editors' note By 1981 s 105 the declaration will also be effective if made on the date of the passing of the resolution for winding-up but before such resolution is passed.

FORMS

DECLARATION OF SOLVENCY

We,..

....

....

....

of..

....

(a) " all the "
or " the maj-
ority of the "
as the case
may be.

being(ᵃ)..............................Directors of..............................
....Limited,

do solemnly and sincerely declare that we have made a full enquiry into the affairs of this company, and that, having so done, we have formed the opinion that this company will be able to pay its debts in full within

(b) Insert
a period of
months not
exceeding
twelve.

a period of(ᵇ)..............................months, from the commencement of the winding up, and we append a statement of the company's assets and liabilities as at..............................19.........., being the latest practicable date before the making of this declaration. And we make this solemn declaration, conscientiously believing the same to be true, and by virtue of the provisions of the Statutory Declarations Act, 1835.

Declared at..............................

One thousand nine hundred and

(c) or Notary
Public or
Justice of the
Peace.

(ᶜ) *A Solicitor*

NOTE.—This margin is reserved for binding, and must not be written across.

Statement as at .... **19**........

showing Assets at estimated realisable values and Liabilities expected to rank.

ASSETS AND LIABILITIES	Estimated to realise or to rank for payment (to nearest £)
ASSETS :—	£
Balance at Bank	
Cash in Hand	
Marketable Securities	
Bills Receivable	
Trade Debtors	
Loans and Advances	
Unpaid Calls	
Stock in Trade	
Work in Progress	
....	
....	
....	
Freehold Property	
Leasehold Property	
Plant and Machinery	
Furniture, Fittings, Utensils, etc.	
Patents, Trade Marks, etc.	
Investments other than marketable securities	
Other property, viz. :	
....	
....	
....	
LIABILITIES :— Estimated realisable value of Assets £	
Secured on specific assets, viz. :— £	
....	
Secured by Floating Charge(s)	
Estimated Cost of Liquidation and other expenses including interest accruing until payment of debts in full	
Unsecured Creditors (amounts estimated £ to rank for payment) :—	
Trade Accounts	
Bills Payable	
Accrued Expenses	
Other Liabilities :—	
....	
....	
Contingent Liabilities :—	
....	
....	
Estimated Surplus after paying Debts in full .. .. .. £	
Remarks :	

22 Extraordinary resolution for voluntary winding-up of insolvent company

Number of } ....
Company }

The Companies Acts 1948 to 1981

———

COMPANY LIMITED BY SHARES.

———

Extraordinary Resolution

(*Pursuant to sections* 141 (1) & 278 (1) (c) *of the Companies Act* 1948)

....

....

Passed   19

At an EXTRAORDINARY GENERAL MEETING of the above-named Company, duly convened, and held at

.

.

on the   day of   19   , the subjoined EXTRAORDINARY RESOLUTION was duly passed, viz.:—

RESOLUTION.

"That it has been proved to the satisfaction of this meeting that the Company cannot by reason of its liabilities continue its business, and that it is advisable to wind up the same, and accordingly that the Company be wound up voluntarily, and that

of

be and he is hereby appointed liquidator for the purposes of such winding-up."

*Signature .... } To be signed by the Chairman, a Director or the Secretary of the Company.

*For the *Gazette* the signature to this Notice must be attested in the space below by either a Solicitor of the Supreme Court, a member of any body of Accountants established in the United Kingdom and for the time being recognised by the Department of Trade for the purposes of Section 161 (1) (a) of the Companies Act 1948, or a member of the Institute of Chartered Secretaries and Administrators, if the signatory is neither a Solicitor nor a member of any of the above bodies.

Attested by ....

Description ....

Name of signatory (in block capitals) ....

23 Special resolution for voluntary winding-up of solvent company

Number of |
Company |

The Companies Acts 1948 *to* 1980

COMPANY LIMITED BY SHARES

Special Resolution

(*Pursuant to sections 141 (2) & 278 (1) (b) of the Companies Act 1948*)

_____LIMITED

Passed   19

AT an EXTRAORDINARY GENERAL MEETING of the above-named Company, duly convened, and held at

on the   day of   19   , the subjoined SPECIAL RESOLUTION was duly passed, viz. :—

RESOLUTION

That the Company be wound up voluntarily, and that

of

be and he is hereby appointed Liquidator for the purposes of such winding-up.

*Signature_____

To be signed by the Chairman, a Director, or the Secretary of the Company.

*For the *London Gazette* the signature to this form must be attested in the space below by either a solicitor, a member of a body of accountants recognised by the Department of Trade for the purpose of section 161 (1) (a) of the Companies Act 1948 or a member of The Institute of Chartered Secretaries and Administrators if the signatory is neither a solicitor nor a member of any of the above bodies.

Witness to the above signature _____

Description _____

In order to prevent any possibility of error in printing the signature, the name of the signatory should be written below in block capitals.

*Name of signatory of resolution (in block capitals)_____

INDEX